STRUCTURAL DESIGN OF BOX CULVERTS

PER AASHTO LRFD DESIGN SPECIFICATIONS

PRACTICAL AND SIMPLE

U.S. Customary Units

STRUCTURAL DESIGN OF BOX CULVERTS

PER AASHTO LRFD DESIGN SPECIFICATIONS

PRACTICAL AND SIMPLE

U.S. Customary Units

HATEM M. ELBADRY, P.E.

CWP

Central West Publishing

This edition has been published by Central West Publishing, Australia

For more information about the books published by Central West Publishing, please visit https://centralwestpublishing.com

Disclaimer

Every effort has been made by the publisher, editors and authors while preparing this book, however, no warranties are made regarding the accuracy and completeness of the content. The publisher, editors and authors disclaim without any limitation all warranties as well as any implied warranties about sales, along with fitness of the content for a particular purpose. Citation of any website and other information sources does not mean any endorsement from the publisher, editors and authors. For ascertaining the suitability of the contents contained herein for a particular lab or commercial use, consultation with the subject expert is needed. In addition, while using the information and methods contained herein, the practitioners and researchers need to be mindful for their own safety, along with the safety of others, including the professional parties and premises for whom they have professional responsibility. To the fullest extent of law, the publisher, editors and authors are not liable in all circumstances (special, incidental, and consequential) for any injury and/or damage to persons and property, along with any potential loss of profit and other commercial damages due to the use of any methods, products, guidelines, procedures contained in the material herein.

NATIONAL LIBRARY OF AUSTRALIA

A catalogue record for this book is available from the National Library of Australia

ISBN (print): 978-1-922617-55-2

Table of Contents

1

Introduction

This manual was issued to simplify and facilitate the structural design of box culverts and keep pace with developments in structural analysis technologies and employ them to reach the best use, one of the recent technologies used for structural analysis and design is the finite element programs. The structural engineer should not rely entirely on those programs and focus on understanding the behavior of the structure and the manual design before going to use the programs on. In any case, programs are just tools, but they do not replace the engineer's role. Therefore, the author intends to employ these programs to facilitate design while keeping the role of the engineer active.

This manual is not considered purely as academic or scientific, and it is considered as a practical book suitable for the current methods used in the design, and since the finite element programs have become a basic requirement for design in most of professional companies, so it is necessary to link these programs to the manual solutions and understand the loads, analysis and outputs to reach the worst case scenarios without forgetting the economic factors which is located in the second place after safety.

The author considers this manual just a tool to facilitate the design in a simple practical way so that it is a suitable reference for the structural engineer without the need to search a large number of references and standards, and the author is keen to compose scientific material in a practical manner suitable for accomplishing the task of designing a culvert in an accurate, simple and professional manner. Therefore, the author has done this manual to reflect what he does himself as a designer in his practical life.

The author relied on the basic AASHTO LRFD Bridge Design Specification, Seventh Edition, 2014 with the use of some states specifications and employed them for an accurate and safe design, he did not add scientific study or research, but it is just an arrangement of information and its compilation in a simple manner for the use of the structural designer.

2

Definitions

2.1 Barrel Length

Barrel length is the distance between the inside faces of culvert headwalls.

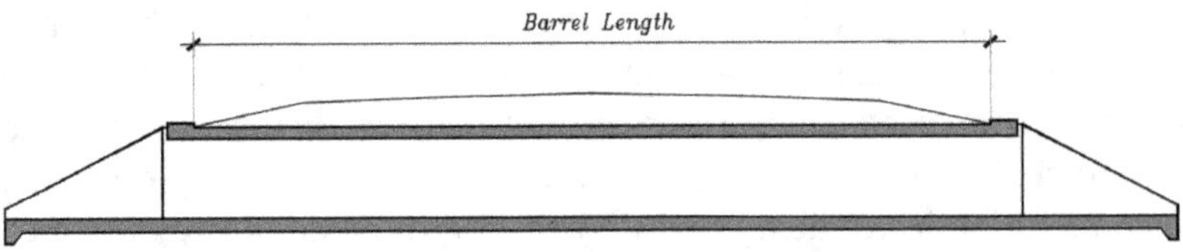

Figure 1. Culvert barrel length

2.2 Axle Spacing

The spacing between vehicle axles in the longitudinal direction (traffic direction).

2.3 Culvert Skew Angle

The angle between culvert's barrel alignment and a line perpendicular to direction of traffic.

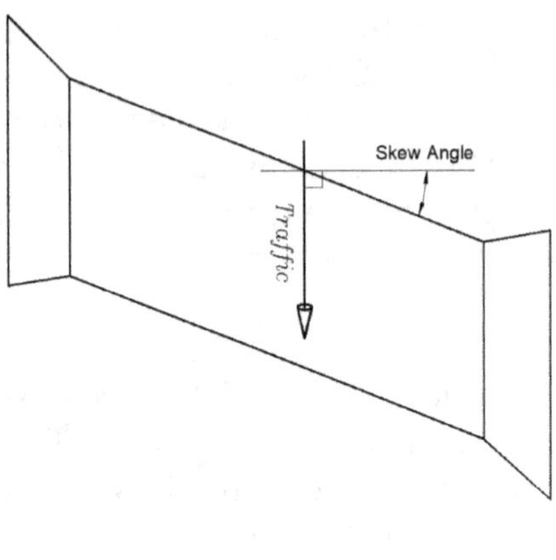

Figure 2. Culvert Skew Angle

2.4 Wheel (Tire) Contact Area

Reference to AASHTO LRFD Article **3.6.1.2.5,** the considered contact area of tire is Lt=10in. and Wt=20in.

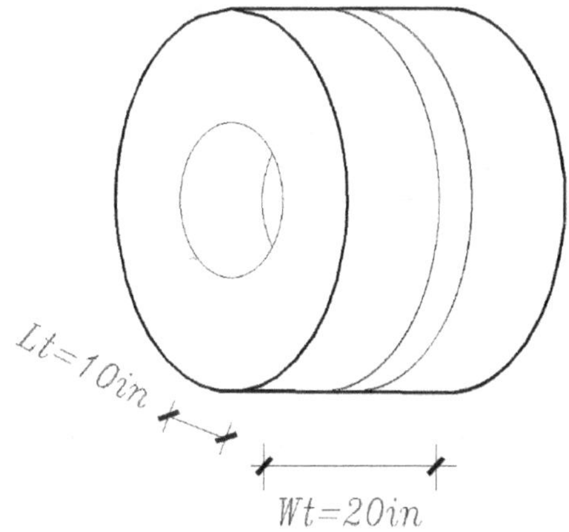

Figure 3. Wheel Contact Area

2.5 Culvert Span (S)

The clear distance between culvert walls.

2.6 Culvert Rise (R)

The clear distance between culvert top and bottom slabs.

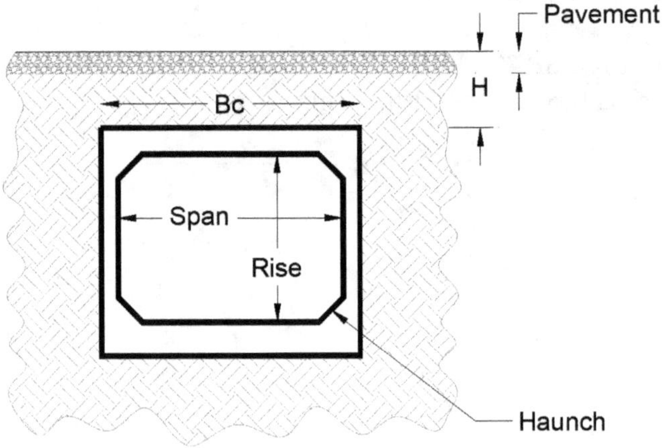

Figure 4. Box Culvert Cross Section

2.7 Box culvert Components

See figures 5, 6 and 7

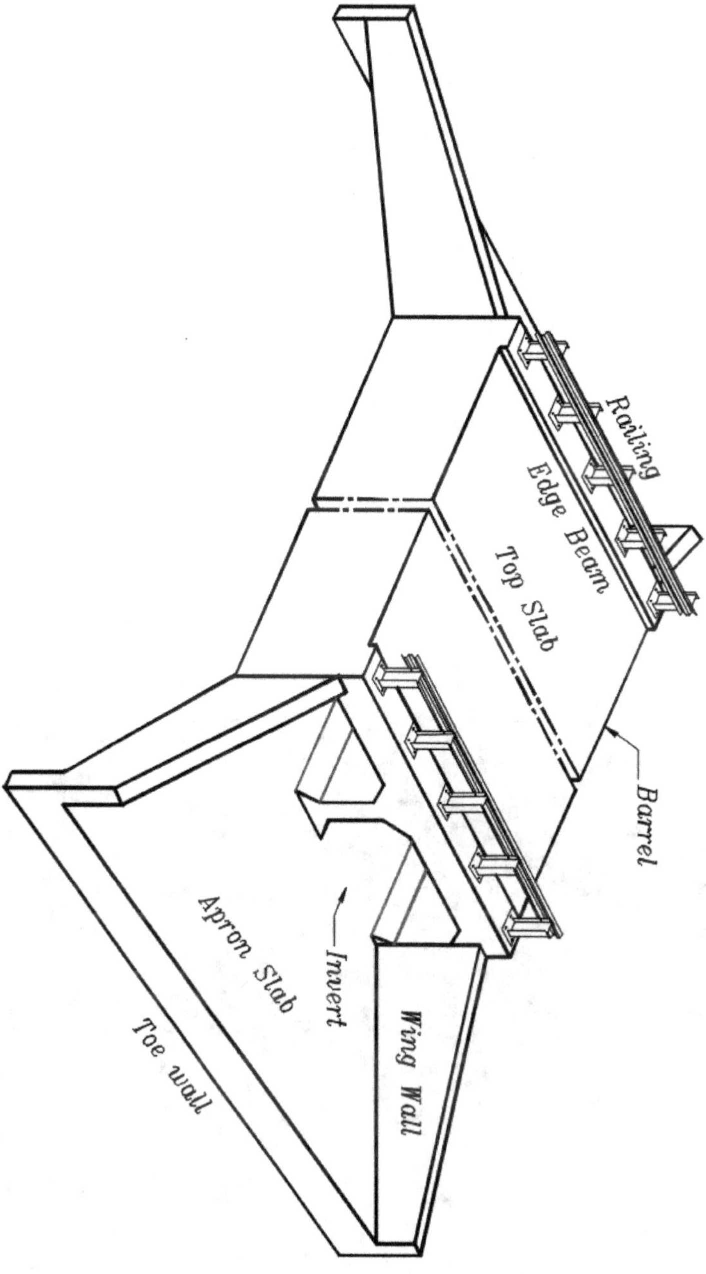

Figure 5. Box Culvert Components

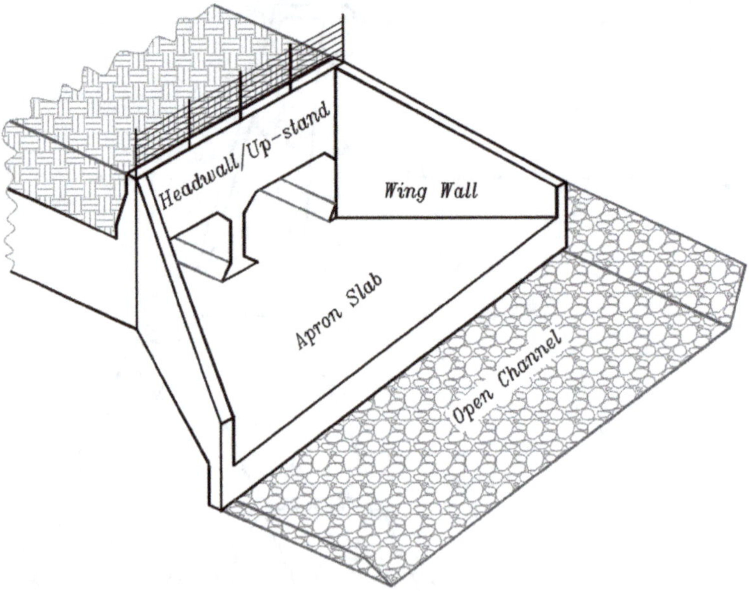

Figure 6. Box Culvert Inlet Components

Figure 7. Box Culvert - Realistic Picture

2.8 Culverts on Rock

A special type of culverts where the walls are keyed into the rock and no bottom slab is used. It is a special system which is not widespread and has some special conditions in design and construction. The minimum embedment depth as per MoDOT is 6".

Figure 8. Culvert on Rock

2.9 Collar Beam

Where a box culvert is likely to settle in the expansion joint locations, either using collar beams or to use the doweled expansion joints to prevent large differential settlement between adjacent sections.

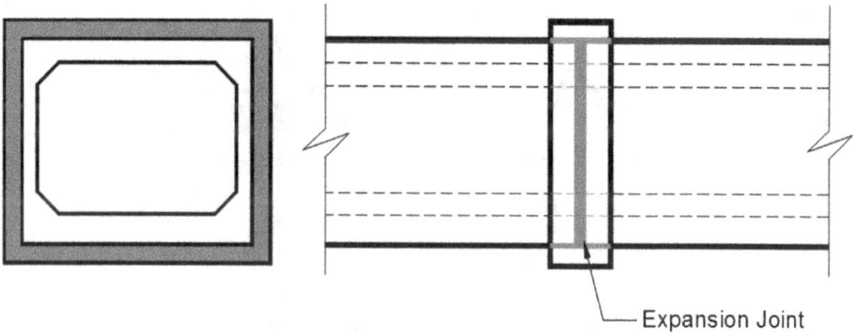

Figure 9. Collar Beam

2.10 Approach Slab

Named also with reliving slab, run-on slab or transition slab. Used for transitioning from the culvert zone to the general embankment zone to reduce local settlement and to accommodate global settlement. Reference to AASHTO LRFD article **11.2**, a structural approach slab or end span design must bridge the space over the fill slope. And per AASHTO LRFD article **11.6.1.3**, the approach slab should be connected directly to the culvert (not to wing walls)

It is recommended to provide approach slabs on both ends of box culvert where the cover between the top of culvert's structure and the finish road pavement is less than 2.0 feet at any location and where distance from the bottom of the base slab to the very top of the culvert exceed 10 feet. The approach slab length is within 13 to 24 feet as per the normal practice.

Slope changes between the culvert and approach slab often develop due to the differential settlement between the two ends of the approach slab.

There is no certain methodology to identify the exact slope, the allowable slope changes recommended in some studies, which are usually based on the survey results of ride comfort only.

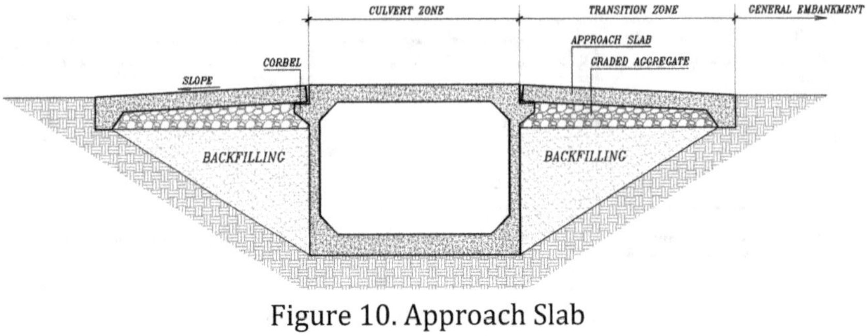

Figure 10. Approach Slab

3

Applicable Loads for Box Culvert

Illinois Department of Transportation "culver manual" is the best material that explained the culvert loads according to AASHTO LRFD. Therefore, it was used as a reference to facilitate understanding of the loads herein.

3.1 Permanent Loads

3.1.1 Dead Load of Structural Components (DC)

The self-weight of structure is based on the reinforced concrete unit weight and volume. For the structural analysis, the top slab carries its self-weight applied uniformly across the top slab. The self-weight for top slab, walls, and haunches are applied as upward reaction from the soil to the bottom slab. The bottom slab weight is not applied in the model because its load is assumed to be directly resisted by the soil. However, the author has a different opinion based on his experience will be explained later in this manual within the structural analysis chapter.

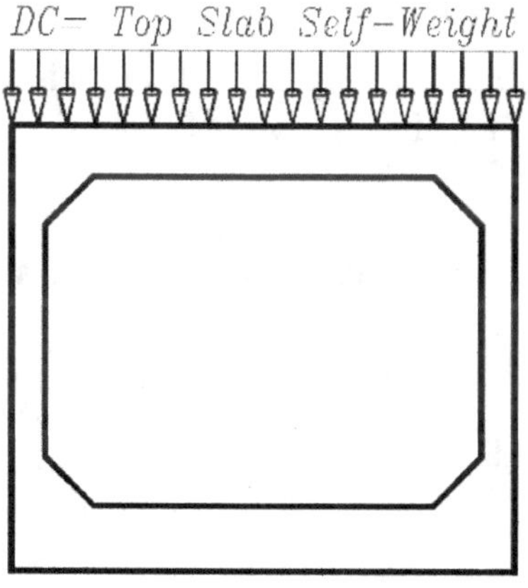

Figure 11. DC Load

3.1.2 Dead Load of Wearing Surfaces and Utilities (DW)

Paving, utilities and the future wearing surface loads shall be considered within the dead load of wearing surfaces DW. The future wearing might be considered as zero if there is backfilling over the culvert's top slab. If there is no fill on the top slab, the future wearing to be considered as per project specification or state regulation requirements. Unless otherwise specified, it is supposed to assume the load as 20 to 50 psf.

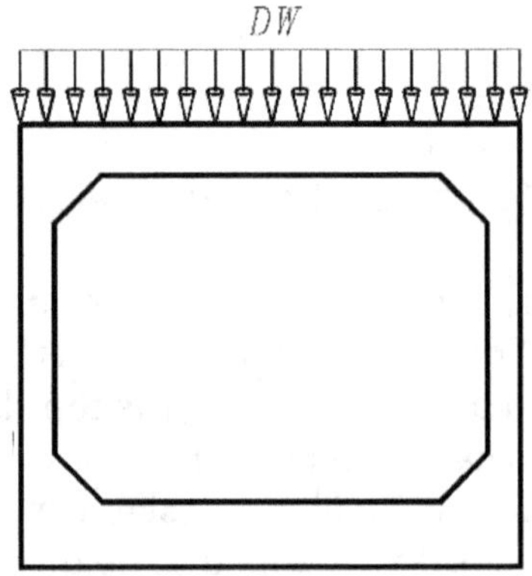

Figure 12. DW Load

Example 1:

-Given:

Pavement Thickness= 12"

Weight per unit volume (γ) for paving= 150 pcf

Future Wearing Surface (FWS) = 50 psf

Utilities load = 15 psf

-Required:

Determine the Dead Load of Wearing Surfaces and Utilities (DW)

-Solution:

$$DW= \frac{T\ paving*\gamma(paving)}{12} + FWS + Utilities\ load$$

$$DW= \frac{12*150}{12} + 50 + 15 = 215\ psf$$

3.1.3 Earth Surcharge Load (ES)

Reference to AASHTO LRFD article **3.11.6.1**, In case of uniform surcharge, a constant horizontal earth pressure shall be added to the basic earth pressure as per the following formula:

$\Delta p = ks*qs$

Where:

Δp = constant horizontal earth pressure due to uniform surcharge (ksf)

ks = coefficient of earth pressure due to surcharge (0.5 for at-rest pressure case)

qs = uniform surcharge applied to the upper surface of the active earth wedge (ksf)

Pavement and future wearing surface are treated as surcharge loads. Therefore, the DW shall be used as uniform surcharge (qs).

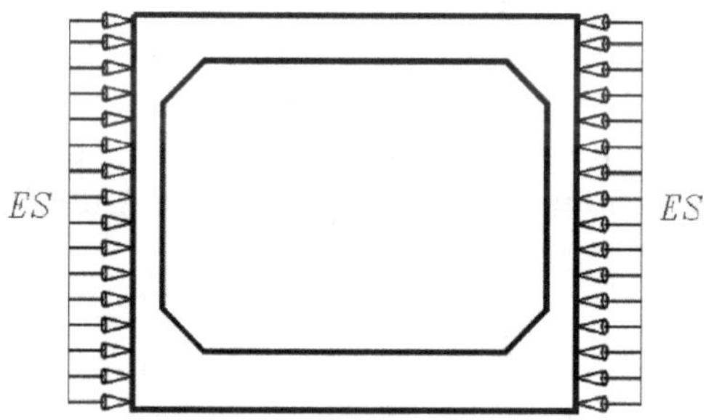

Figure 13. ES Load

Example 2:

-Given:

DW= 50 psf

-Required:

Uniform Earth Surcharge Load

-Solution:

$\Delta p = ks*qs$

$\Delta p = 0.5*215 = 107.5$ psf

3.1.4 Horizontal Earth Pressure Load (EH)

The horizontal earth pressure acting on the culvert will create bending moment on the culvert walls and axial force on the top and bottom slabs. AASHTO LRFD Article **3.11.5.1**, stated that the horizontal soil pressure is assumed to be linearly proportional to the depth of earth. This earth pressure shall be taken as:

$P = k \gamma s\ z$

Where:

p = lateral earth pressure (ksf)

k = Reference to AASHTO LRFD Article **3.11.5.2** & **3.11.5.3,** coefficient of lateral earth pressure.

For at-rest pressure:

$k_o = 1 - \sin\varphi$. Based on $\varphi = 30°$; k_o can be assumed as 0.5

γs = unit weight of soil (kcf)

z = depth below the bottom of the pavement (ft)

AASHTO LRFD Article **3.11.7,** for culverts where earth pressure may reduce effects caused by other loads. In lieu of more precise information, a 50 percent reduction may be used, but need not be combined with the minimum load factor of 0.90 for strength limit state and 1.0 for s service limit state as specified in AASHTO LRFD **Table 3.4.1-2.**

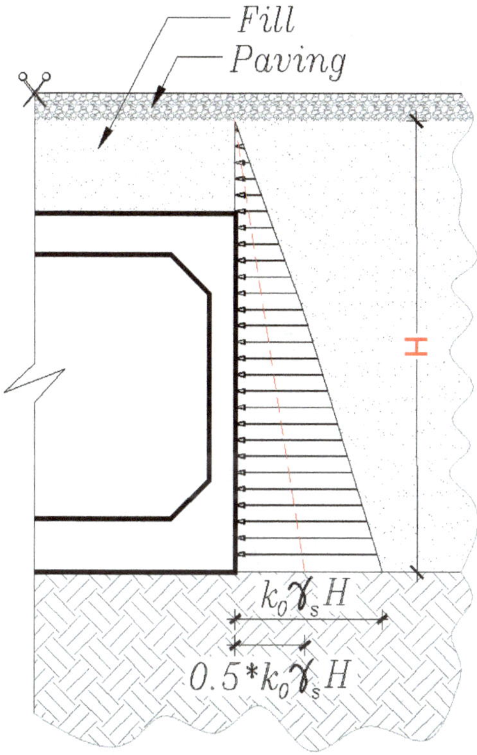

Figure 14. EH Load

AASHTO LRFD Article **3.11.3,** if the water is expected in the soil, the wall shall be designed to withstand the hydrostatic water pressure plus the earth pressure and Submerged unit weights of the soil shall be used to determine the lateral earth pressure below the groundwater table.

$$\gamma_{sat} = \frac{G_S + e}{1+e}\gamma_W \qquad S=1$$

$$\gamma_{dry} = \frac{G_S}{1+e}\gamma_W \qquad S=0$$

$$\gamma_{sub} = \gamma_{sat} - \gamma_w$$

Where:

γ_{sat} = saturated unit weight of soil

γ_{sub} = submerged unit weight of soil

γ_{dry} = dry unit weight of soil
S= degree of saturation
e= void ratio

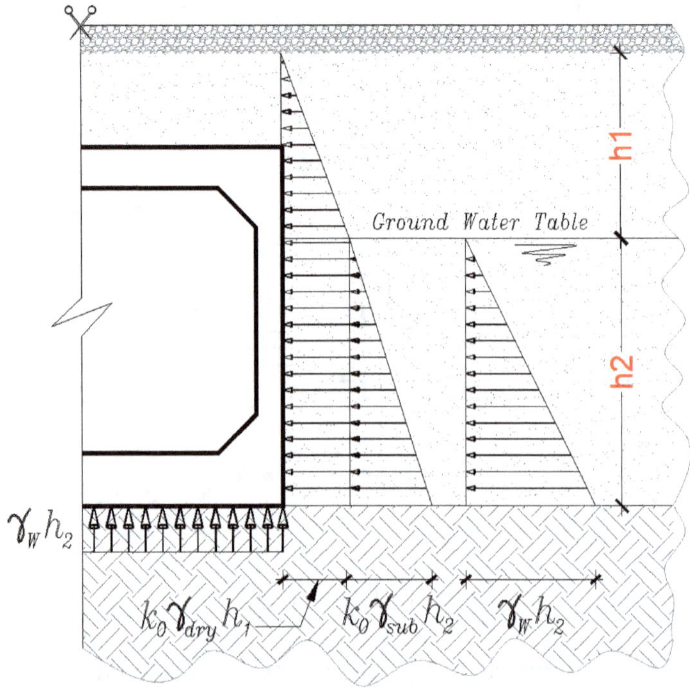

Figure 15. Lateral Soil Pressure Distribution with Hydrostatic Pressure

EH for Wing Walls

Wing walls are designed to withstand the lateral external soil pressure as the self-weight, water pressure, and live load surcharge are usually neglected. The lateral soil loads is calculated using the same procedure of EH. However, the load factors of wings will be different than barrels as explained in section **5.3** in this manual.

Due to the slope of the wing wall, the designer might design the wall as variable section for every linear foot considering the wall as a vertical cantilever retaining wall with vertical main reinforcement.

In the following Figure, the blue lines are referring to the vertical strips for designing the wing wall:

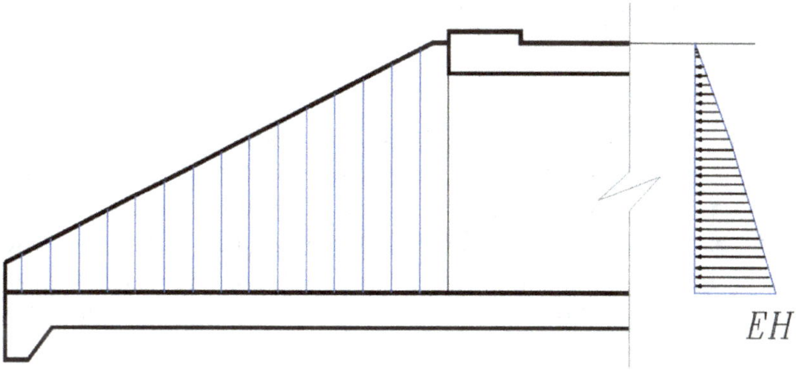

Figure 16. Vertical Variable Design Strips

For wing walls on rock, the vertical reinforcement shall be designed with the same procedure and the horizontal reinforcement shall be designed as a horizontal cantilever beam considering the soil triangular load and distribute it as a trapezoidal load for every linear foot from bottom and triangle for the last foot in the top of wing wall as per the following Figure.

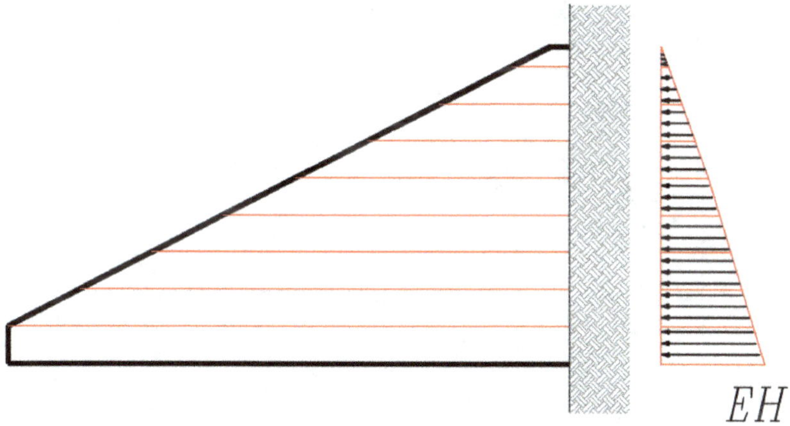

Figure 17. Horizontal Variable Design Strips

Loads of Headwalls and Edge Beams

The up-stand headwalls, when required, are loaded with soil lateral earth pressure EH with the same wing wall load factors. In addition to the vehicular collision load if applicable per AASHTO LRFD Article **3.6.5.1.**

The edge beams are designed to consider its self-weight considering the minimum reinforcing ratios. Mostly, the top slab loads are carried by the walls. However, when the culvert is skewed, the edge beam, approximately, might carry out half of a triangular load due to the skew as per the tributary area (See the following Figure). The load value is easier and more accurate to be calculated by finite element method.

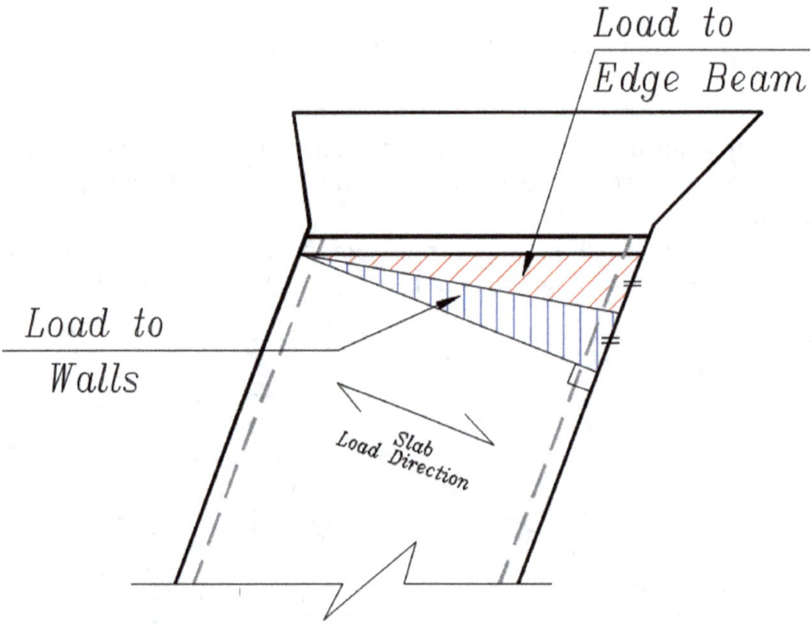

Figure 18. Edge Beam Load Configuration

Example 3:
-Given:
The box culvert in figure No.19
γs = 120 pcf.
-Required:
Lateral earth pressure

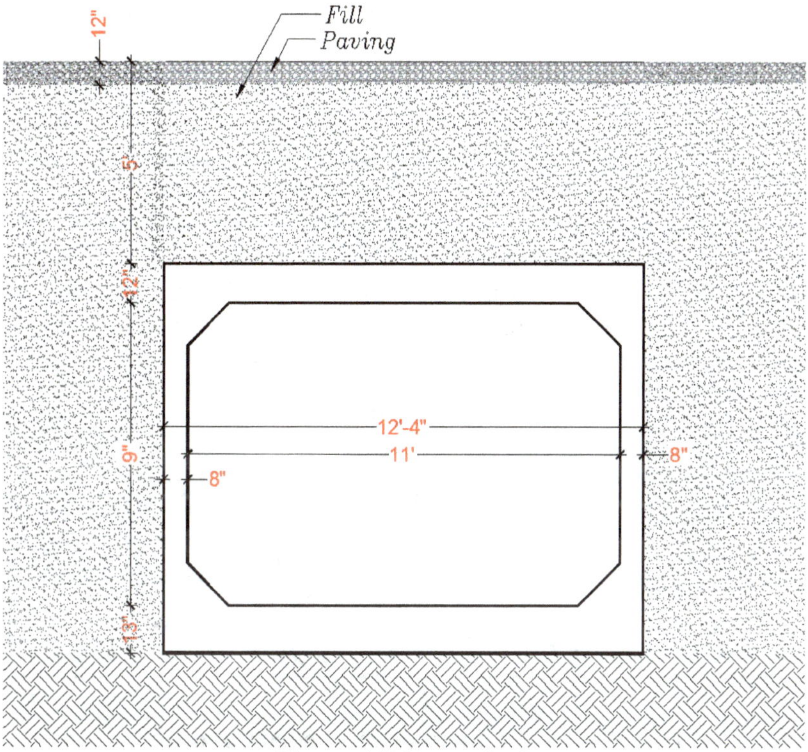

Figure 19. Example 3

-Solution:

As per AASHTO LRFD Article **3.11.5.1**

At the bottom of culvert:

Pb = k γs z = 0.5* (120/1000) *(4+(12/12) +9+(13/12) = 0.905 ksf.

At the top of culvert:

Pt = k γs z = 0.5* (120/1000) *4= 0.24 ksf.

As per AASHTO LRFD Article **3.11.7**

At the bottom of culvert:

P = 0.5* Pb= 0.5*0.905 =0.45 ksf.

At the top of culvert:

P = 0.5* Pt= 0.5*0.24 =0.12 ksf.

3.1.5 Vertical Pressure from Dead Load of Earth Fill (EV)

The presence of a backfill above the culvert results in a vertical load. However, vertical soil pressure shall be increased for soil-structure interaction. AASHTO LRFD Article **12.11.2.2**, Classifies the total modified un-factored vertical earth pressure on the top of box culverts according to the installation method of box culvert, embankment and trench condition. Since the trench condition is different than the common normal practice for box culvert construction and the strict requirements for such method, embankment installation condition is usually assumed for box culvert design.

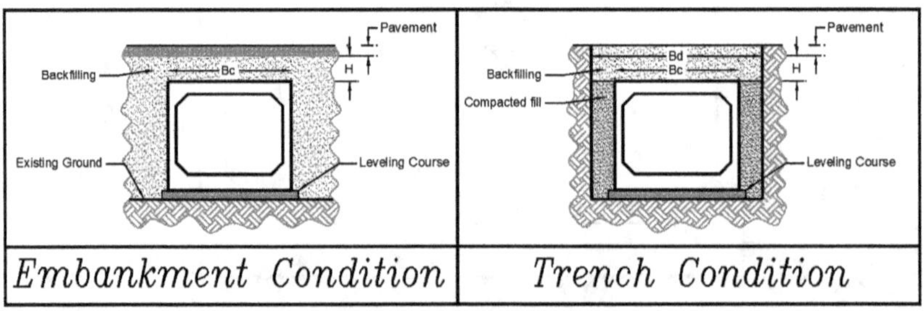

Figure 20. Embankment VS Trench Condition

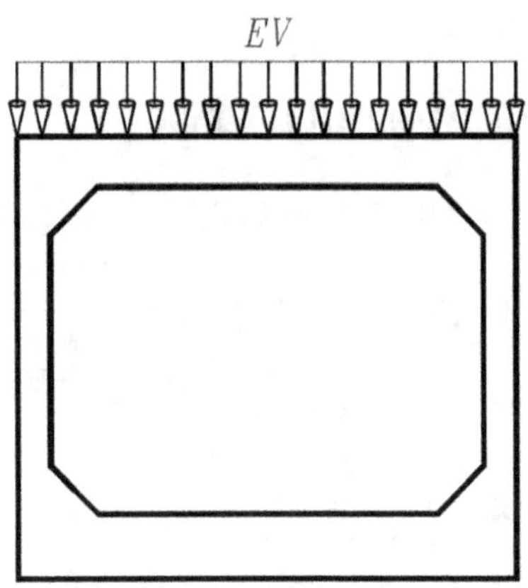

Figure 21. EV Loads

3.1.5.1 For embankment installations

$WEv = F e \gamma s B C$

And,

$$F e = 1 + 0.20 \frac{H}{B C}$$

$F e \leq 1.15$ for compacted fill
$F e \leq 1.40$ for un-compacted fill

3.1.5.2 For Trench installations:

$WEv = F t \gamma s B C H$

And,

$$F t = \frac{C d B^2 d}{HB C} \leq Fe$$

where:
WE = total un-factored earth load (klf)
Bc = outside width of culvert
H = depth of backfill (excluding pavement thickness)
Fe = soil-structure interaction factor for embankment installation
Ft = soil-structure interaction factor for trench installations
γs = unit weight of backfill
B d = horizontal width of trench
C d = a coefficient specified in Figure No.22

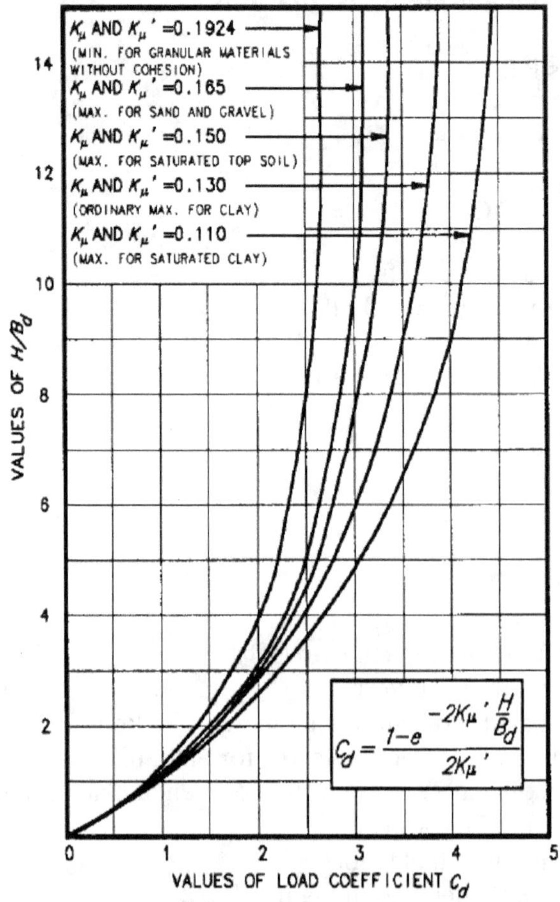

Figure 22. Coefficient C d for Trench Installations

As mentioned, the embankment condition is always followed as per the following example:

Example 4:
-Given:
The box culvert in the figure No.23
Pavement thickness= 12 in.
γs = 120 pcf

-Required:
Total modified un-factored vertical earth pressure

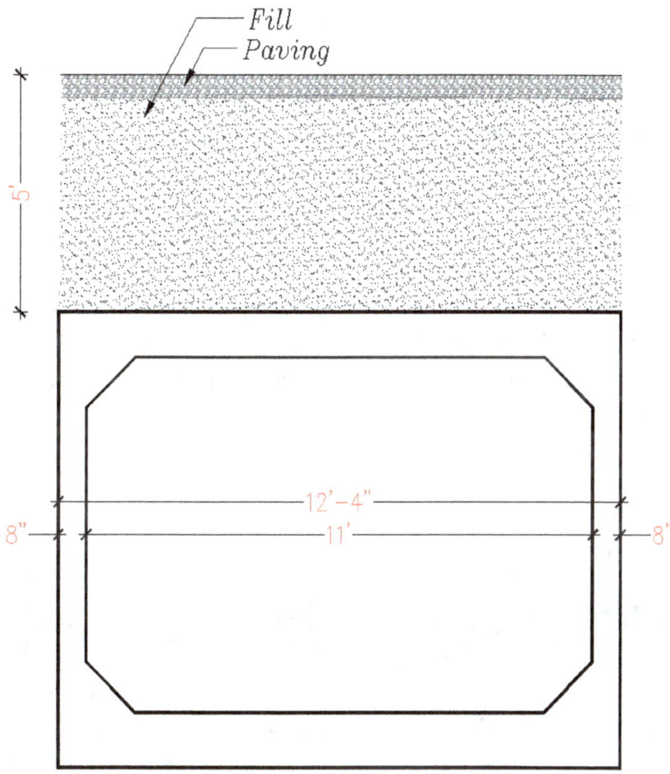

Figure 23. Example 4

-Solution:
H= 5-1 = 4 ft.

$$Fe = 1 + 0.20\frac{H}{BC} = 1 + 0.20\frac{4}{12.33} = 1.06 < 1.15 \text{ OK}$$

WEv = F e γs H = 1.06 *(120/1000) * 4 = 0.51 ksf.

Note:
If the soil filling above the culvert is saturated with underground water, the load of water and soil to be considered on the top slab and the proper soil unit weight to be used.

3.2 Transient Loads

3.2.1 Vehicular Live Load (LL) + Vehicular Dynamic Load Allowance (IM)

Obviously, live loads will be generated as a result of vehicles crossing over the culvert. Reference to AASHTO LRFD Article **12.11.2.1,** the Article **3.6.1.3.3** shall be used for live load of box culverts. Where span does not exceed 15 ft., only axle load for truck or tandem per Articles **3.6.1.2.2** and **3.6.1.2.3** to be applied, and the lane load is not required.

As per AASHTO LRFD Article **3.6.1.2.4,** the design lane load consists of a load of 0.64 klf uniformly distributed over an area of 1 foot (parallel to the culvert span) by 10 feet perpendicular to the culvert span.

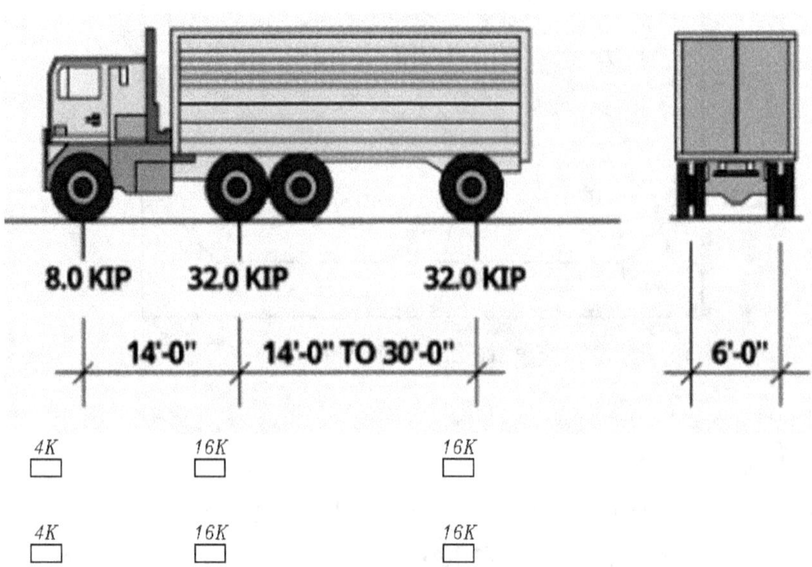

Figure 24. Truck Axle Load per Article **3.6.1.2.2**

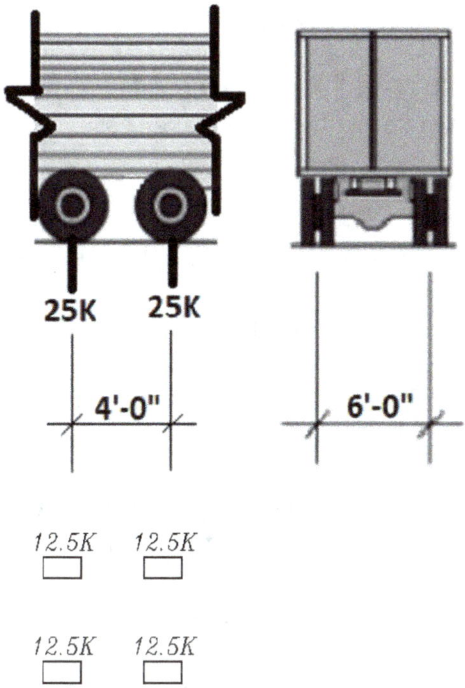

Figure 25. Tandem Axle Load per Article **3.6.1.2.3**

Exceptions

As per AASHTO LRFD Article **3.6.1.2.6a,** the effect of live load may be neglected in the following cases (see figure No.26)

1) For single span culverts, where the fill depth exceeds 8 ft. and exceed span length.

2) For multiple span culverts, where the depth of fill exceeds the distance between inside faces of end walls

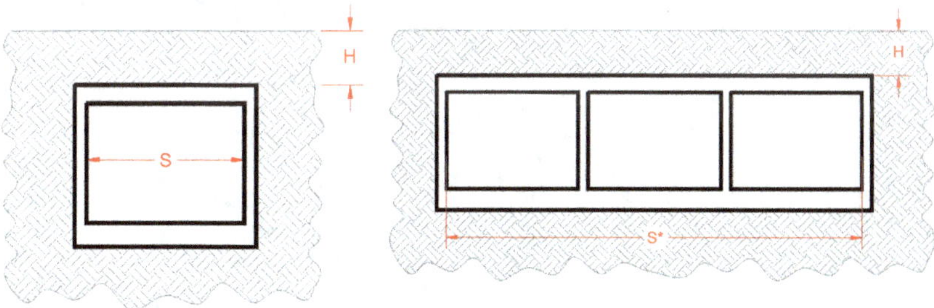

H>8ft and H>S H>S*

Figure 26. Exceptions of Live Load on the Top Slab of Box Culvert

Dynamic Load Allowance (IM)

Reference to AASHTO LRFD Article **3.6.2.2,** the dynamic load allowance for culverts in percent, shall be taken as:

$IM = 33(1.0 - 0.125DE) \geq 0\%$

DE = the minimum depth of earth cover above the structure.

Multiple Presence of Live Load

Reference to AASHTO LRFD Article **3.6.1.1.2,** per **Table 3.6.1.1.2-1** Multiple Presence Factors, m:

Number of loaded lanes	**Multiple Presence Factors, m**
1	1.20
2	1.00
3	0.85
>3	0.65

Reference to AASHTO LRFD Article **12.11.2.1,** For traffic traveling parallel to the span, box culverts shall be designed for a single loaded lane with the single lane multiple presence factor (m= 1.2)

3.2.1.1 Where the depth of fill is less than 2 ft.

AASHTO LRFD Article **4.6.2.10.1,** shall be applied to box culverts with depths of fill less than 2.0 ft. there are two cases according to the traffic direction to span.

3.2.1.1.1 Traffic parallel to span

AASHTO LRFD Article **4.6.2.10.2** shall be applied to calculate the vehicular live load parallel to span for H<2 ft. as follow:
Live load distribution length perpendicular to the span:
E = (96 + 1.44(S))
Live load distribution length parallel to the span:
Espan = (LT + LLDF (H))
Where:
E = Equivalent distribution width perpendicular to span (in.)
S = Clear span (ft)
Espan = Equivalent distribution length parallel to span (in.)
LT = Length of tire contact area parallel to span, as per AASHTO LRFD Article **3.6.1.2.5** (10 in.)
LLDF = Factor for distribution of live load with depth of fill, (1.15), as per AASHTO LRFD **Table 3.6.1.2.6a-1**.
H = Depth of fill from top of culvert to top of pavement (in.)

Truck loads are considered according to the available space, the number of axles which will be accommodated at the roof depends on the width of the top slab parallel to span. The axle spacing might be considered as 14' which is the worst case scenario. However, the clear distance between influence areas to be calculated to check whether there is load interaction or not.

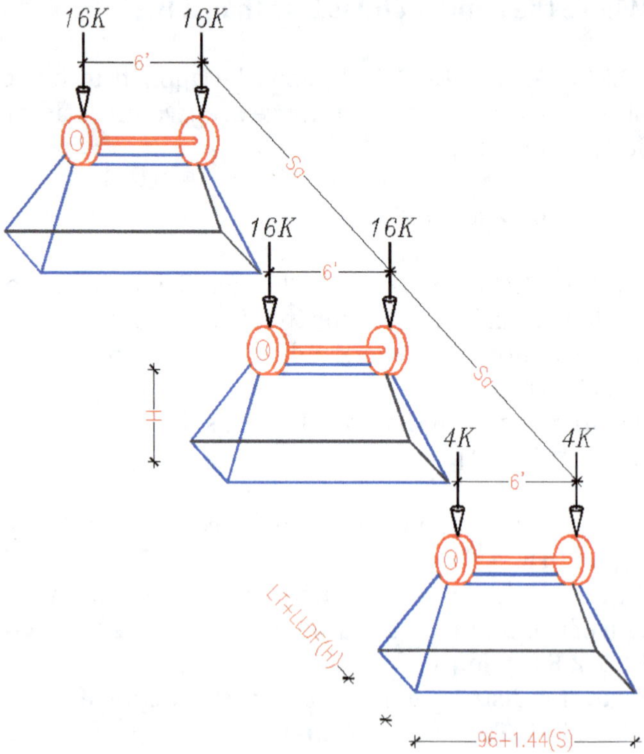

Figure 27. Truck Live Load Distribution for Traffic Parallel to Span H<2ft.

Note: if the filling thickness above the culvert's top slab equals to zero, the Espan equation to be:

Espan = LT

In the case of single axle load, the (32Kips) axle shall be considered as per the following Figure:

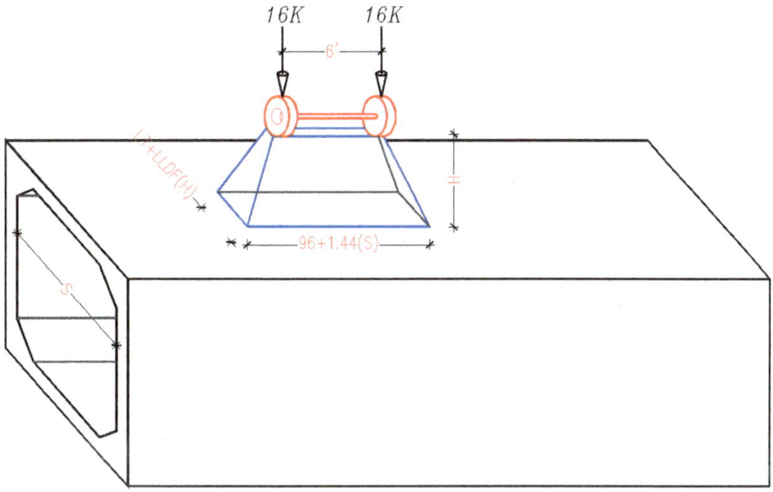

Figure 28. Single Axle Truck Live Load Distribution for Traffic Parallel to Span H<2ft.

The Tandem two axles are usually considered to be interacting, and axle spacing equals to 4'. Therefore, the live load distribution for traffic parallel to Span H<2ft shall be calculated as per the following Figure:

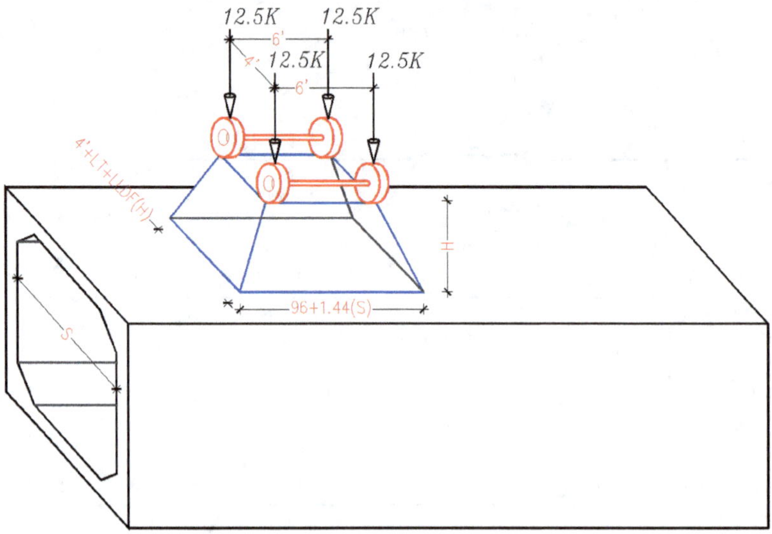

Figure 29. Tandem Live Load Distribution for Traffic Parallel to Span H<2ft.

Example 5:
-Given:
The following box culvert and the shown dimensions in Figure No.30
The skew angle equals zero
-Required:
Determine the vehicular live load on the top slab of the box culvert

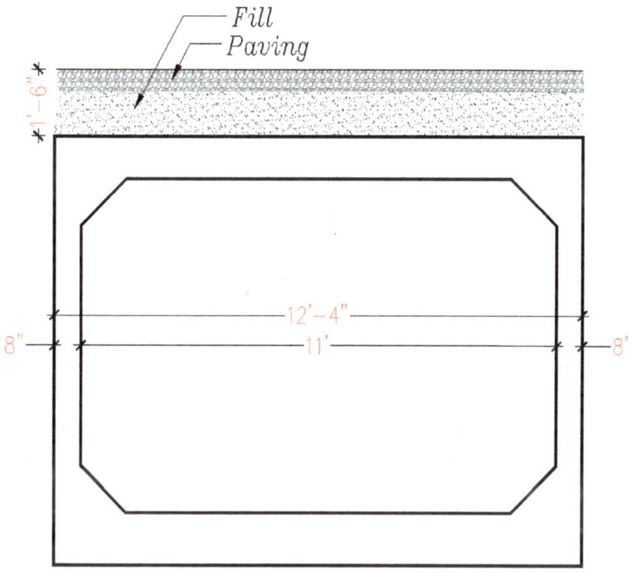

Figure 30. Example 5. Cross Section

-Solution:

Since the culvert is not skewed, the live load shall be considered parallel to span.

Dynamic Load Allowance, IM, (AASHTO LRFD Article **3.6.2.2**):

The fill thickness DE = 1.5 ft.

IM = 0.33(1.0 - 0.125*1.5) = 0.268

Multiple presence factor, m, (AASHTO LRFD Article **3.6.1.1.2):**

For traffic traveling parallel to the span, consider a single loaded lane with m= 1.2

The span does not exceed 15 feet. Therefore, the lane load is not included, and Article **3.6.1.2.4** is not applied.

<u>For Truck</u>

Live load distribution area:

Live load distribution length perpendicular to the span:

E = (96 + 1.44(S)) = (96 + 1.44(11)) = 111.84 in = 9.32 ft.

Live load distribution length parallel to the span:

Espan = (LT + LLDF (H)) = (10+1.15(1.5*12)) = 30.7 in = 2.56 ft.

Check of axle interaction:

Clear distance between axles= 14-2.56= 11.44' (Positive number, thus: No interaction)

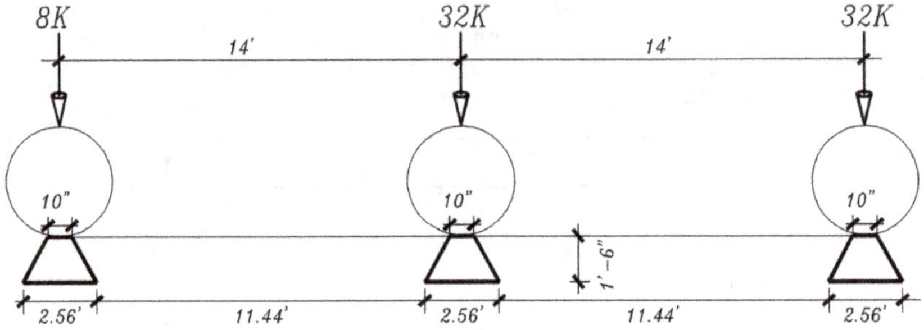

Figure 31. Example 5. Load Distribution in Axle Direction

According to culvert dimensions, there no probability to have more than one axle on the top slab. Therefore, consider (32Kips) single axles load as per following figure:

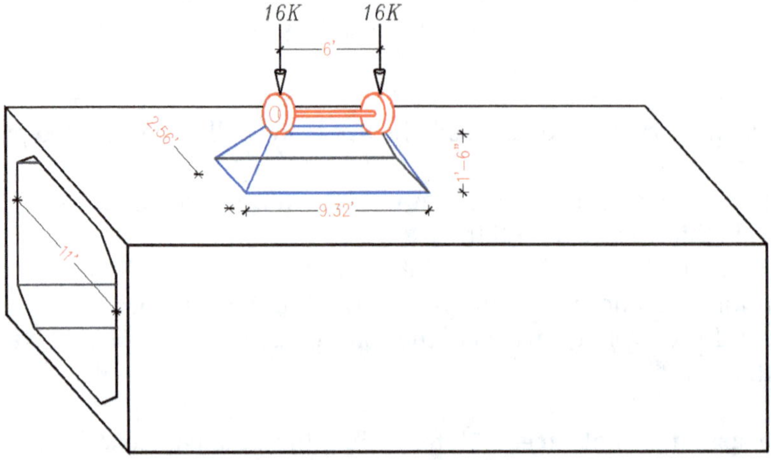

Figure 32. Example 5. Isometric for Truck Live Load Distribution

Live load Magnitude:

$$Wll = \frac{\text{Axle load}}{\text{Distribution Area}} = \frac{32}{9.32*2.56} = 1.34 \text{ ksf}$$

Wll+IM = Wlltruck(1+IM) *m =1.34(1+0.268) *1.2=2.04 ksf

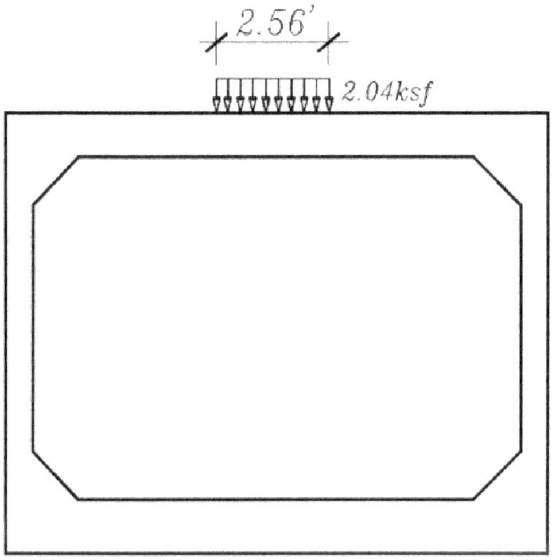

Figure 33. Example 5. Truck Live Load

<u>For Tandem</u>
Assume that the two axles will overlap
Live load distribution area:
Live load distribution length perpendicular to the span:
E= Same as Truck = 9.32 ft.
Live load distribution length parallel to the span:
Espan = Same as Truck + 4'= 2.56+4= 6.56 ft.

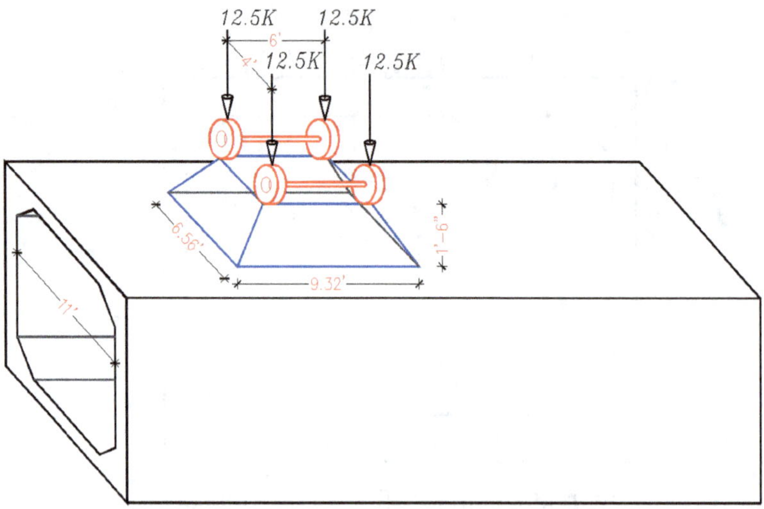

Figure 34. Example 5. Isometric for Tandem Live Load Distribution

Live load Magnitude:

$$Wll= \frac{\text{Axle load}}{\text{Distribution Area}} = \frac{50}{9.32*6.56} = 0.82 \text{ ksf}$$

Wll+IM = Wlltandem(1+IM) *m =0.82(1+0.268) *1.2=1.25 ksf

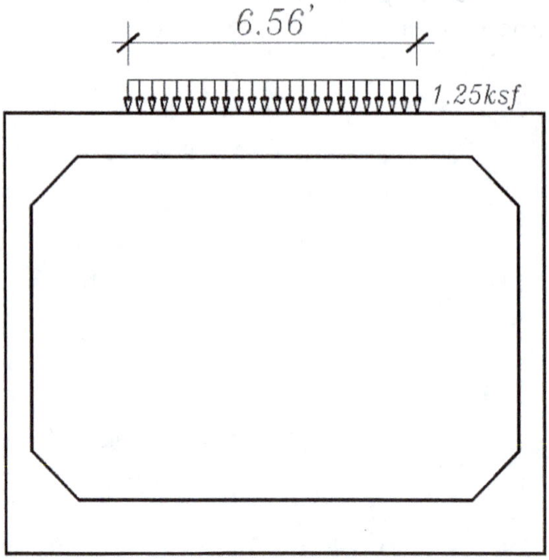

Figure 35. Example 5. Tandem Live Load

Conclusion:

The vehicular live load on the top slab has two different values and distribution areas. The most critical effect shall be considered for design.
Since the load distribution width is less than top slab width, the load may act in unsymmetrical way on the top slab. The worst case shall be considered to ensure the safe design.

3.2.1.1.2 Traffic perpendicular to span

Most of highway box culverts are loaded parallel to span as per AASHTO LRFD Article **C3.6.1.2.6b.** Furthermore, Research (McGrath, et al. 2004) has shown that in design of box sections allowing distribution of live load through fill in the direction parallel to the span provides a more accurate design model to predict moment, and shear forces as per Article **C3.6.1.2.6a**. However, application of both perpendicular and parallel vehicular live loads which is greater is required in the following cases:

- Single box culvert with 90 degrees' skew
- Multiple box culvert with skew angle exceeds 30 degrees

For the patch dimension parallel to movement direction, as per AASHTO LRFD Article **4.6.2.10.3** which refers to **Table 4.6.2.1.3-1**-Equivalent Strips. The equations are:

For Positive Moment: 26.0 + 6.6S
For Negative Moment: 48.0 + 3.0S

In the following table, the equations are rearranged considering spacing in feet and adding 4' to tandem equation since the two axles are always considered to be overlapped:

Case	For Positive Moment	For Negative Moment
TRUCK	E = 2.17 + 0.55S	E = 4.00 + 0.25S
TANDEM	E = 6.17 + 0.55S	E = 8.00 + 0.25S

Where:
S = clear span (ft.)

E = patch dimension parallel to movement direction (ft.)
For the patch dimension perpendicular to movement direction, as per AASHTO LRFD Article **3.6.1.2.6b:**

For Truck:
Without Interaction: Wt+LLDF(H)+0.06(S)
With Interaction: Wt+Sw+LLDF(H)+0.06(S)
For Tandem:
Wt+Sw+LLDF(H)+0.06(S)
Where:
S = Clear span of the culvert
H = Depth of fill from top of culvert to top of pavement
LLDF = Live load distribution factor per AASHTO LRFD **Table 3.6.1.2.6a-1**; (1.15)
Wt = Width of tire contact area, per AASHTO LRFD **3.6.1.2.5**; (20 in)
Sw = Wheel spacing; (6.0 ft)

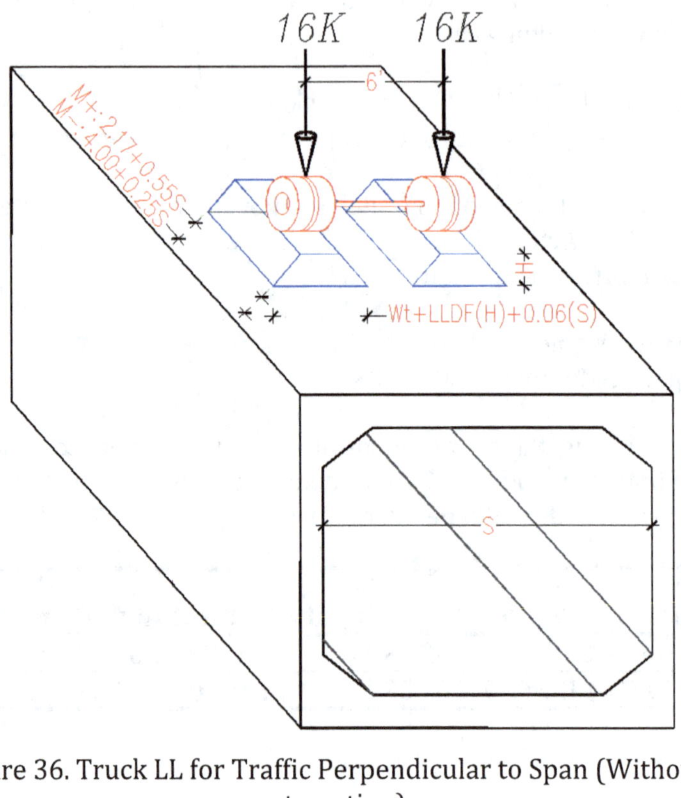

Figure 36. Truck LL for Traffic Perpendicular to Span (Without interaction)

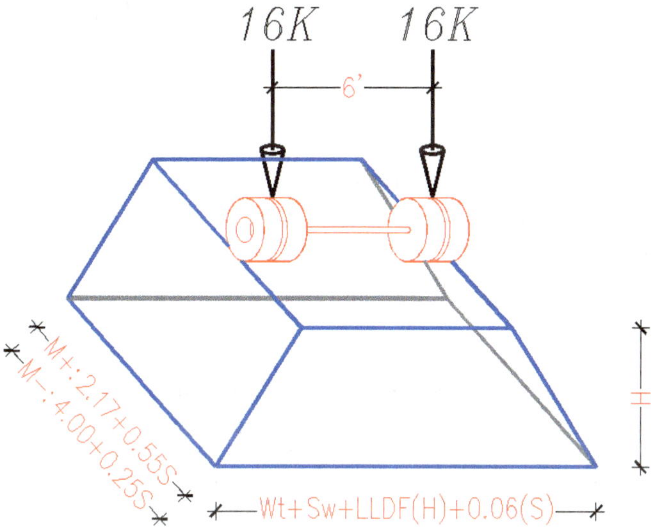

Figure 37. Truck LL for Traffic Perpendicular to Span (With interaction)

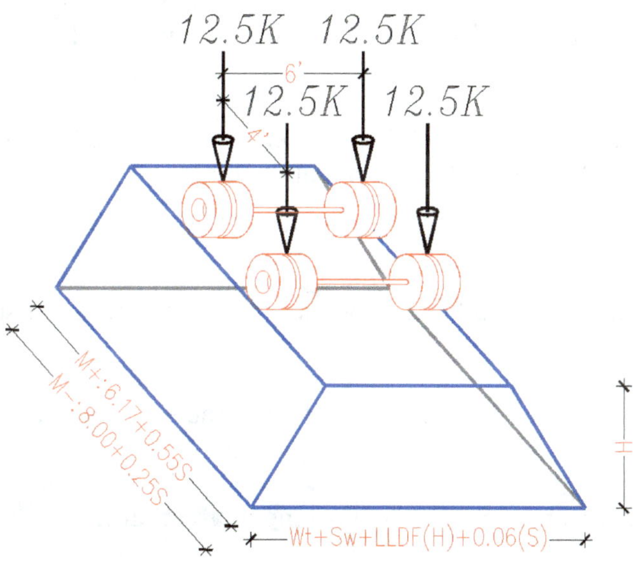

Figure 38. Tandem LL for Traffic Perpendicular to Span

Note: If the filling thickness above the top slab equals zero, the term LLDF(H) will be excluded from the previous equations.

Note: As per AASHTO LRFD article **3.6.1.3.1**, center of any wheel load might not be closer than 2 ft. from the edge of lane. Therefore, for two lanes, the minimum spacing shall be 4 ft.

Example 6:
-Given:
The same box culvert in Example No.5
The skew angle equals 90°
-Required:
Determine the vehicular live load on the top slab of the box culvert
-Solution:
Since the culvert is single spanned and skewed, the live load shall be considered primarily perpendicular to span. And the greater of parallel and perpendicular to span loads shall be considered.
Dynamic Load Allowance, IM, (AASHTO LRFD Article **3.6.2.2**):
The fill thickness DE = 1.5 ft.
IM = 0.33(1.0 - 0.125*1.5) = 0.268
Multiple presence factor, m, (AASHTO LRFD Article **3.6.1.1.2):**
The maximum applicable lanes are two. Therefore, m= 1.2 (for one lane) and m=1(for two lanes)
Since the traffic travels primarily perpendicular to span and H<2 ft., Article **4.6.2.10.3** shall be considered to calculate the LL distribution dimensions.

The span does not exceed 15 feet. Therefore, the lane load is not included, and Article **3.6.1.2.4** is not applied.

<u>For Truck:</u>
One Lane:
Patch dimension parallel to movement direction (+M to be used for single culvert)
= 2.17+0.55S
= 2.17+(0.55*11) = 8.22 ft. < 14 ft. No interaction, single axle will be considered

Patch dimension transverse to movement direction of vehicle for one lane:
Assume without Interaction: Wt+LLDF(H)+0.06(S)
= 20/12 + (1.15*1.5) + (0.06*11) = 4.05 ft.
Check the interaction:
6-4.05= 1.95 ft. Positive, No interaction

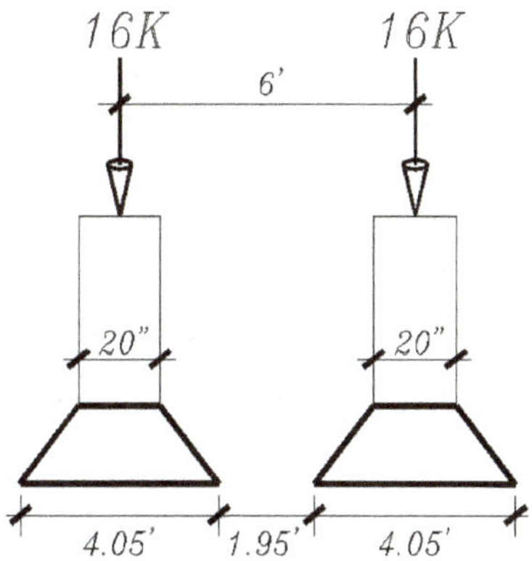

Figure 39. Example 6. Truck Load Distribution for One Lane

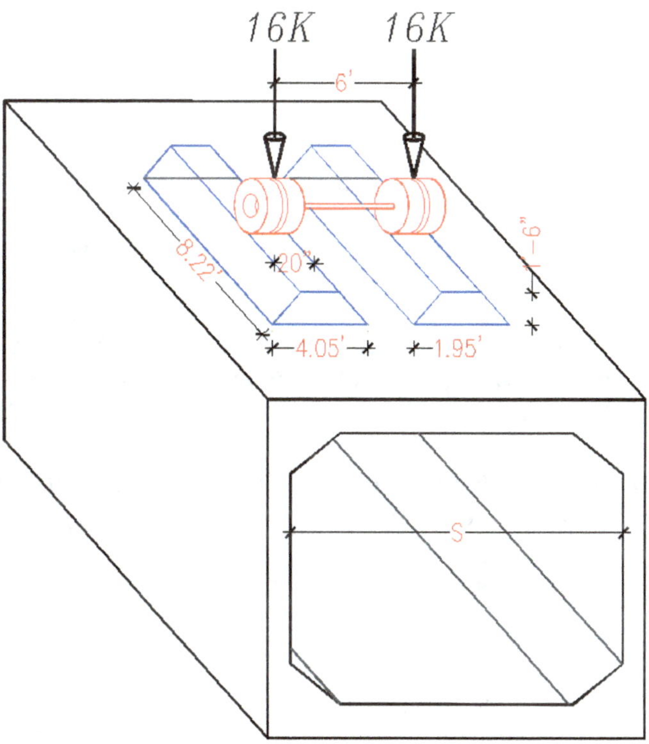

Figure 40. Example 6. Isometric for Truck Load Distribution (One Lane)

Live load Magnitude:

$$Wll = \frac{\text{Axle load}}{\text{Distribution Area}} = \frac{16}{8.22*4.05} = 0.48 \text{ ksf}$$

m=1.2

Wll+IM = Wlltruck(1+IM) *m =0.48 (1+0.268) *1.2=0.73 ksf

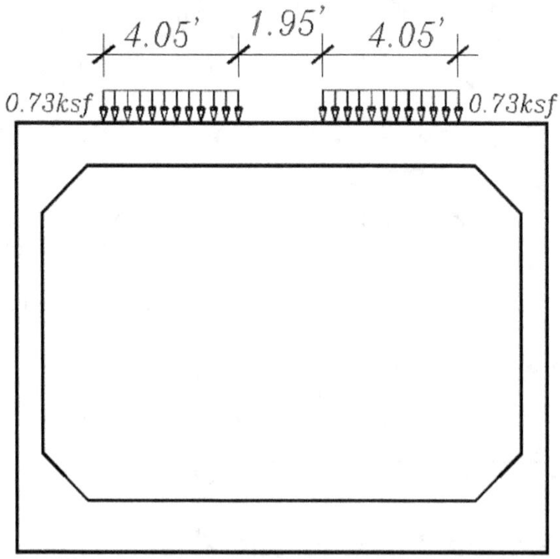

Figure 41. Example 6. Truck Load for One Lane

Two Lanes:

The same patch dimensions for one lane will be considered and as per AASHTO LRFD Article **3.6.1.3.1**, the minimum spacing from center of wheels shall be 4 ft. the two lanes interaction to be calculated as follow:

Clear space between loads distribution areas = 4-4.05= -0.05 ft. Negative, hence there is 0.05 ft. interaction.

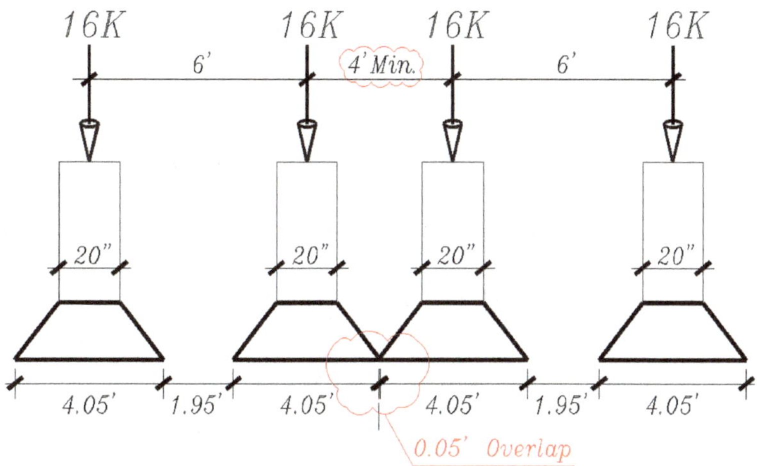

Figure 42. Example 6. Truck Load Distribution for Two Lanes

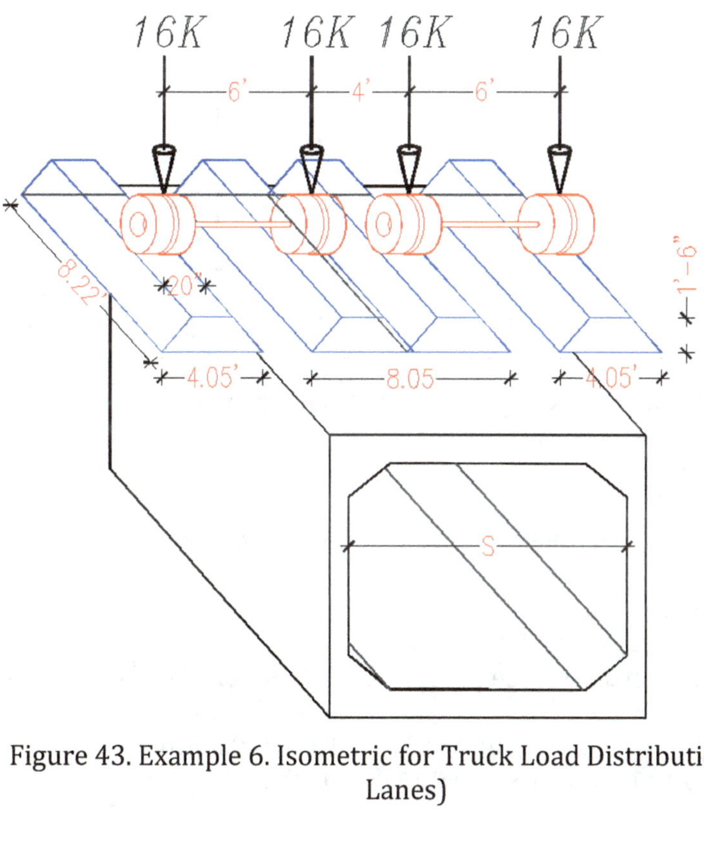

Figure 43. Example 6. Isometric for Truck Load Distribution (Two Lanes)

Live load Magnitude:
For external wheels:

$$Wll = \frac{\text{Axle load}}{\text{Distribution Area}} = \frac{16}{8.22*4.05} = 0.48 \text{ ksf}$$

m= 1.0
Wll+IM = Wlltruck(1+IM) *m =0.48(1+0.268) *1.0=0.61 ksf
For internal wheels:
The internal wheels are overlapped, the overall width = (4.05*2)-0.05= 8.05 ft.

$$Wll = \frac{\text{Axle load}}{\text{Distribution Area}} = \frac{32}{8.22*8.05} = 0.48 \text{ ksf}$$

m= 1.0
Wll+IM = Wlltruck(1+IM) *m =0.48(1+0.268) *1.0=0.61 ksf

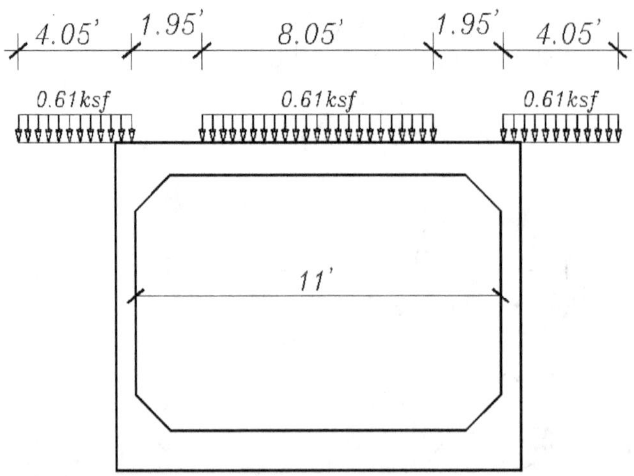

Figure 44. Example 6. Truck Load for Two Lanes

For Tandem:
One lane:
Patch dimension parallel to movement direction (+M to be used for single culvert)
= 6.17+0.55S
= 6.17+(0.55*11) = 12.22 ft.
Patch dimension transverse to movement direction of vehicle for one lane:
Assume without Interaction: Wt+Sw+LLDF(H)+0.06(S)
= 20/12 + 6 + (1.15*1.5) + (0.06*11) = 10.05 ft.

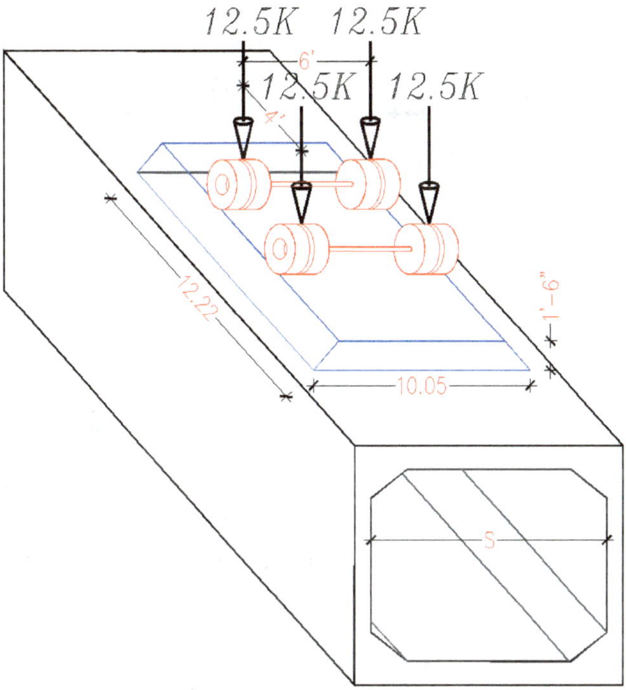

Figure 45. Example 6. Isometric for Tandem Load Distribution (One Lane)

Live load Magnitude:

$$\text{Wll}= \frac{\text{Axle load}}{\text{Distribution Area}} = \frac{50}{12.22*10.05} = 0.41 \text{ ksf}$$

m= 1.2

Wll+IM = Wlltandem(1+IM) *m =0.41(1+0.268) *1.2=0.62 ksf

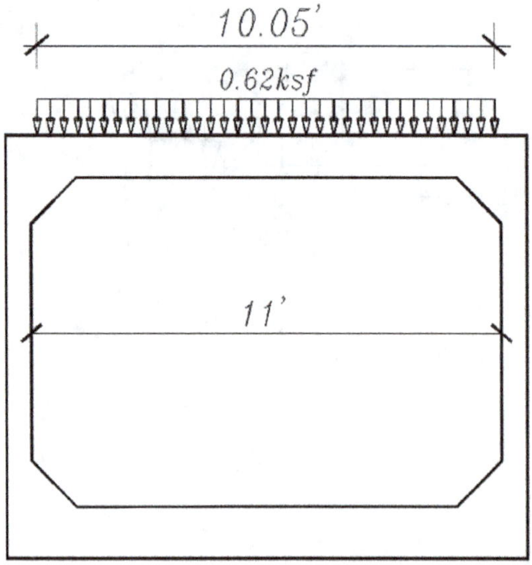

Figure 46. Example 6. Tandem Load for One Lane

Two lanes:
Patch dimensions will remain the same
The same patch dimensions for one lane will be considered and as per AASHTO LRFD Article **3.6.1.3.1**, the minimum spacing from center of wheels shall be 4 ft. the two lanes interaction to be calculated as follow:
Clear space between loads distribution areas = 4-(10.05-6) = -0.05 ft.
Negative, hence there is 0.05 ft. interaction.

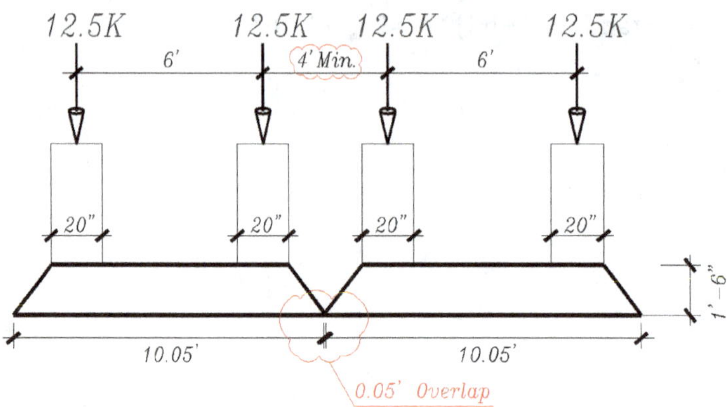

Figure 47. Example 6. Tandem Load Distribution for Two Lanes

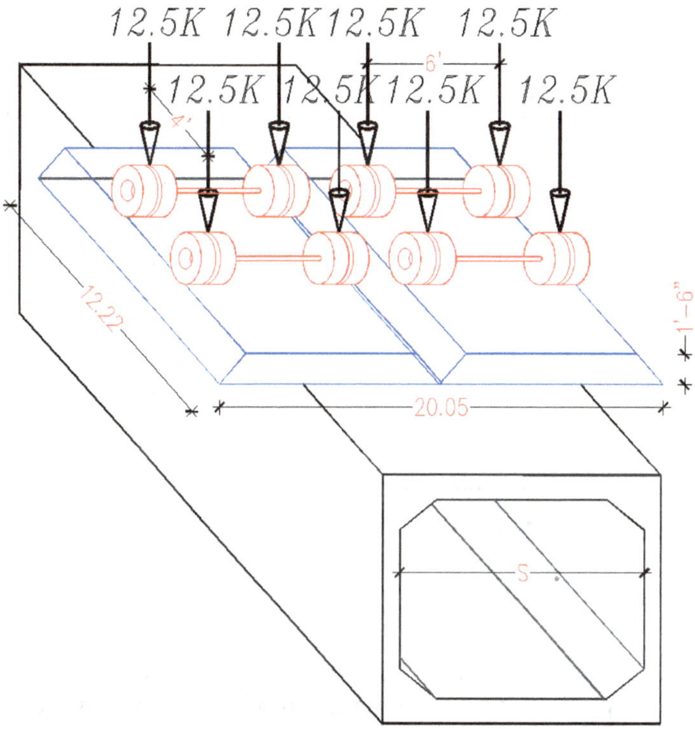

Figure 48. Example 6. Isometric for Tandem Load Distribution (Two Lanes)

Live load Magnitude:

$$Wll= \frac{\text{Axle load}}{\text{Distribution Area}} = \frac{100}{12.22*20.05} = 0.41 \text{ ksf}$$

m= 1.0

Wll+IM = Wlltandem(1+IM) *m =0.41(1+0.268) *1.0 =0.52 ksf

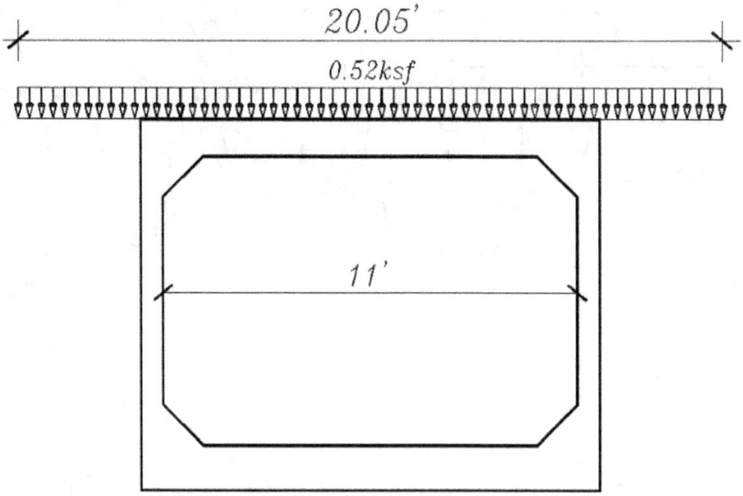

Figure 49. Example 6. Tandem Load for Two Lanes

Conclusion:

Maximum load will govern. However, the live load parallel to span (in the example No.5 shall be compared with this load and consider which is greater.

3.2.1.2 Where the depth of fill is greater than or equal 2 ft.

3.2.1.2.1 Traffic parallel to span

AASHTO LRFD Article **3.6.1.2.6b** shall be used to calculate the vehicular live load over box culvert top slab for traffic parallel to span with H≥ 2 ft.

For the patch dimension perpendicular to movement direction:

<u>For Truck</u>:
Without Interaction: Wt+LLDF(H)+0.06(S)
With Interaction: Wt+Sw+LLDF(H)+0.06(S)

<u>For Tandem</u>:
Wt+Sw+LLDF(H)+0.06(S)

For the patch dimension parallel to movement direction:
<u>For Truck</u>:
(Interaction in movement direction must be checked)
Without Interaction: Lt+LLDF(H)
With Interaction: Lt+Sa+LLDF(H)
<u>For Tandem</u>:
Lt+Sa+LLDF(H)

Where:
S = Clear span of the culvert
H = Depth of fill from top of culvert to top of pavement
LLDF = Live load distribution factor per AASHTO LRFD **Table 3.6.1.2.6a-1**; (1.15)
Wt = Width of tire contact area, per AASHTO LRFD Article **3.6.1.2.5**; (20 in)
Lt = Length of tire contact area, per AASHTO LRFD Article **3.6.1.2.5**; (10 in)
Sa = Axle spacing
Sw = Wheel spacing; (6.0 ft)

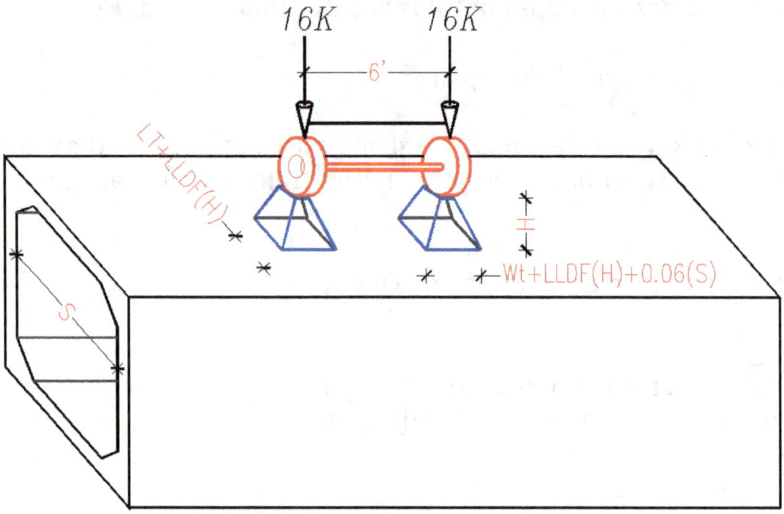

Figure 50. Truck LL for Traffic Parallel to Span without Interaction & H≥2 ft.

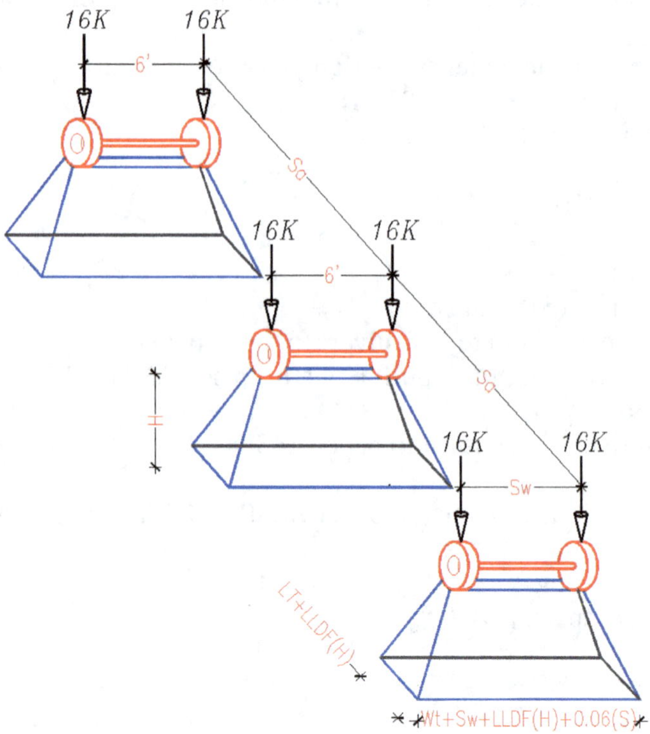

Figure 51. Truck LL for Traffic Parallel to Span with Interaction & H≥2 ft.

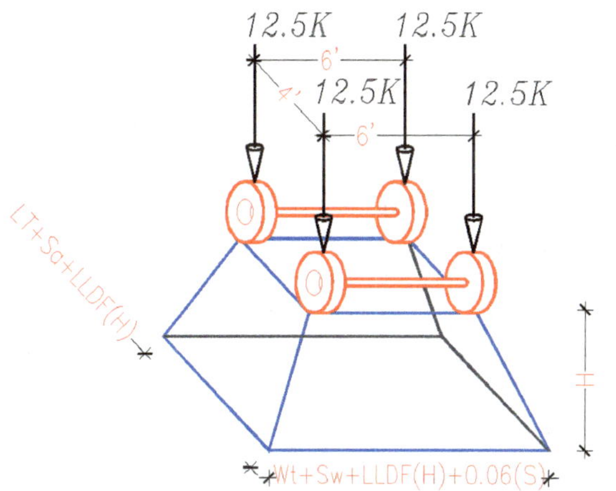

Figure 52. Tandem LL for Traffic Parallel to Span & H≥2 ft.

Example 7:

-Given:

The shown box culvert in figure No.53 & The culvert is not skewed.

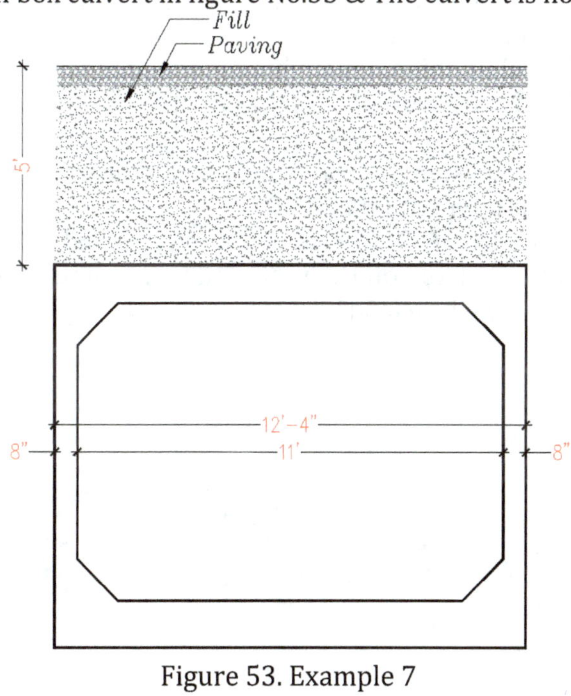

Figure 53. Example 7

-Required:
Determine the vehicular live load on the top slab of the box culvert
-Solution:
Since the culvert is not skewed, the live load shall be considered parallel to span.
Dynamic Load Allowance, IM, (AASHTO LRFD Article **3.6.2.2**):
The fill thickness DE = 5 ft.
IM = 0.33(1.0 - 0.125*5) = 0.12
Multiple presence factor, m, (AASHTO LRFD Article **3.6.1.1.2):**
For traffic traveling parallel to the span per Article **12.11.2.1**:
m=1.2

The span does not exceed is less than 15 feet. Therefore, the lane load is not included.

<u>For Truck</u>:
As per AASHTO LRFD Article **3.6.1.2.6b**:
For the patch dimension perpendicular to movement direction:
Assume without Interaction: Wt+LLDF(H)+0.06(S)
= 20/12 + (1.15*5) +(0.06*11) = 8.08 ft. > 6 ft. Interaction shall be considered as follow:
Wt+Sw+LLDF(H)+0.06(S)
= 20/12 + 6 + (1.15*5) +(0.06*11) = 14.08 ft.

For the patch dimension parallel to movement direction:
Assume without Interaction: Lt+LLDF(H)
= 10/12 + (1.15*5) = 6.58 ft. < 14 ft. No overlap and no more axles might be accommodated on the roof with these dimensions. Therefore, consider single axle load.

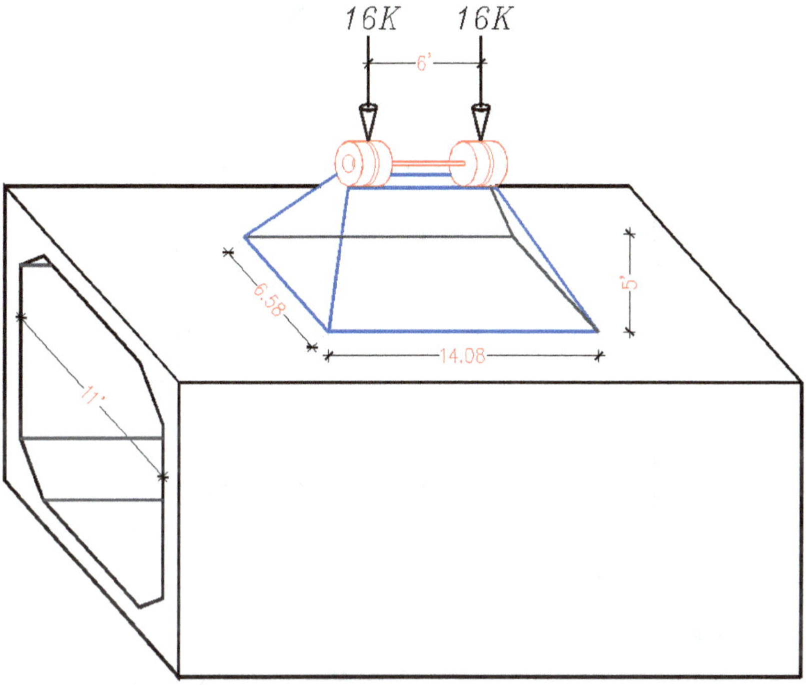

Figure 54. Example 7. Isometric for Truck Live load

Live load Magnitude:

$$Wll = \frac{\text{Axle load}}{\text{Distribution Area}} = \frac{32}{14.08*6.58} = 0.34 \text{ ksf}$$

m= 1.2

Wll+IM = Wlltruck(1+IM) *m =0.34(1+0.12) *1.2 = 0.46 ksf

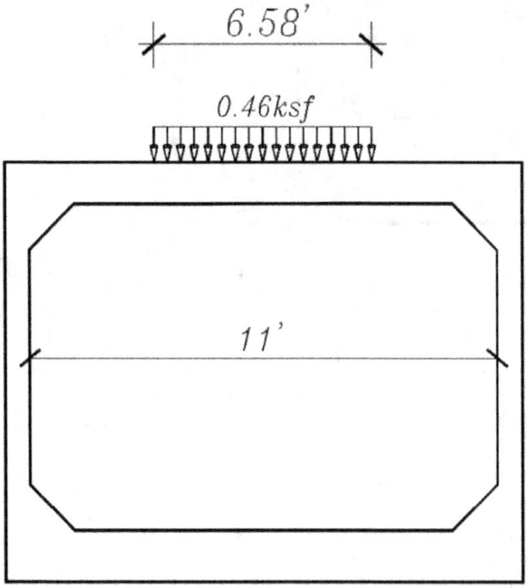

Figure 55. Example 7. Truck Live load

<u>For Tandem</u>:
As per AASHTO LRFD Article **3.6.1.2.6b**:
For the patch dimension perpendicular to movement direction:
Same as the Truck = 14.08 ft.

For the patch dimension parallel to movement direction:
Assume without Interaction: Lt+Sa+LLDF(H)
= 10/12 + 4 + (1.15*5) = 10.58 ft.

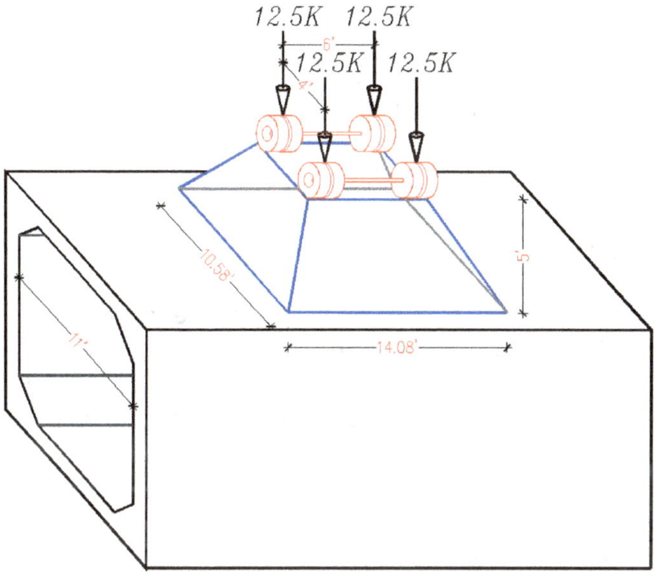

Figure 56. Example 7. Isometric for Tandem Live load

Live load Magnitude:

$$Wll= \frac{\text{Axle load}}{\text{Distribution Area}} = \frac{50}{14.08*10.58} = 0.33 \text{ ksf}$$

m= 1.2

Wll+IM = Wlltandem(1+IM) *m =0.33(1+0.12) *1.2 = 0.44 ksf

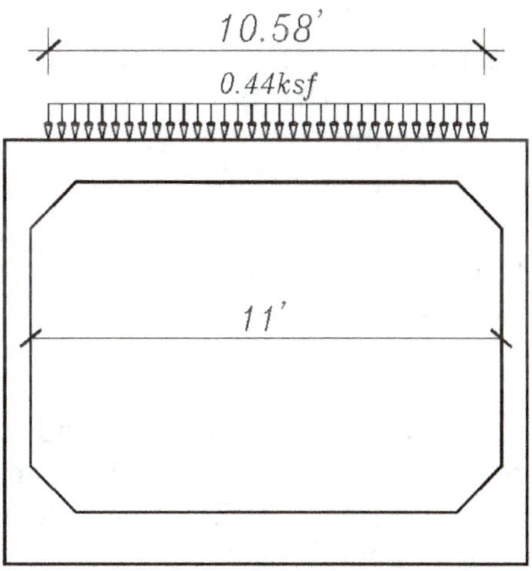

Figure 57. Example 7. Tandem Live load

Conclusion:

The tandem load value seems greater than truck. Which means that the tandem case will govern.

3.2.1.2.2 Traffic perpendicular to span

Same as 2.2.1.1.2

Note: When the traffic travels primarily perpendicular to the span, the patch dimension parallel to the direction of vehicle movement will be calculated according to AASHTO LRFD Article **3.6.1.2.6** and Article **4.6.2.1** and the larger of the two dimensions will be used.

Example 8:
-Given:
The same box culvert in Example No.7
The skew angle equals 90°
-Required:
Determine the vehicular live load on the top slab of the box culvert
-Solution:
Since the culvert is single spanned and skewed, the live load shall be considered primarily perpendicular to span. And the greater of parallel and perpendicular to span loads shall be considered.
Dynamic Load Allowance, IM, (AASHTO LRFD Article **3.6.2.2**):
The fill thickness DE = 5 ft.
IM = 0.33(1.0 - 0.125*5) = 0.12
Multiple presence factor, m, (AASHTO LRFD Article **3.6.1.1.2):**
The maximum applicable lanes are two. Therefore, m= 1.2 (for one lane) and m=1(for two lanes)

The span does not exceed 15 feet. Therefore, the lane load is not included and Article **3.6.1.2.4** is not applied.

For Truck:
When the traffic travels primarily perpendicular to the span, the patch dimension parallel to the direction of vehicle movement will be calculated according to AASHTO LRFD Article **3.6.1.2.6** and Article **4.6.2.1** and the larger of the two dimensions will be used.

One Lane:
For the patch dimension parallel to movement direction as per Article **3.6.1.2.6**:
Assume without Interaction: Lt+LLDF(H)
= 10/12 + (1.15*5) = 6.58 ft.
Patch dimension parallel to movement direction as per Article **4.6.2.1** (+M to be used for single culvert)
= 2.17+0.55S
= 2.17+(0.55*11) = 8.22 ft. >6.58 ft.
Article 4.6.2.10.3 controls; use (8.22 ft.)

Patch dimension transverse to movement direction of vehicle for one lane:
Assume without Interaction: Wt+LLDF(H)+0.06(S)
= 20/12 + (1.15*5) + (0.06*11) = 8.07 ft. > 6 ft. Interaction is there
Patch dimensions= Wt+Sw+LLDF(H)+0.06(S)
= 20/12 + 6 + (1.15*5) + (0.06*11) = 14.07 ft.

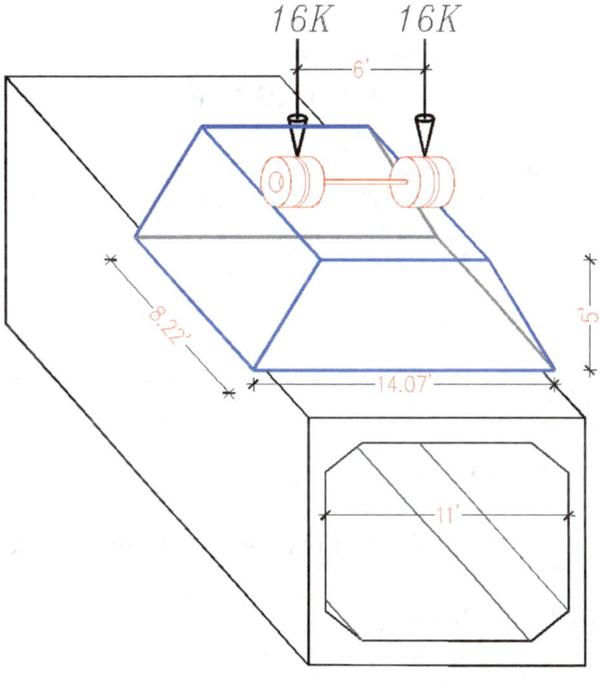

Figure 58. Example 8. Isometric for Truck Live load (One Lane)

Live load Magnitude:

$$Wll = \frac{\text{Axle load}}{\text{Distribution Area}} = \frac{32}{8.22*14.07} = 0.28 \text{ ksf}$$

m=1.2

Wll+IM = Wlltruck(1+IM) *m =0.28 (1+0.12) *1.2=0.38 ksf

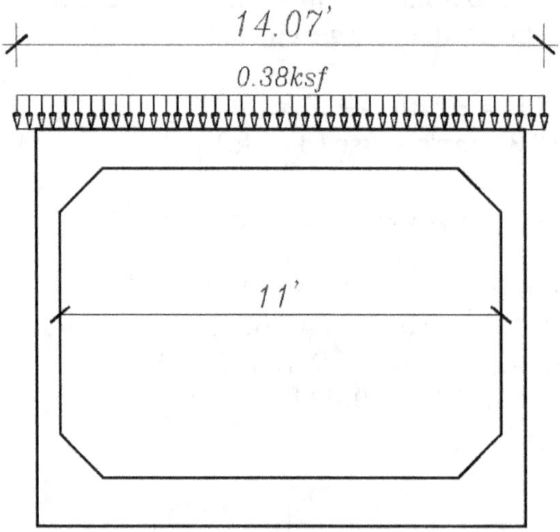

Figure 59. Example 8. Truck Load for One Lane

Since Truck load for one lane exceeded the width of culvert, the two lanes case will not govern. Therefore, no need to consider multiple lanes in this example.

For Tandem:

One lane:

Patch dimension parallel to movement direction (+M to be used for single culvert)

= 6.17+0.55S

= 6.17+(0.55*11) = 12.22 ft.

Patch dimension transverse to movement direction of vehicle for one lane:

Same as Truck = 14.07 ft.

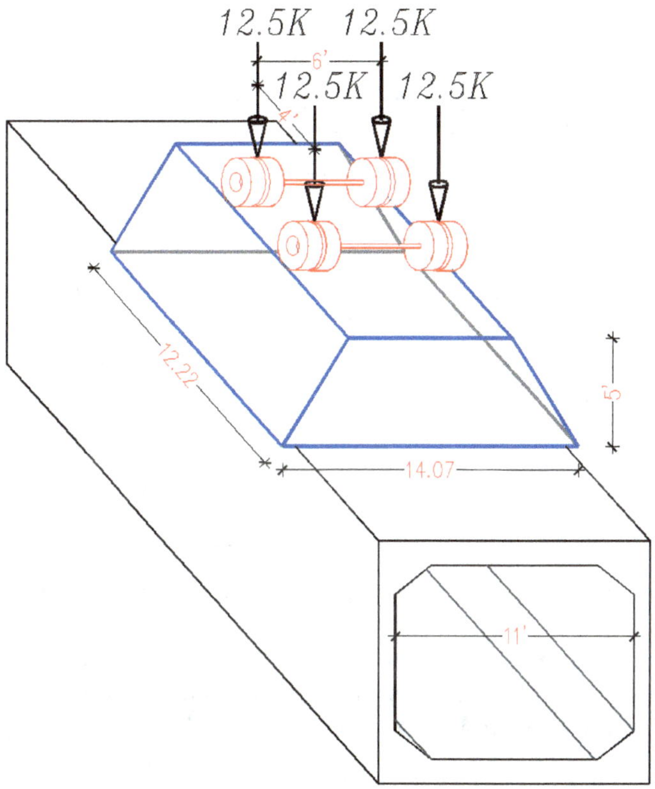

Figure 60. Example 8. Isometric for Tandem Load Distribution (One Lane)

Live load Magnitude:

$$\text{Wll}= \frac{\text{Axle load}}{\text{Distribution Area}} = \frac{50}{12.22*14.07} = 0.29 \text{ ksf}$$

m= 1.2

Wll+IM = Wlltandem(1+IM) *m =0.29(1+0.12) *1.2=0.39 ksf

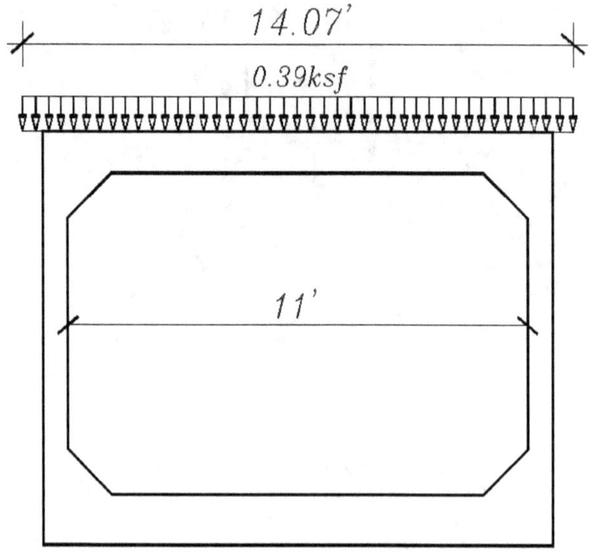

Figure 61. Example 8. Tandem Load for One Lane

Since Tandem load for one lane exceeded the width of culvert, the two lanes case will not govern. Therefore, no need to consider multiple lanes in this example.

Conclusion:

As per the calculations, the Tandem load will govern. However, the live load parallel to span (in the example No.7) shall be compared with this load and consider which is greater.

3.2.2 Live Load Surcharge (LS)

As per AASHTO LRFD Article **3.11.6.4**, a live load surcharge shall be applied where vehicular load is expected (LS is neglected when LL is neglected) to act on the surface of the backfill within a distance equal to one-half (0.5) the distance from top of pavement to bottom of the box culvert

The increase in horizontal pressure due to live load surcharge may be estimated as:

$\Delta p = k \gamma s \, heq$

Where:

Δp = constant horizontal earth pressure due to live load surcharge (ksf)

γs = total unit weight of the backfill, $\gamma soil$

k = coefficient of lateral earth pressure, assumed to be 0.5 for at-rest pressure

heq = equivalent height of soil for vehicular load from AASHTO LRFD **Table 3.11.6.4-1** or **Table 3.11.6.4-2** (ft)

Abutment Height	**Heq (ft)**
5	**4**
10	**3**
>20	**2**

AASHTO LRFD **Table 3.11.6.4-1**—Equivalent Height of Soil for Vehicular Loading on Abutments Perpendicular to Traffic

Retaining wall height (ft)	**heq (ft) Distance from wall backface to edge of traffic**	
	0 ft.	**1 ft. or further**
5	**5**	2
10	**3.5**	2
>20	**2**	2

AASHTO LRFD **Table 3.11.6.4-2**—Equivalent Height of Soil for Vehicular Loading on Retaining Walls Parallel to Traffic

It is recommended that, for culverts with skew ≤ 30 degrees, AASHTO LRFD **Table 3.11.6.4-1** Equivalent Height of Soil for Vehicular Loading on Abutments Perpendicular to Traffic might be used. For culverts with skew > 30 degrees, AASHTO LRFD **Table 3.11.6.4-2** Equivalent Height of Soil for Vehicular Loading on Retaining Walls Parallel to Traffic shall be used with the distance from the back face of the wall to the edge of traffic equal to 0.0 feet. Therefore, the two tables might be combined as follow:

Distance from Top of Pavement to Bottom of Bottom Slab (ft)	**heq (ft)**	
	Skew Angle	
	≤ 30°	**> 30°**
5	4	5
10	3	3.5
>20	2	2

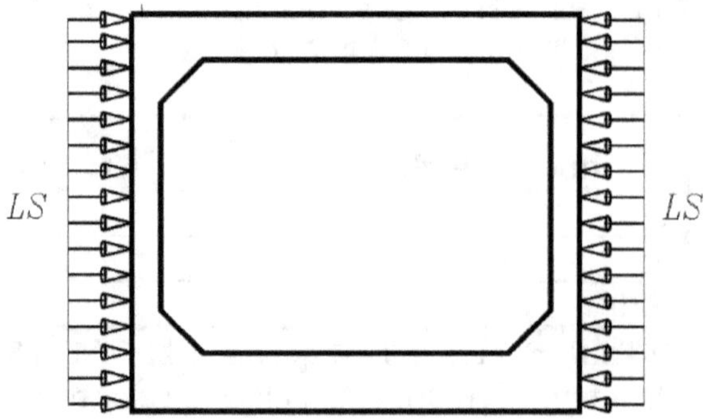

Figure 62. LS Load

Example 9:
-Given:
The following box culvert in figure No.63
The culvert is not skewed
$\gamma s = 120$ pcf.

-Required:
Determine the live load surcharge considering vehicular load is expected to act on the surface of the backfill within a distance equal to

one-half the distance from top of pavement to bottom of the box culvert.

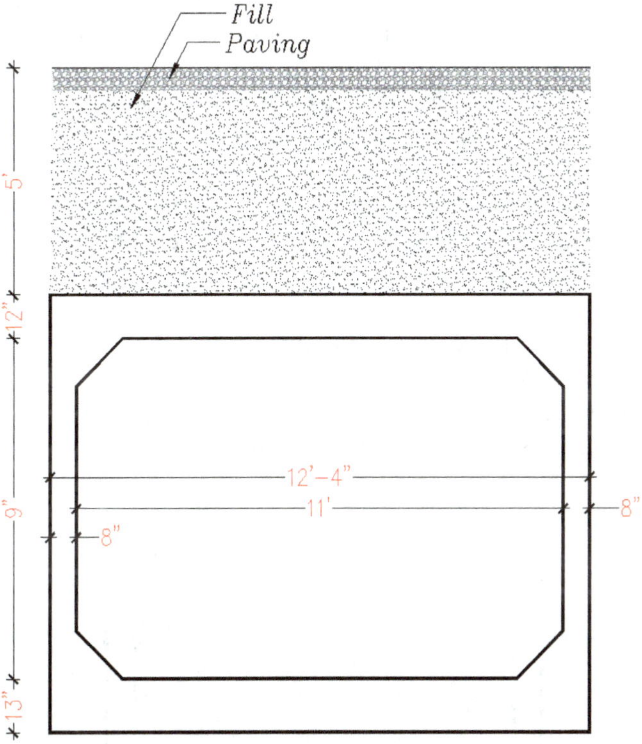

Figure 63. Example No.9

-Solution:

Distance form top of pavement to bottom of box culvert = 5+ (12/12) + 9 + (13/12) =16.08 ft.

Using the table for skew ≤ 30° and linear interpolation:

$heq = 2 + \frac{20-16.08}{20-10} * (3-2) = 2.39$ ft

$\Delta p = k\, \gamma s\, heq$

$\Delta p = 0.5*0.120*2.39 = 0.14$ ksf.

3.2.3 Water Load (WA)

As per AASHTO LRFD Article **3.7.1**, Water Pressure shall be calculated as the product of height of water above the point of consideration and the specific weight of water.
Designers need to consider load cases where the culvert is full of water as well as cases where the culvert is empty.

A simple hydrostatic distribution is used for the water load:
The lateral water pressure inside the culvert (at the bottom) is:
WA = γw * rise * width
Where:
WA= lateral water pressure at the bottom of the culvert (plf)
γw = specific weight of water (62.4 pcf)
Rise= as specified in **2.6**
Width= can be assumed as 1.0 linear feet.

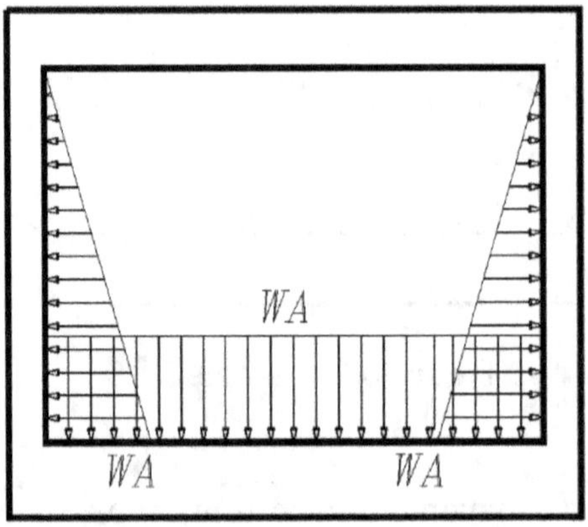

Figure 64. WA Load

Buoyancy: AASHTO LRFD Article **3.7.2**, states that, Buoyancy shall be considered to be an uplift force, taken as the sum of the vertical components of static pressures, as specified in Article **3.7.1**, acting on all components below design water level.

Example 10:

-Given:
The same box culvert in example No.9

-Required:
Lateral water pressure at the bottom of the culvert
-Solution:
WA = γw * rise * 1.0 ft. = (62.4/1000) *9.0 *1.0 = 0.56 klf.

4

Structural Analysis

Structural analysis was a previously complex process prior to the use of finite element method (FEM). The principle was the ultimate possible proximity of the structure to end up with a rough and simple analysis. However, simplification always entails a lack of precision in the structural analysis. With the advent of finite element, structural analysis has become easier, more accurate and faster. The Author will focus on contemporary systems and use them to access accurate and easy analysis. There are different ways to analyze the box culverts, and the approximate strip method will be explained which is one of the methods used to analyze culverts.

Traditional Method: Two-dimensional modeling is one of the methods used to analyze the box culvert, the structure will be assumed as rigid frame with one-foot strip, loads to be multiplied by 1.0 ft. to convert the units to klf, and the free body diagram (FBD) used for the analysis will represent the geometrical centerline of slabs and walls but mid thicknesses can be assumed to be easier for the designers.
The model is assumed to be externally supported by a pinned support on one end and a roller support on the other. However, for culverts keyed on rock, a pinned supports might be considered in both ends. The boundary conditions are:

1) Lateral and vertical displacements are restricted at the pinned end and,
2) Vertical displacements is restricted at the other (roller) end.

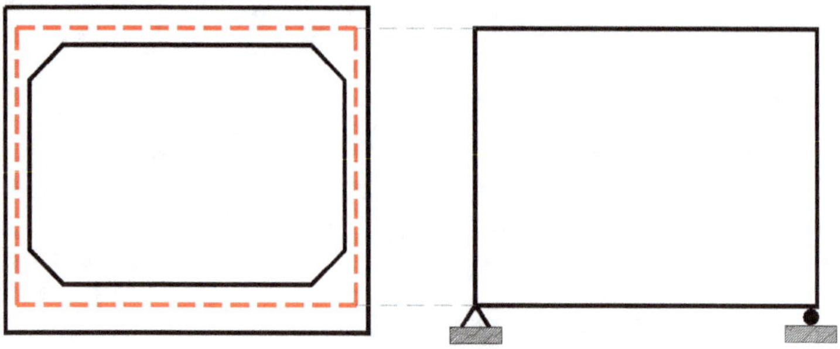

Figure 65. Free Body Diagram (FBD)

The model is always assumed to be in equilibrium so external reactions to loads applied to the structure were assumed to act equal and opposite. Therefore, DC, DW, EV, WA (vertical) and live load shall be applied in the bottom direction distributed on the whole bottom length. The bottom loads to be calculated as follow (FBD is in red in the center of culvert walls and slabs):

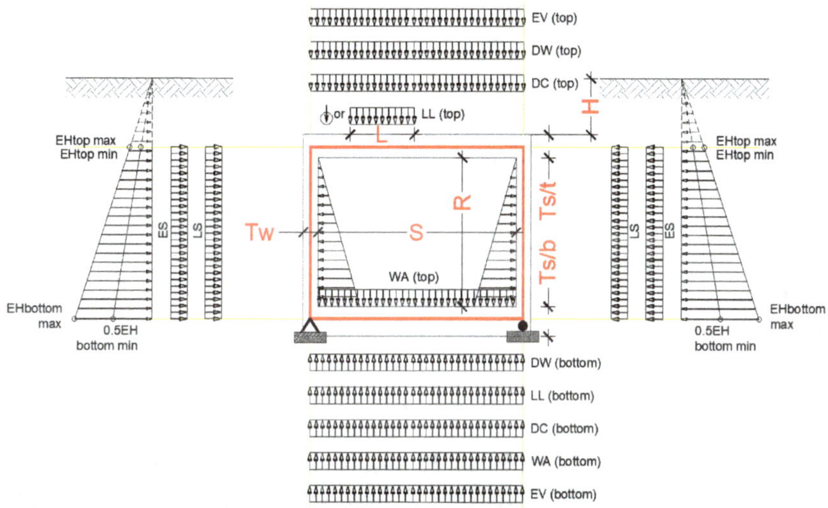

Figure 66. Structural Model Loads (method 1)

<u>Loads calculation:</u>

(DC):

DCtop distributed on the top slab (klf.) = γ concrete *Ts/t *1 ft.

Calculate the distributed DCbottom as follow:

DCtop (kips) = γ concrete *Ts/t *1 ft. *(S+Tw)

DCwall (kips) = γ concrete *Tw *1 ft. *(R+0.5Ts/t+0.5Ts/b)

DChaunch (kips, if any) = 0.5 *haunch width *haunch depth * γ concrete*1 ft.

Considering that bottom slab's self-weight will be transferred directly to soil:

DCbottom (klf.) = (DCtop + 2DCwall + 4DChaunch) / (S+Tw)

(DW):

DWtop = as calculated in 3.1.2.

DWbottom = as calculated in 3.1.2. *1 ft

(WA):

Assume that the culvert is flowing full

WAtop for both wall and base = γ water *R *1 ft

WAbottom = (WAtop*S) / (S+Tw)

(LL):

LLtop = as calculated in 3.2.1. *1 ft.

LLbottom = (LLtop*L) / (S+Tw)

(EH):

At centerline & H does not include paving thickness.

EHtop max. = γ soil *(H+0.5Ts/t) *ko *1 ft

EHtop min. = 0.5 *γ soil *(H+0.5Ts/t) *ko *1 ft

EHbottom max. = γ soil *(H+Ts/t+R+0.5Ts/b) *ko *1 ft

EHbottom min. = 0.5 * γ soil *(H+Ts/t+R+0.5Ts/b) *ko *1 ft

(EV):

EVtop = as calculated in 3.1.5.

EVbottom = as calculated in 3.1.5. *1 ft

(ES):

ES = as calculated in 3.1.3. *1 ft

(LS):

LS = as calculated in 3.2.2. *1 ft

Recommended Method

The manual structural analysis depends on the simplification of the structure to facilitate the structural analysis in one of the previously used methods, such as moment distribution, slope deflection and three moment equation method or analyzing through simplified matrices which might be solved manually. However, with the use of the finite element method (FEM), the software solves a huge number of complex matrices in a very short time and with high accuracy which never been achieved by manual methods. Therefore, FEM has become one of the most important tools for the structural engineer, and accordingly, this method will be used in this manual to obtain the best results from the author's point of view, with different attempts to explain the different methods of analysis.

There are different ways to model the box culvert structure using FEM. The same way explained previously might be modeled in the software with the same conditions. But the author recommends making a realistic model as per the actual conditions by modeling the box culvert as frame or shell elements, add bottom springs to express the soil behavior and apply the actual loads as per the following figure:

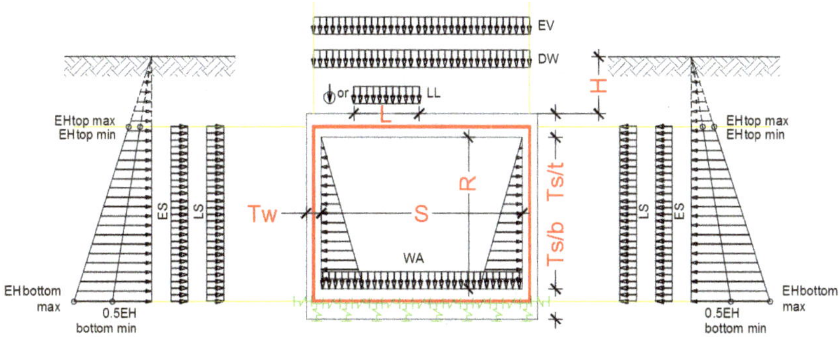

Figure 67. Structural Model Loads (method 2)

For the multi cell box culverts, the software will be faster and much more accurate to analyze the structure by making multiple loading trials or apply moving loads as will be explained later in this manual. For the purpose of showing the difference between method 1(traditional method) & method 2(recommended by the Author), the following simple single span box culvert has been modeled in a finite element software using the two methods. This culvert was used in the previous load calculation examples.

Example 11:

γ concrete = 150 pcf. & fc'= 4 ksi
γ soil = 120 pcf. & qa= 2 ksf.
γ water = 62.4 pcf.
γ(paving)= 150 pcf. & Pavement Thickness= 12"
Future Wearing Surface (FWS)= 50 psf

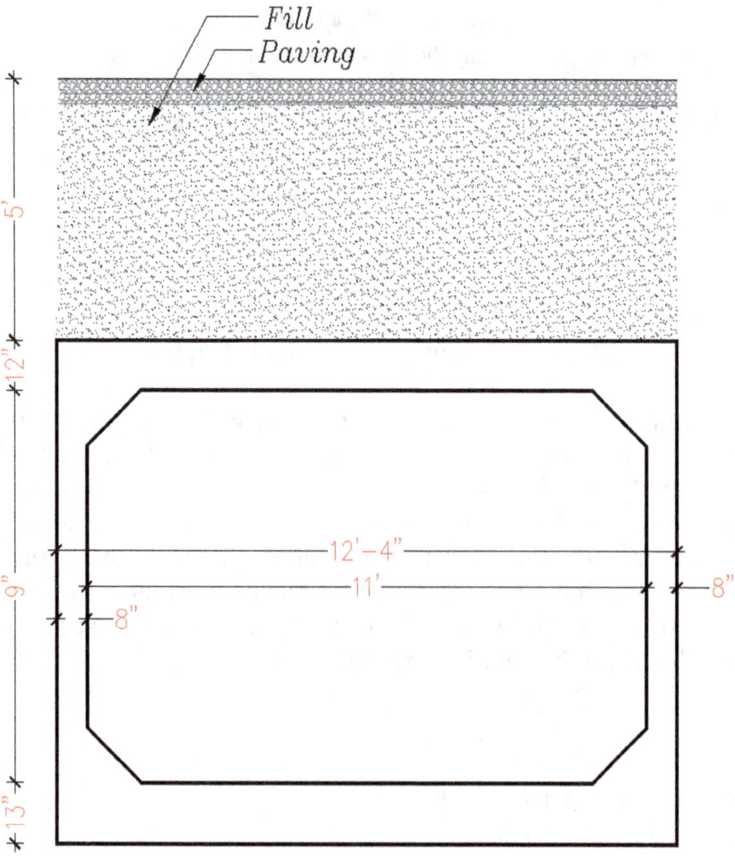

Figure 68. Box Culvert's Geometry

Calculating Loads:

The loads will be calculated as per figures 66 & 67 as follow:

(DC):

DCtop distributed on the top slab (klf.) = γ concrete *Ts/t *1 ft.
=0.15*1.0*1.0 = 0.15 klf.
Calculate the distributed DCbottom as follow:
DCtop = γ concrete *Ts/t *1 ft. *(S+Tw)
= 0.15*1.0*1.0 *(11+(8/12)) = 1.75 kips
DCwall = γ concrete *Tw *1 ft. *(R+0.5Ts/t+0.5Ts/b)
= 0.15 *(8/12) *1.0 *(9+0.5+(13/(12*2)) = 1.0 kip
Assume haunch width = depth = 1.0 ft.
DChaunch = 0.5 *haunch width *haunch depth * γ concrete*1 ft.

= 0.5 *1.0 *1.0 *0.15 *1.0 = 0.075 kips

Considering that bottom slab's self-weight will be transferred directly to soil:

DCbottom = (DCtop + 2DCwall + 4DChaunch) / (S+Tw)

= (1.75 +(2*1.0) +(4*0.075)) / (11+(8/12)) = 0.35 klf.

(DW):

Since there is filling above the culvert, DW might be neglected but it is mentioned in the given data. Therefore, DW will be calculated as follow:

DWtop = as calculated in 3.1.2.

DWbottom = as calculated in 3.1.2. *1 ft

DW = $\frac{T\ paving * \gamma(paving)}{12} + FWS + Utilities\ load$

DWtop & bottom= $\frac{12*0.15}{12} + 0.050 + 0 = 0.2$ klf

(WA):

Assume that the culvert is flowing full

WAtop for both wall and base = γ water *R *1 ft = (62.4/1000) *9 *1.0 = 0.56 klf.

WAbottom = (WAtop*S) / (S+Tw)

= (0.56*11) / (11+(8/12)) = 0.53 klf.

(LL):

LLtop = as calculated in Example 7, the live load is as follow:

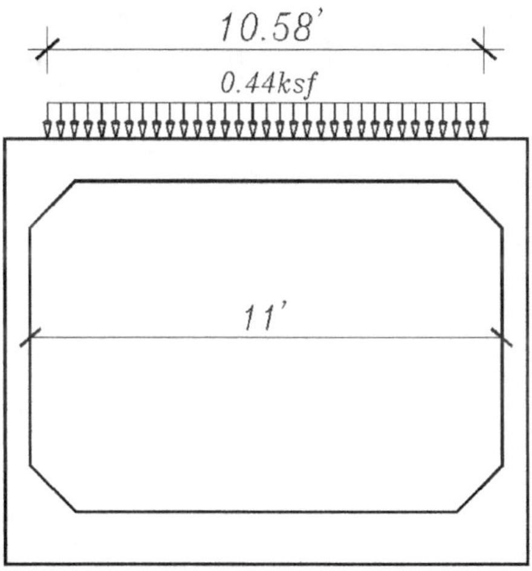

LLbottom = (LLtop*L) / (S+Tw)

= (0.44*10.58) / (11+(8/12)) = 0.40 klf.

(EH):
(At centerline)
EHtop max. = γ soil *(H+0.5Ts/t) *ko *1 ft
= 0.12 *(4+ (0.5*1.0) *0.5 * 1ft = 0.27 klf.
EHtop min. = 0.5 *γ soil *(H+0.5Ts/t) *ko *1 ft = 0.135 klf.
EHbottom max. = γ soil *(H+Ts/t+R+0.5Ts/b) *ko *1 ft
= 0.12*(4+1.0+9+(13/12*2)) *0.5 * 1ft = 0.87 klf.
EHbottom min. = 0.5 * γ soil *(H+Ts/t+R+0.5Ts/b) *ko *1 ft = 0.44 klf.
(EV):
As per Example No.4, EVtop = 6.27/12.33 = 0.51 ksf.
EVbottom = EVtop *1 ft = 0.51 klf.
(ES):
Since DW is considered: Δp = ks*qs *1 ft
Δp = 0.5*0.2*1 = 0.10 ksf.
(LS):
As per Example No.9, LS = 0.14 ksf.
LS = 0.14 *1 ft = 0.14 ksf.

Structural Finite Element Models:

SAP2000 software has been used for structural analysis. The load combinations for strength I (explained in load factors and load combinations, in structural design chapter) were used. The following table shows the comparison between the two models:

Point of Comparison	Model 1	Model 2
Model FBD		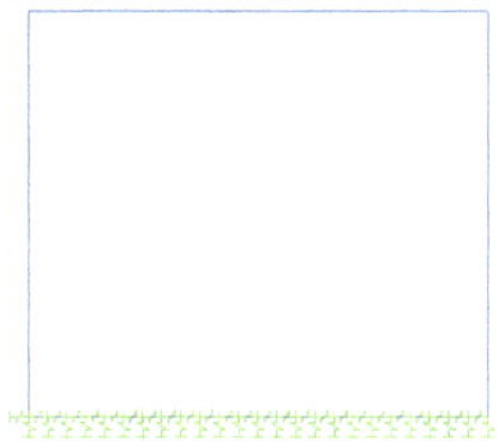
Method used	Method 1	Method 2
Support	Real Supports	X, Y &Z Springs
Material properties	Material properties are not assigned to the software	Material properties are assigned
Sections	Sections are not assigned to software	Sections assigned as per geometry of structure
Loads	-Assigned on the top and bottom. See figure No.66 -DC load is assigned manually	-On the top only. See figure No.67 -DC load is calculated automatically by software

Analysis Results:

The aim of doing this exercise is to show the results of the analysis for both of methods 1&2. The results differ between the two methods as follows:

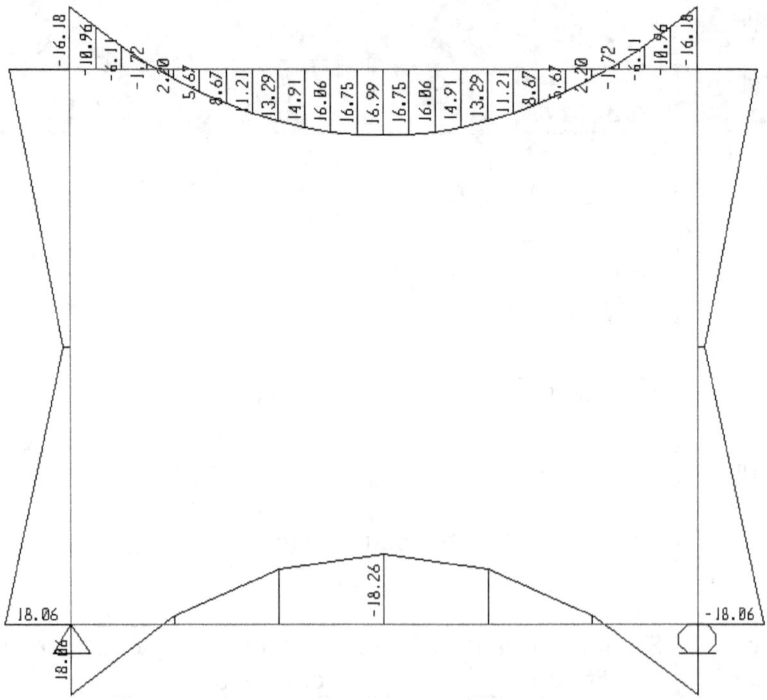

Figure 69. B.M.D. Strength I.a Combination (method 1)

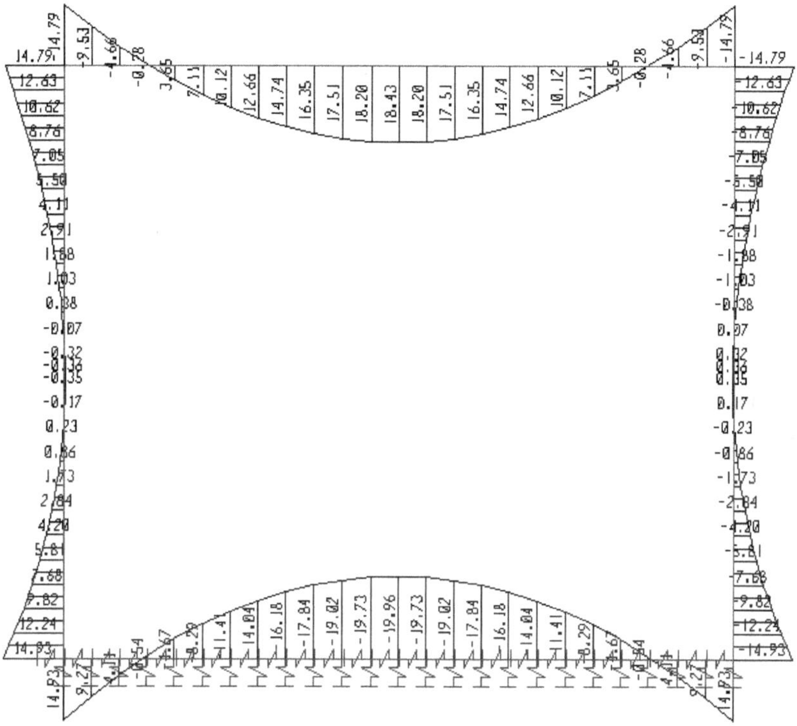

Figure 70. B.M.D. Strength I.a Combination (method 2)

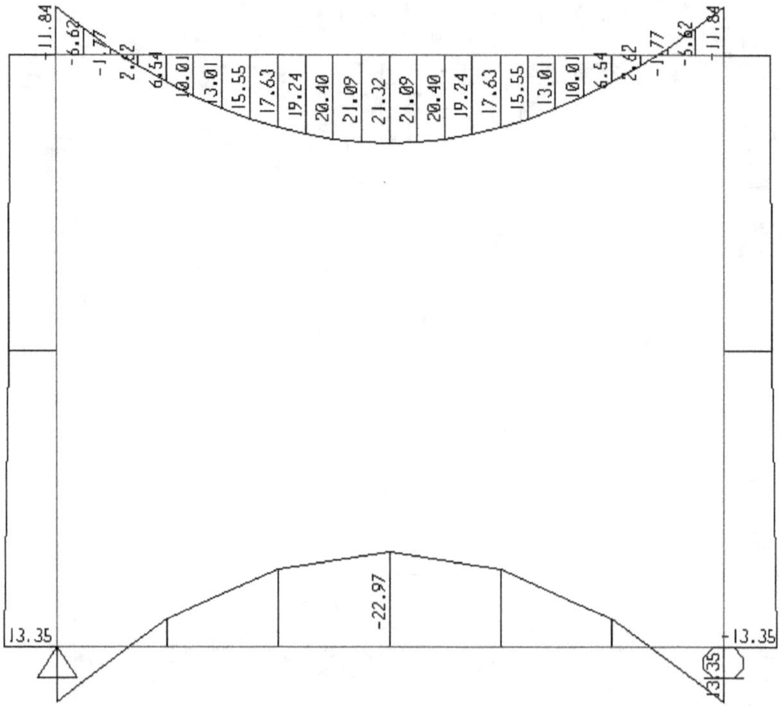

Figure 71. B.M.D. Strength I.b Combination (method 1)

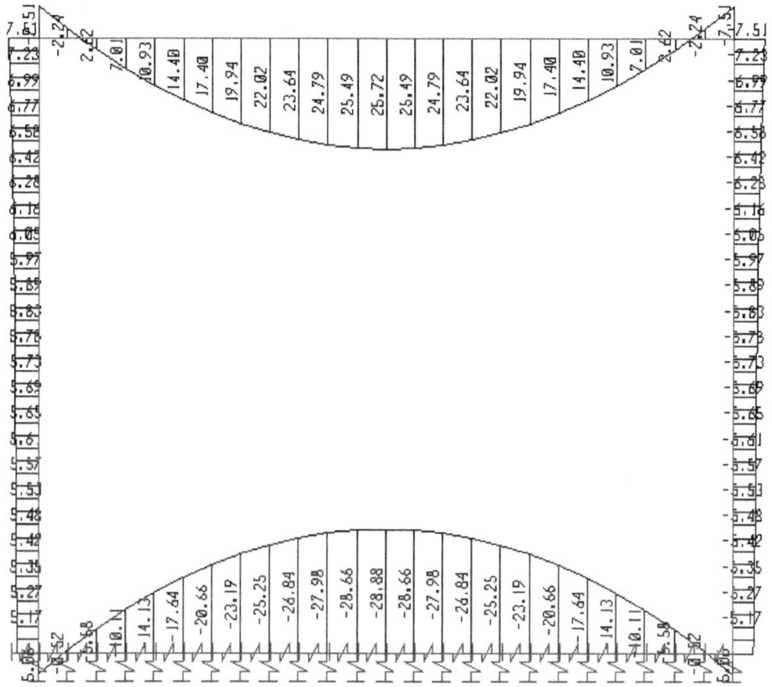

Figure 72. B.M.D. Strength I.b Combination (method 2)

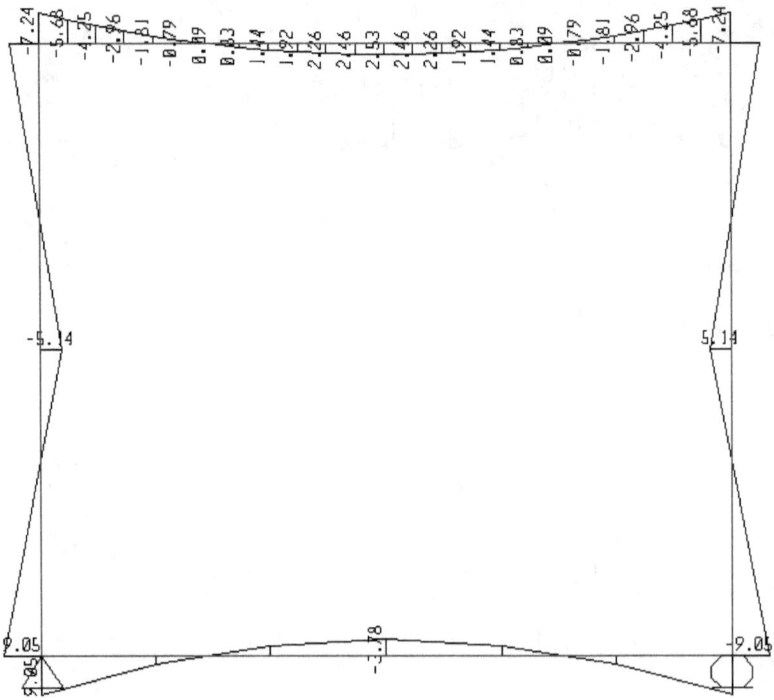

Figure 73. B.M.D. Strength I.c Combination (method 1)

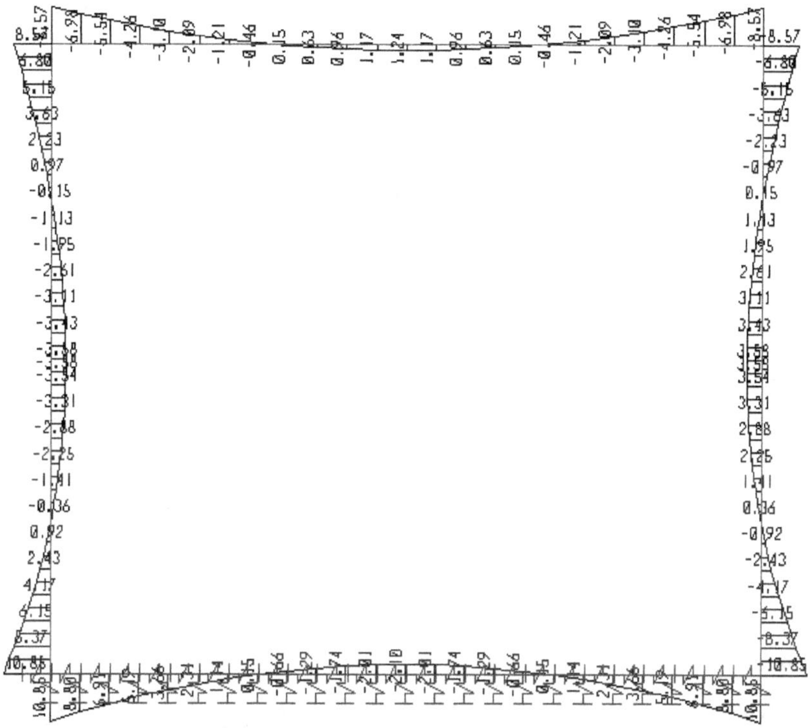

Figure 74. B.M.D. Strength I.c Combination (method 2)

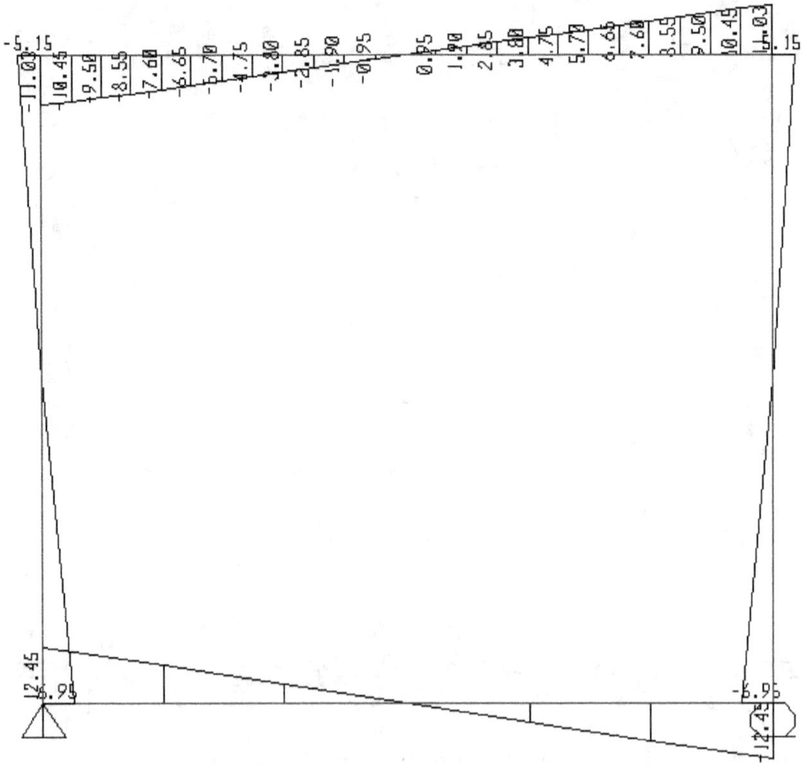

Figure 75. S.F.D. Strength I.a Combination (method 1)

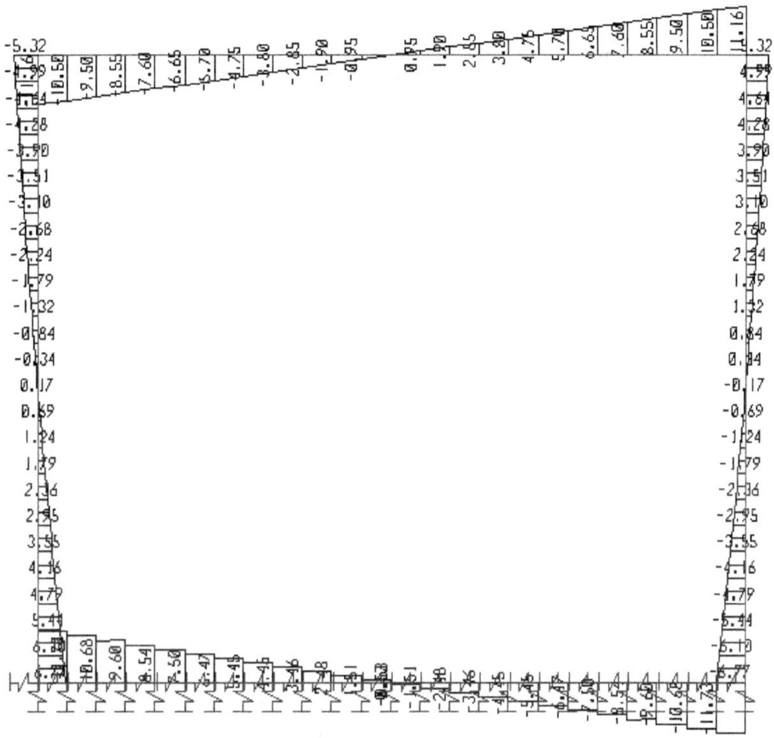

Figure 76. S.F.D. Strength I.a Combination (method 2)

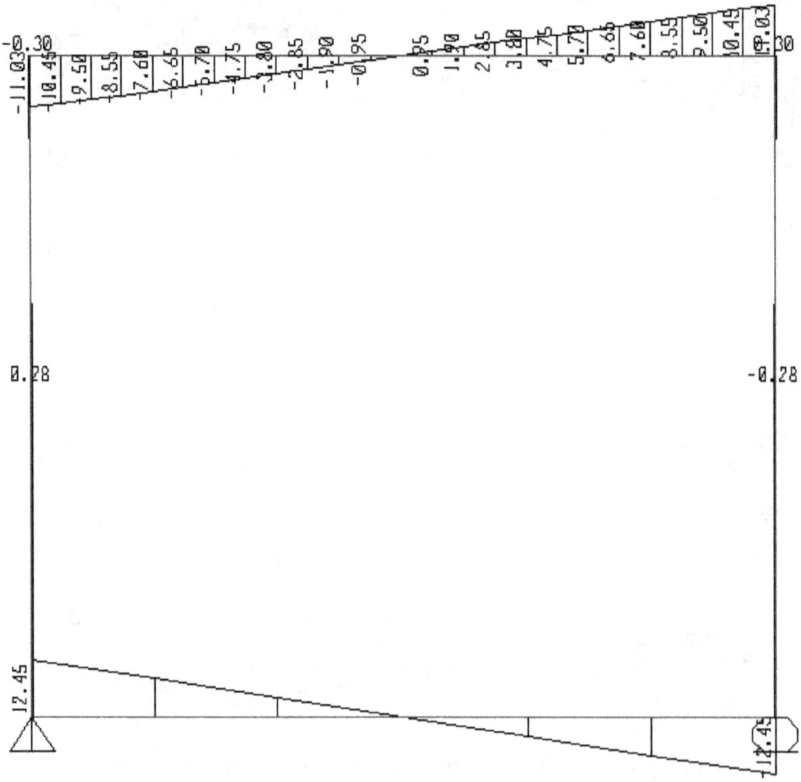

Figure 77. S.F.D. Strength I.b Combination (method 1)

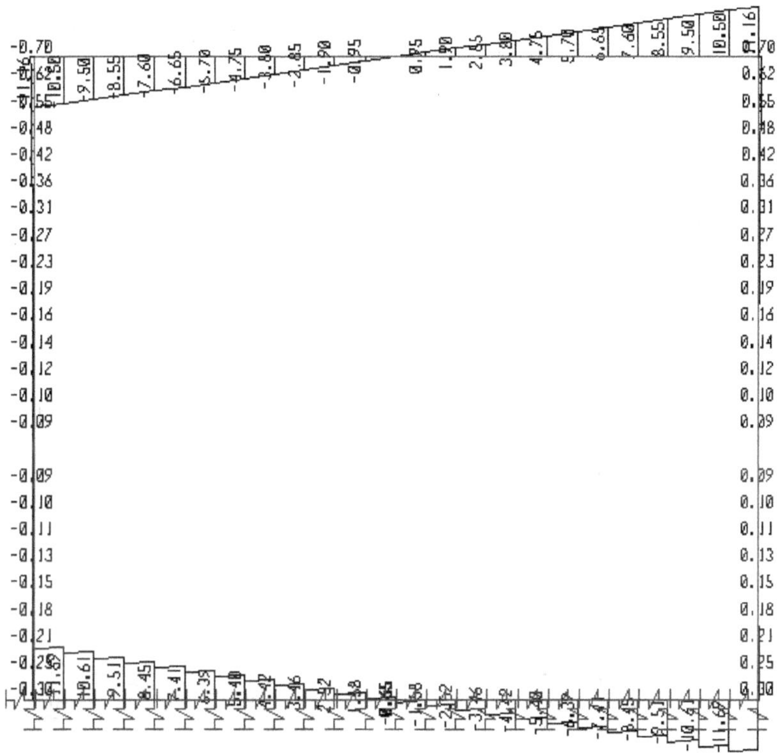

Figure 78. S.F.D. Strength I.b Combination (method 2)

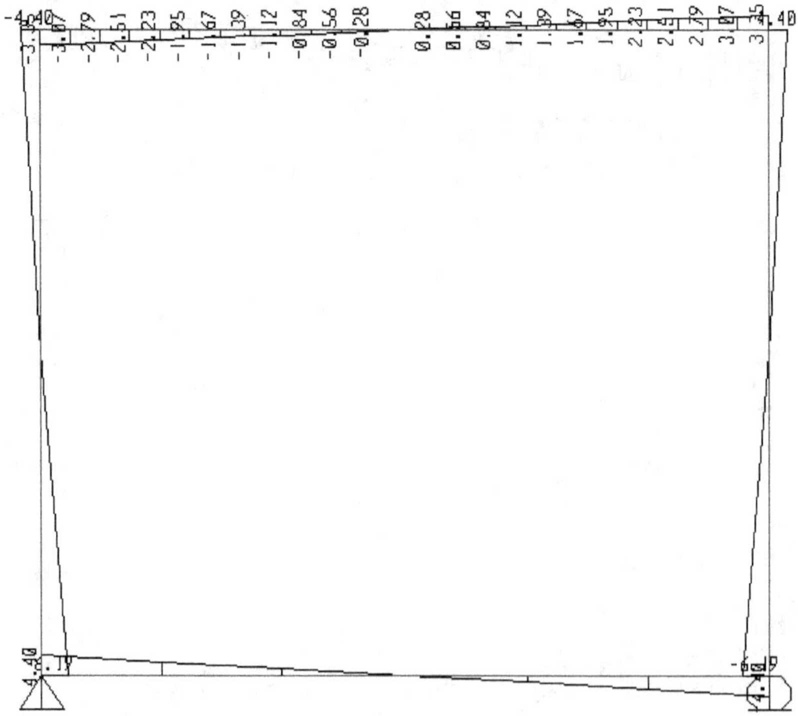

Figure 79. S.F.D. Strength I.c Combination (method 1)

Figure 80. S.F.D. Strength I.c Combination (method 2)

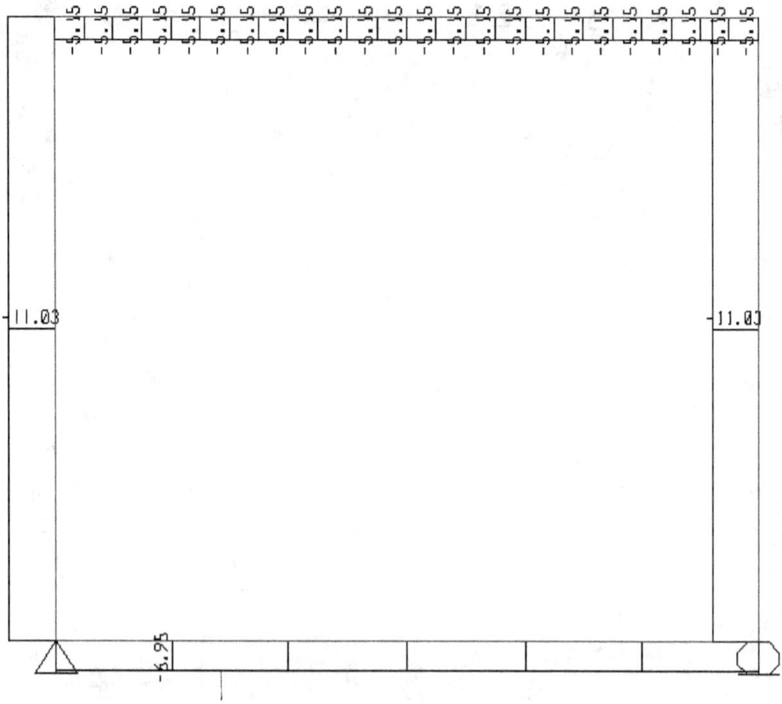

Figure 81. N.F.D. Strength I.a Combination (method 1)

Figure 82. N.F.D. Strength I.a Combination (method 2)

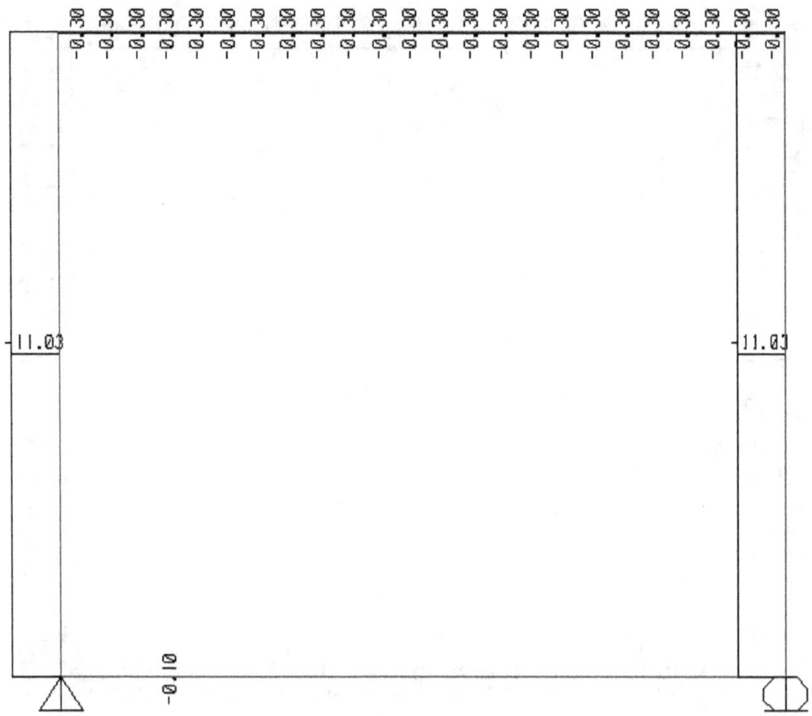

Figure 83. N.F.D. Strength I.b Combination (method 1)

Figure 84. N.F.D. Strength I.b Combination (method 2)

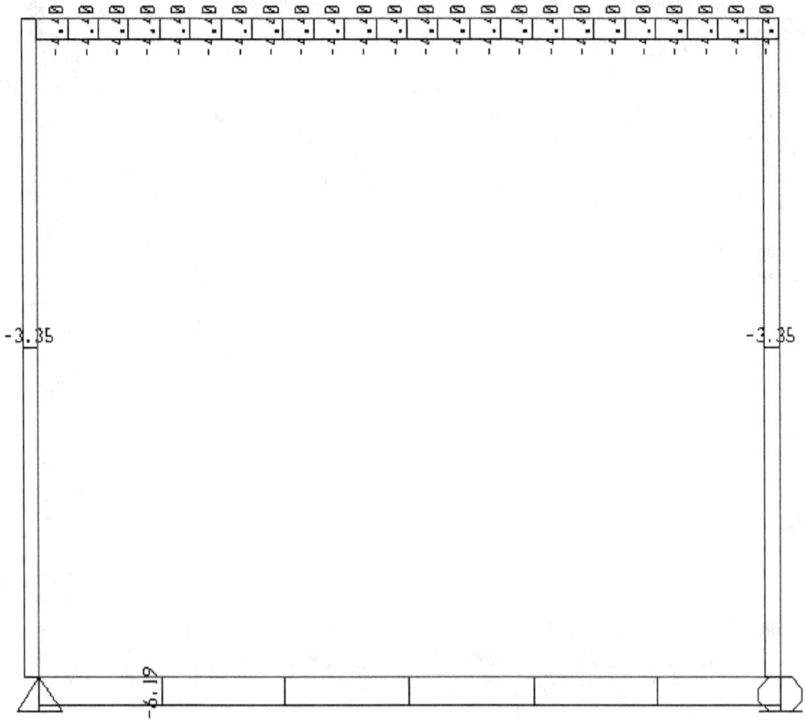

Figure 85. N.F.D. Strength I.c Combination (method 1)

Figure 86. N.F.D. Strength I.c Combination (method 2)

Conclusion of Example 11:

Despite there are some slightly different straining actions on the critical sections (location of critical sections are shown in the structural design chapter) between the two methods but the previous study shows that the two methods are close. However, the second method (method 2) is closer to the behavior of the real structure, and its results are most accurate structurally, as it is evidence of its suitability for the analysis of complex culverts and the advantages of this method are as follows:

1) Express the actual structural behavior as per the real situation
2) The structural stiffness is involved which leads to accurate analysis
3) A practical representation of the behavior of the soil, obtaining the actual forms of settlement and structure/soil relative stiffness. Furthermore, the possibility of checking the soil allowable stresses which is difficult to be done in the method 1.
4) Results actual deformation which is hard to be achieved using method 1
5) The ability to perform the precise serviceability and stability checks for the structure
6) Achieving structural integrity, the possibility of studying the structure as one unit and considering the effect of the structural connection
7) The ability to perform an accurate behavioral analysis in lieu of costly laboratory testing
8) In addition to the analysis, the ability to perform design and checking using the software itself if the program supports the used code which will save a lot of time and efforts.

Therefore, the author is recommending to use method 2. Moreover, as mentioned previously, the structural engineer can use this method with different ways like two/three-dimensional analysis, frame/shell elements and apply the precise vehicular live loads as actual moving loads. Furthermore, the designer can do many trials to ensure the optimum analysis and to obtain the safest economical design in shorter time. Nevertheless, there are conditions for using any software:

1) The user's experience and knowledge about the structural engineering and structure's behavior to be able to expect the results and to make sure the outputs are reasonable as the software might be inaccurate due to any technical issue, the user shall be able to evaluate the outputs
2) The user's knowledge about the software and his ability to direct the software to achieve the desired purpose
3) Ensure using a trustable software which was used in some famous projects or has been tried and tested by licensed/experienced engineers
4) Testing the software by modeling a simple assignment like simply supported beam prior to using it for the analysis or design to ensure the validity of the software and to avoid making mistakes as a result of using a corrupted program due to viruses or installing/activation problems.

Note:
Some designers may model the culvert as full 3D model using shell elements for the most precise analysis to take all culvert components in consideration including the wing walls, headers and apron slabs. Furthermore, the longitudinal behavior of the culvert will be taken in consideration as well. In this case, the vehicular live loads will be applied onto lanes like bridges. However, such complicated and time-consuming method will not give touchable differences than the simple method using linear feet or certain length of the culvert as a frame or shell element which is the normal practice for practical design. The designer shall choose the method and to apply it correctly to get the right outputs and the accurate design.

Exploring the Worst-Case Scenario Due to Vehicular Live Load Using FEM

Using manual analysis, there is a difficulty in identifying the largest effect of moving loads as a result of the vehicles crossing the top of the culverts. In order to calculate the maximum moments and forces, different load cases must be used, and the loading location shall be changed several times to identify the most critical case of the vehicular live load which is difficult. Therefore, create influence lines to determine the location for maximum moments and forces which became easy and fast using finite element method.

In the case of a large thickness backfill, there is a high possibility of overlapping loads, and thus it is easy to represent them statically on the culvert's top slab. However, in the case of shallow installation, there is a possibility of the presence of separate axles load with different values, and it remains necessary to analyze the moving load using FEM software. In the following example No.12; SAP2000 is the tool for performing the analysis to show how the FEM helps to study the moving load effect.

Example 12:

-Given:

Five cells box culvert.

Culvert is not skewed

H = 1'6"

S =11 ft.

R = 9 ft.

T (wall) = 8 in.

T (top slab) = 1.0 ft.

T (bottom slab) = 13 in.

γ concrete = 150 pcf. & fc'= 4 ksi

γ soil = 120 pcf. & qa= 2 ksf.

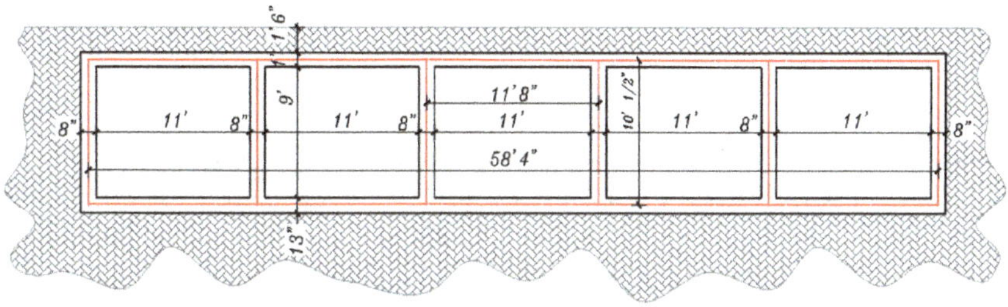

Figure 87. Example 12. Five Cells Box Culvert Dimensions

-Required:
Analysis of vehicular live load on the top slab

-Solution:

Calculation of live load value and distribution area:

Since the culvert is not skewed, the live load shall be considered parallel to span.
Dynamic Load Allowance, IM, (AASHTO LRFD Article **3.6.2.2**):
The fill thickness DE = 1.5 ft.
IM = 0.33(1.0 - 0.125*1.5) = 0.268
Multiple presence factor, m, (AASHTO LRFD Article **3.6.1.1.2):**
For traffic traveling parallel to the span, consider a single loaded lane with m= 1.2
The span does not exceed is less than 15 feet. Therefore, the lane load is not included.

<u>For Truck</u>
Live load distribution area:
Live load distribution length perpendicular to the span:
E = (96 + 1.44(S)) = (96 + 1.44(11)) = 111.84 in = 9.32 ft.
Live load distribution length parallel to the span:
Espan = (LT + LLDF (H)) = (10+1.15(1.5*12)) = 30.7 in = 2.56 ft.
Check of axle interaction:
Clear distance between axles= 14-2.56= 11.44' (Positive number, thus: No interaction)

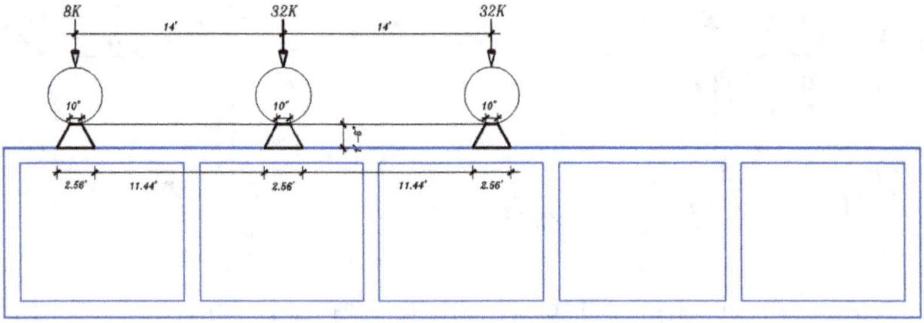

Figure 88. Example 12. Truck Load Distribution in Axle Direction

According to culvert dimensions, all axles can be accommodated on top slab

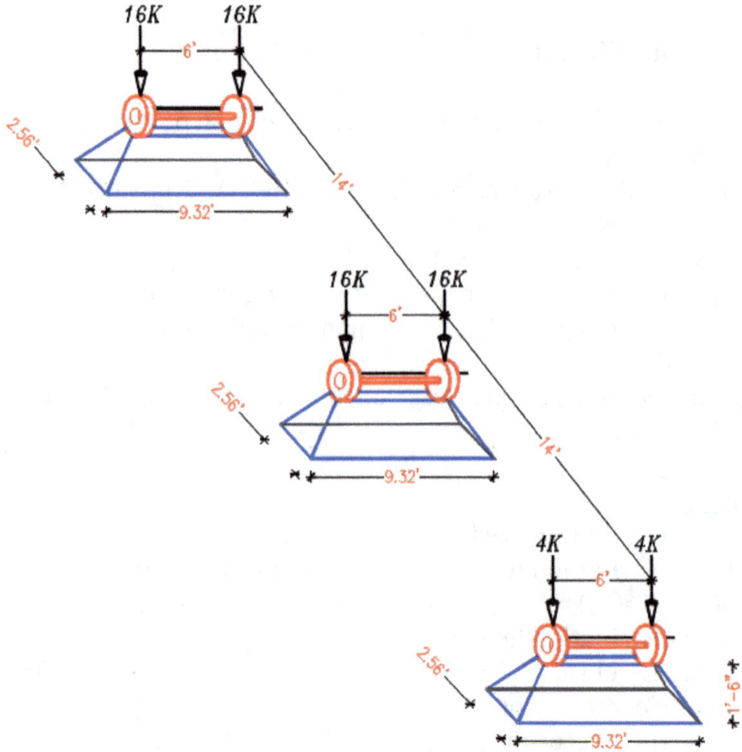

Figure 89. Example 12. Isometric for Truck Live Load Distribution

Live load Magnitude:
For front axle:

$$\text{Wll}= \frac{\text{Axle load}}{\text{Distribution Area}} = \frac{8}{9.32*2.56} = 0.33 \text{ ksf}$$

Wll+IM = Wlltruck(1+IM) *m =0.33(1+0.268) *1.2=0.50 ksf
For rear axles:

$$\text{Wll}= \frac{\text{Axle load}}{\text{Distribution Area}} = \frac{32}{9.32*2.56} = 1.34 \text{ ksf}$$

Wll+IM = Wlltruck(1+IM) *m =1.34(1+0.268) *1.2=2.04 ksf
For structural analysis purpose using the equivalent strip method, the distributed live load shall be converted to an equivalent concentrated load to be applied in the software as axle load to introduce the moving load as follow:
(LL+IM) in ksf. * (Live load distribution length parallel to the span * 1.0 ft.)
For front axle:
LL for SAP2000 model= 0.5*2.56*1.0 = 1.28 kips
For rear axles:
LL for SAP2000 model= 2.04*2.56*1.0 = 5.22 kips

<u>For Tandem</u>
The separate axles will give better moving load distribution. However, assume that the two axles will overlap as a general case for tandem which will result to a conservative design.
Live load distribution area:
Live load distribution length perpendicular to the span:
E= Same as Truck = 9.32 ft.
Live load distribution length parallel to the span:
Espan = Same as Truck + 4'= 2.56+4= 6.56 ft.

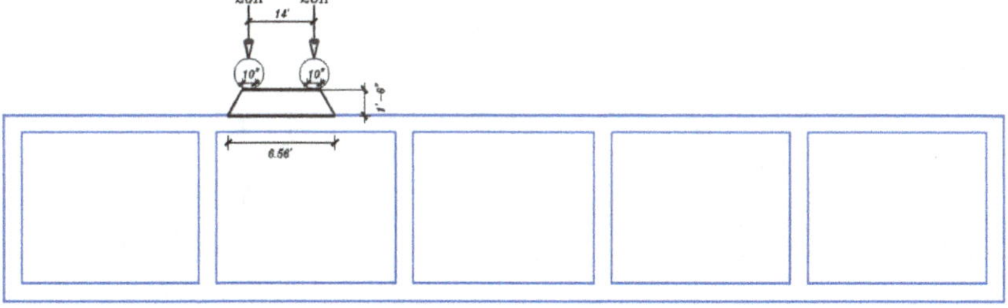

Figure 90. Example 12. Tandem Load Distribution in Axle Direction

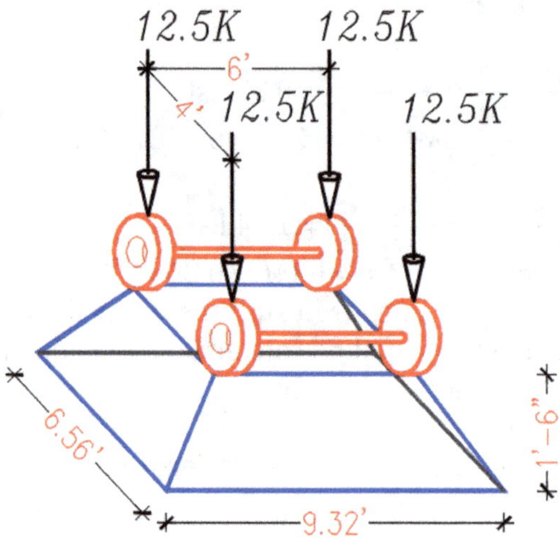

Figure 91. Example 12. Isometric for Tandem Live Load Distribution

Live load Magnitude:

$$Wll = \frac{\text{Axle load}}{\text{Distribution Area}} = \frac{50}{9.32*6.56} = 0.82 \text{ ksf}$$

Wll+IM = Wlltandem(1+IM) *m =0.82(1+0.268) *1.2=1.25 ksf

LL for SAP2000 model= 1.25*6.56*1.0 = 8.2 kips

Structural model in SAP2000:

1) Define the axes as per the red lines in figure No. 92

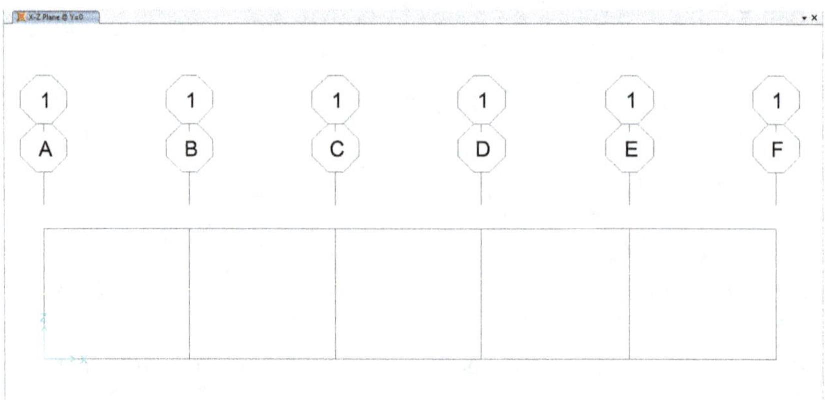

Figure 92. Example 12. Define Axes

2) Draw frame elements in the centerline of slabs and walls

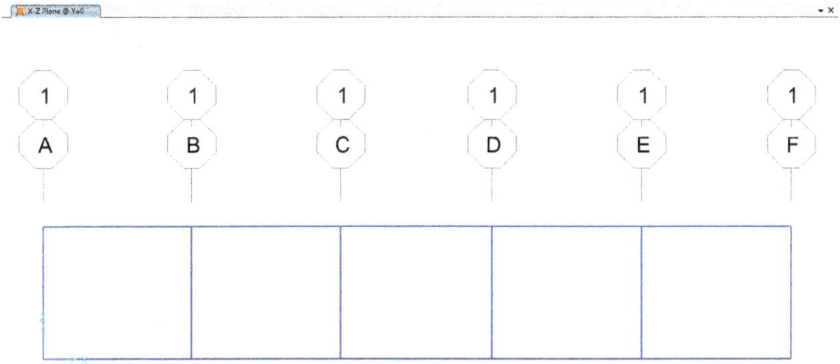

Figure 93. Example 12. Define Frame Elements

3) Define section's material

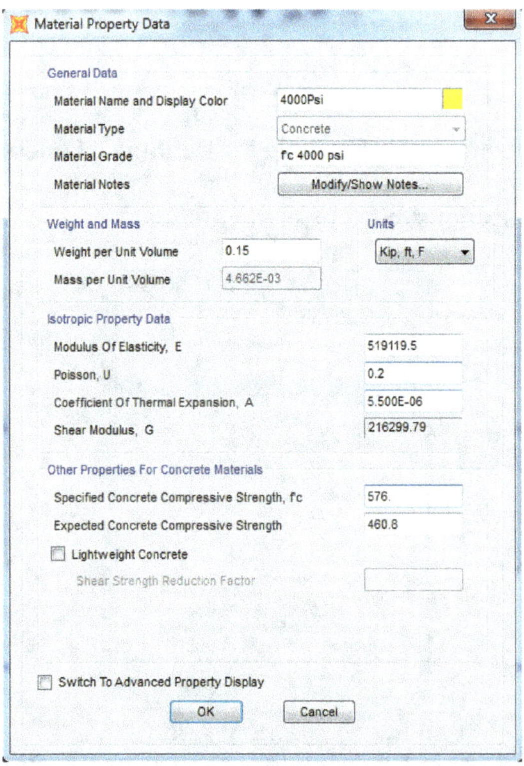

Figure 94. Example 12. Define Concrete Material

4) Define Sections as per structure's geometry

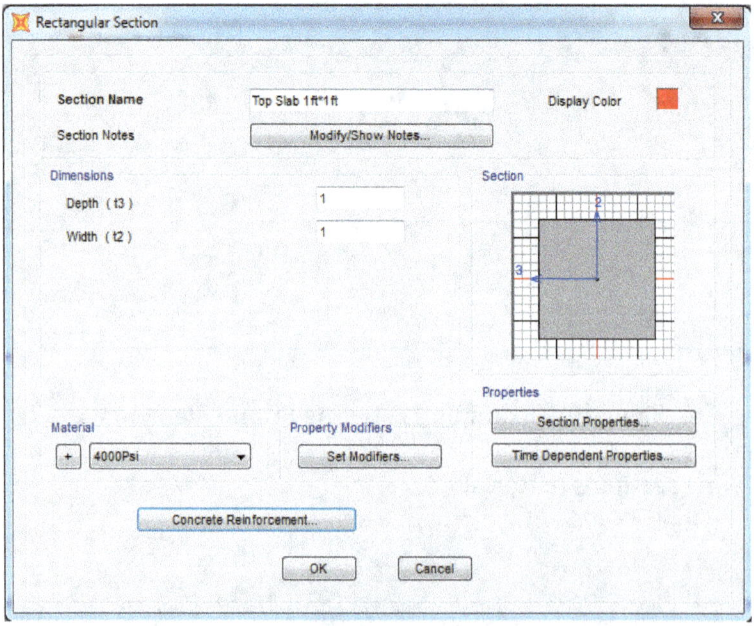

Figure 95. Example 12. Example for Defining a Concrete Section

5) Assign the sections to frame elements

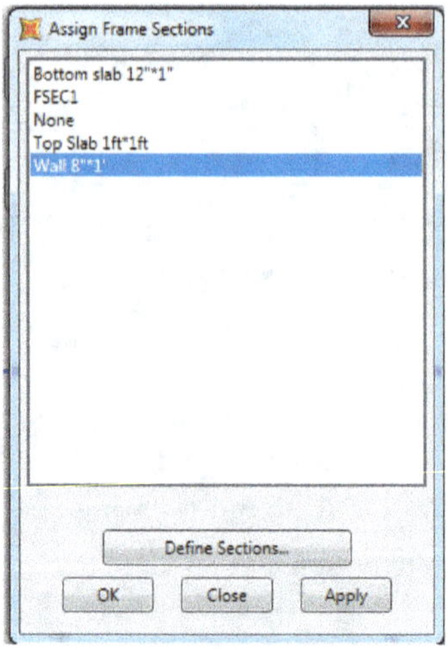

Figure 96. Example 12. Example for assigning a Section to frame element

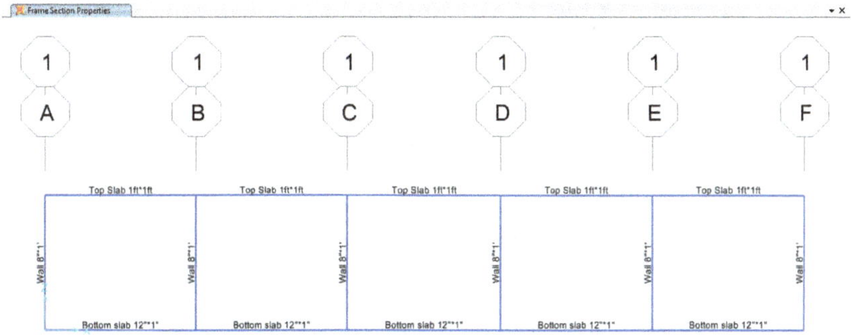

Figure 97. Example 12. Frame Sections

6) Assign X, Y & Z springs for the bottom frame elements to introduce the soil reaction. The reason from applying the spring in the three dimensions is to get a stable model.

The joint spring can be approximately calculated as per Bowles equation (9-9) FOUNDATION ANALYSIS AND DESIGN - Joseph E. Bowles, (Fifth Edition):

Ks = 12 (SF) qa,

, assume SF=2.5, hence Ks = 60

Divide the frame elements to 0.5 feet segments. The tributary area for joints

= 60*0.5*1.0 = 30 kips/ft.

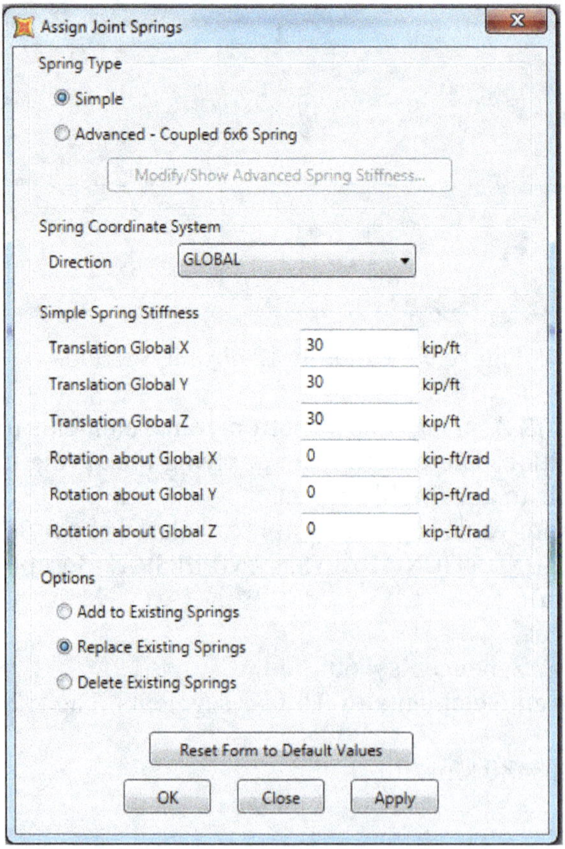

Figure 98. Example 12. Assign Joint Spring

7) Define moving load path

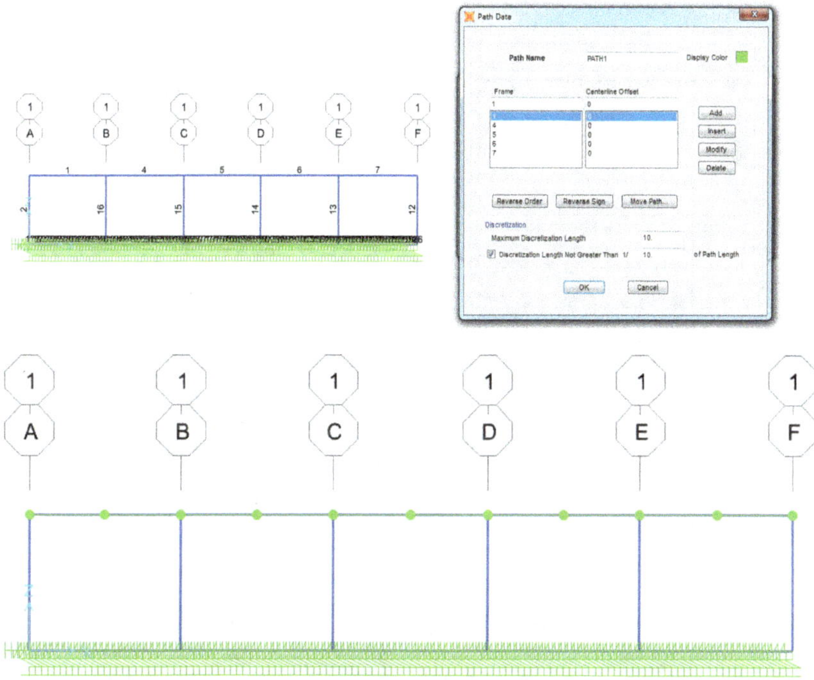

Figure 99. Example 12. Moving Load Path

8) Define moving load vehicle

For Truck

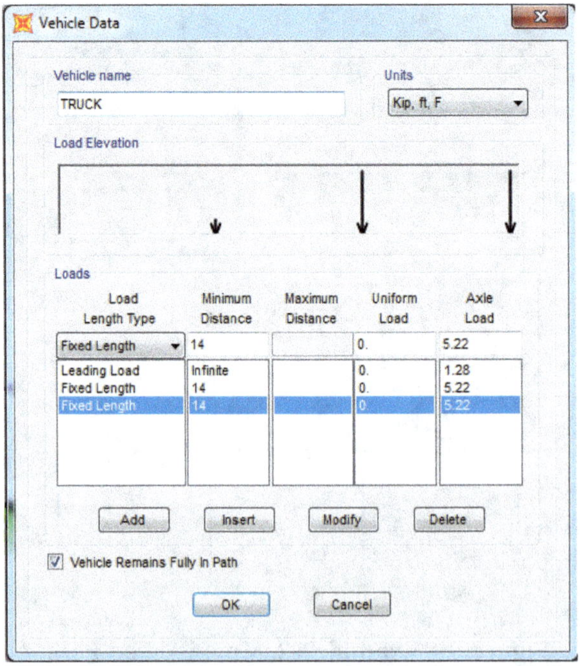

Figure 100. Example 12. Truck Vehicle Load

For Tandem

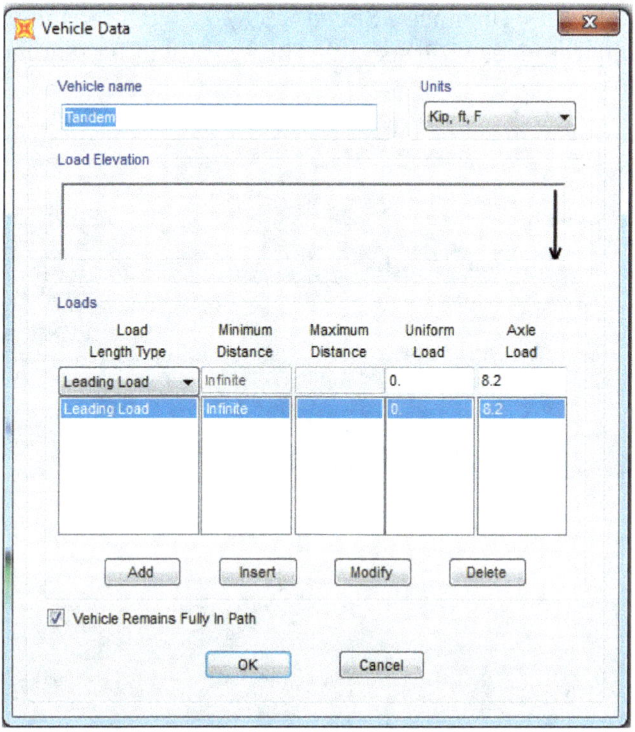

Figure 101. Example 12. Tandem Vehicle Load

9) Define load patterns for vehicular live load
Design speed is 73 ft/s.
Duration of load = Distance / Speed = 59 / 73 = 0.8 seconds.
Consider a step every 0.1 second. The steps will be studied by the software.

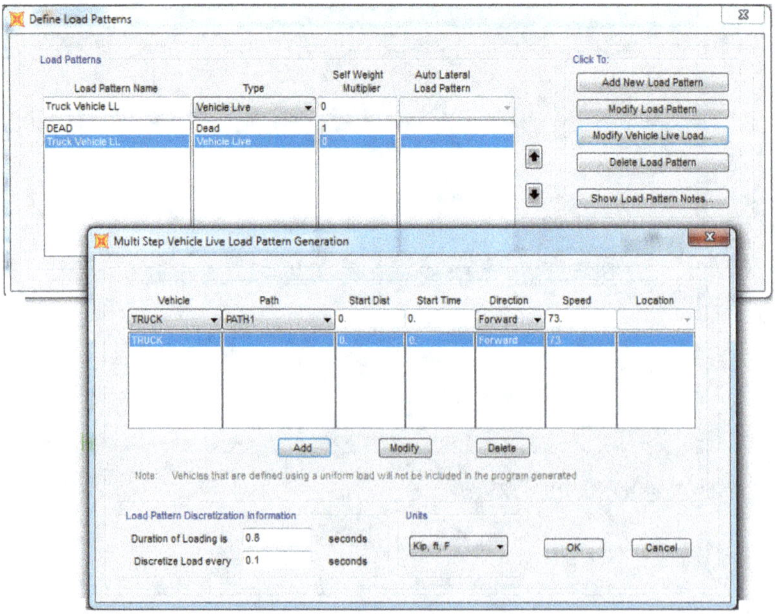

Figure 102. Example 12. Truck Load Pattern

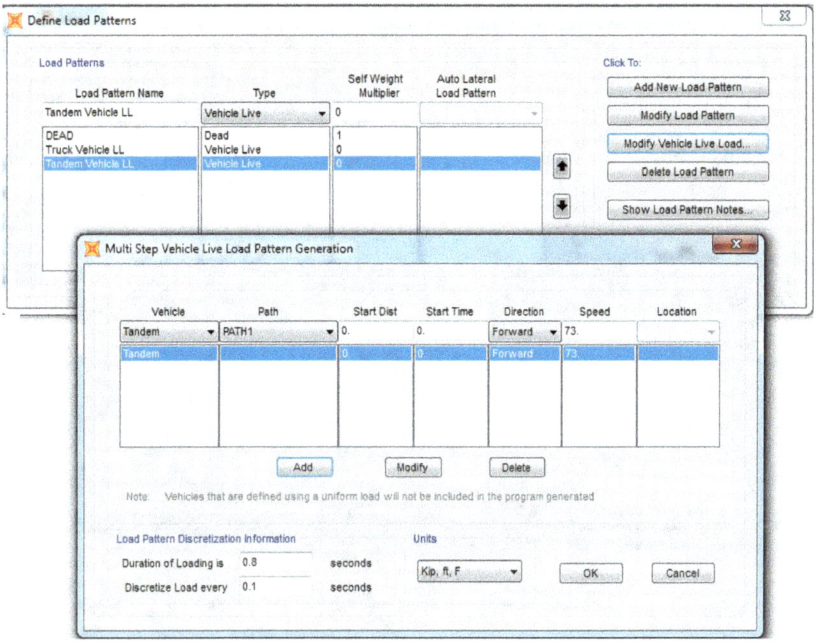

Figure 103. Example 12. Tandem Load Pattern

10) Define multi step static load cases

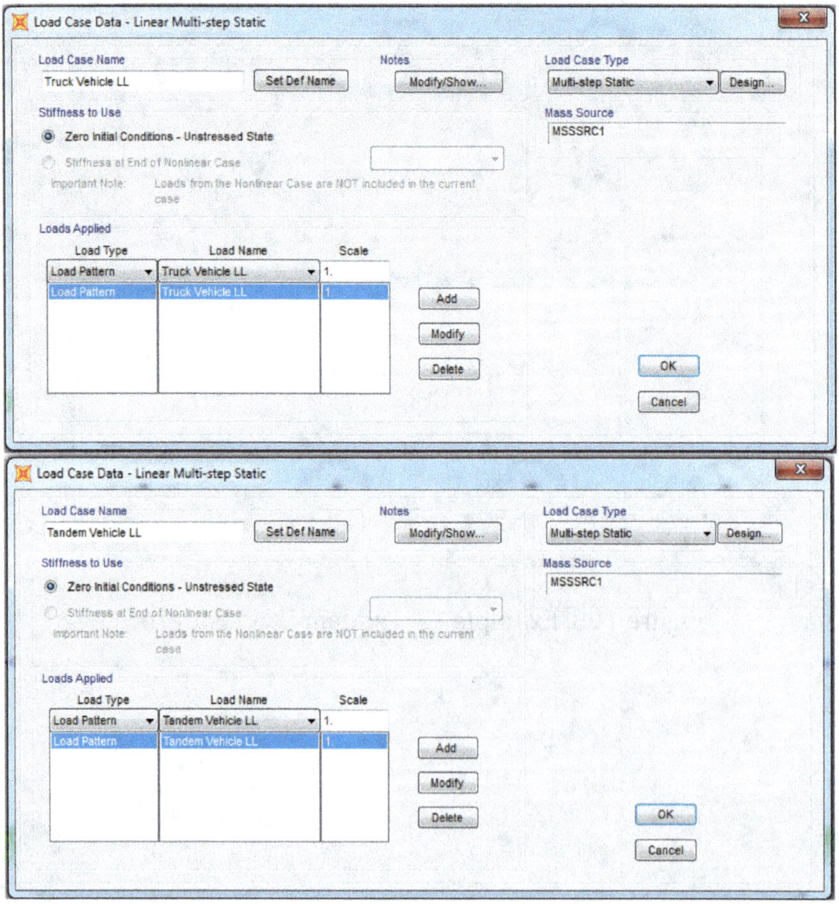

Figure 104. Example 12. Moving Load Cases

11) Run the model and check the straining actions due to moving live load

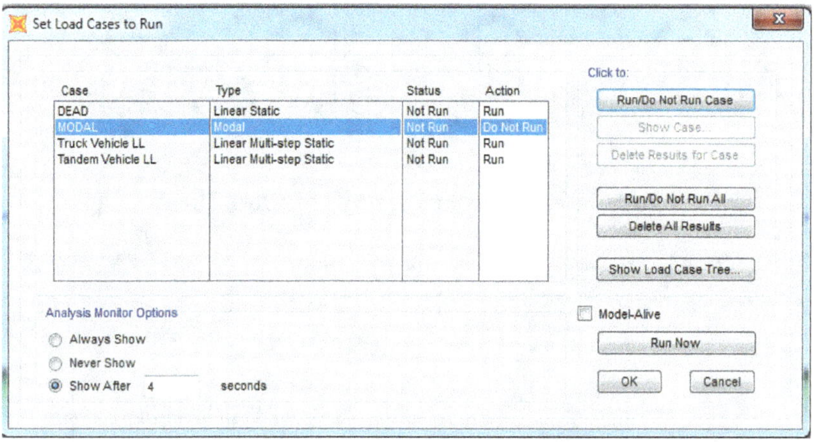

Figure 105. Example 12. Run Model

12) Results

The software will calculate forced and moments for every step. As example, the following figures are showing the bending moment (kips/ft.) due to every step:

<u>For Truck</u>

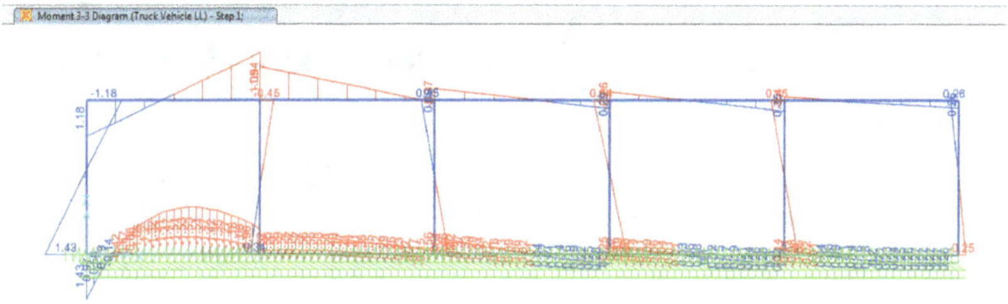

Figure 106. Example 12. BMD for Step No.1

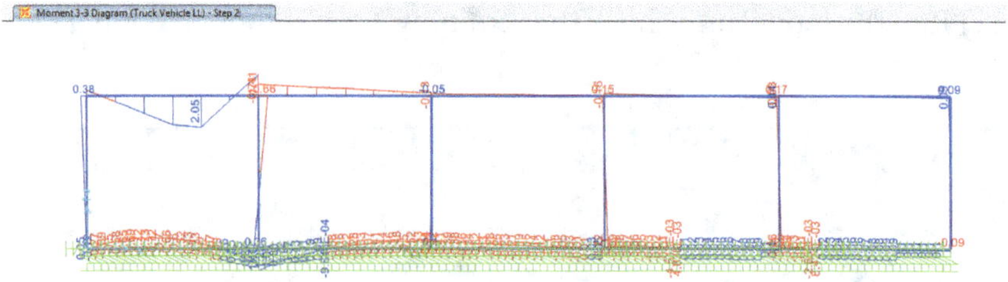

Figure 107. Example 12. BMD for Step No. 2

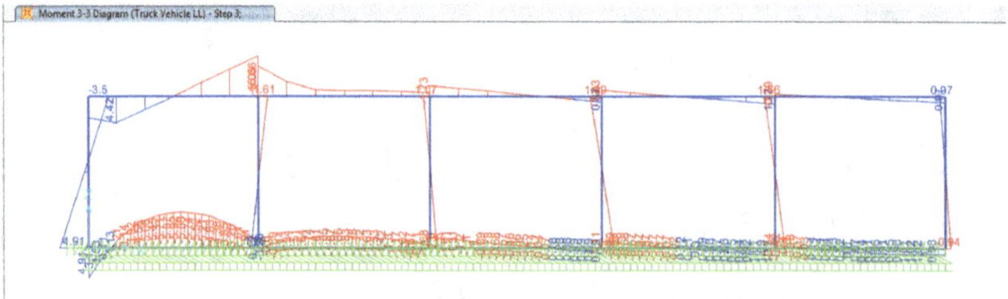

Figure 108. Example 12. BMD for Step No.3

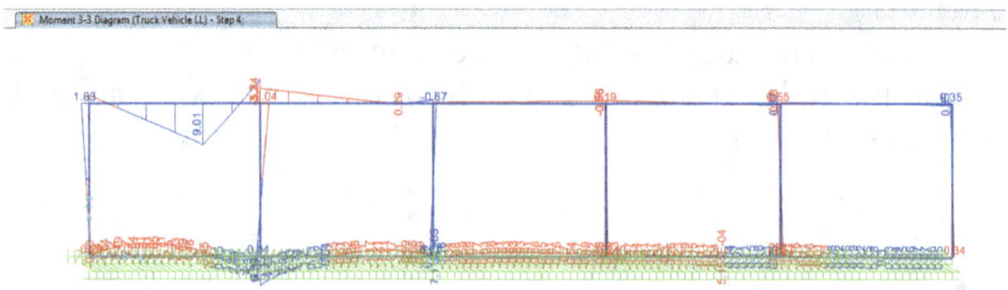

Figure 109. Example 12. BMD for Step No.4

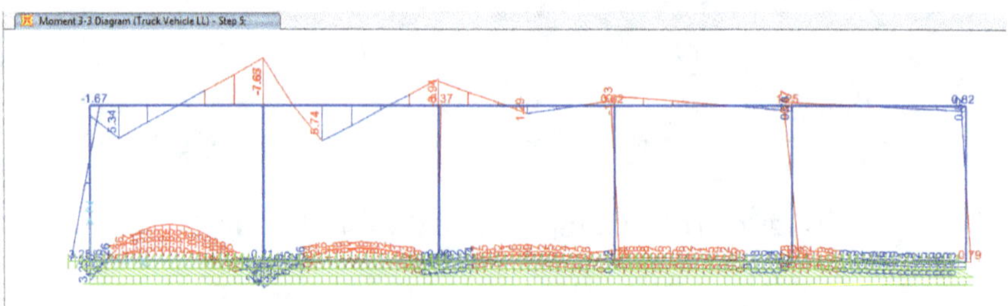

Figure 110. Example 12. BMD for Step No.5

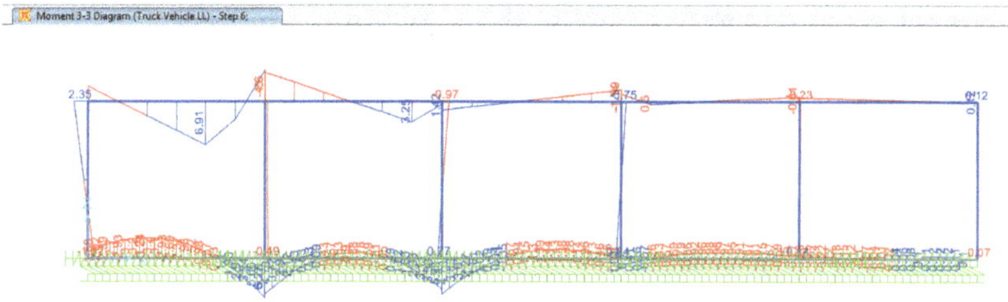

Figure 111. Example 12. BMD for Step No. 6

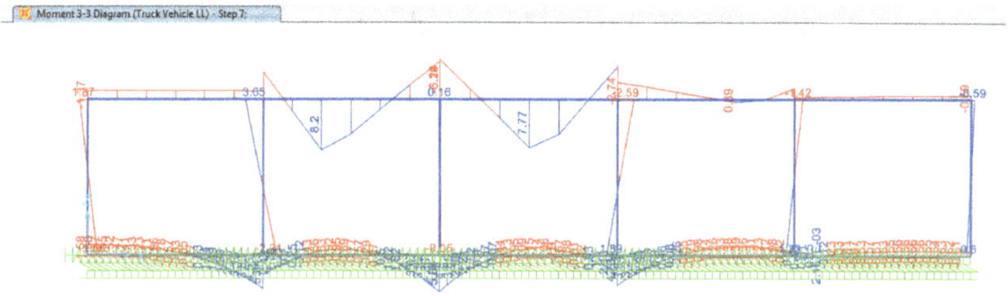

Figure 112. Example 12. BMD for Step No. 7

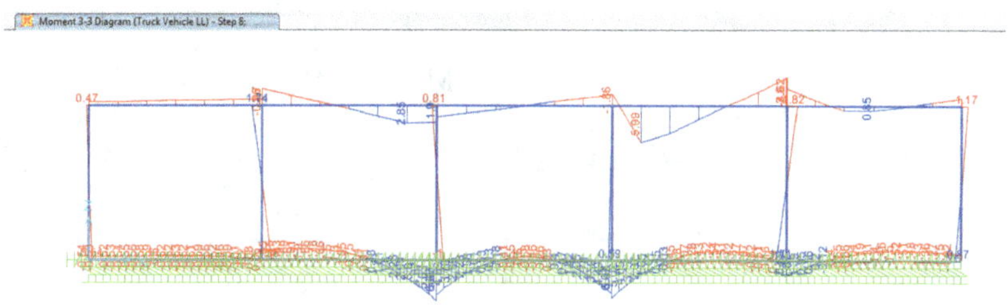

Figure 113. Example 12. BMD for Step No. 8

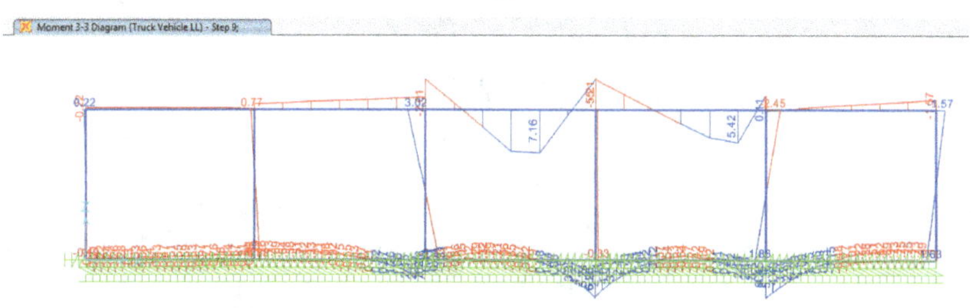

Figure 114. Example 12. BMD for Step No. 9

The truck envelope case showing the maximum moment value from all cases:

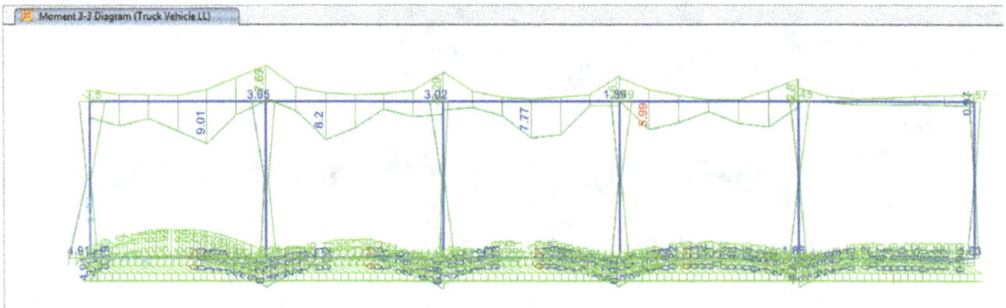

Figure 115. Example 12. Truck Envelope BMD

<u>For Tandem:</u>

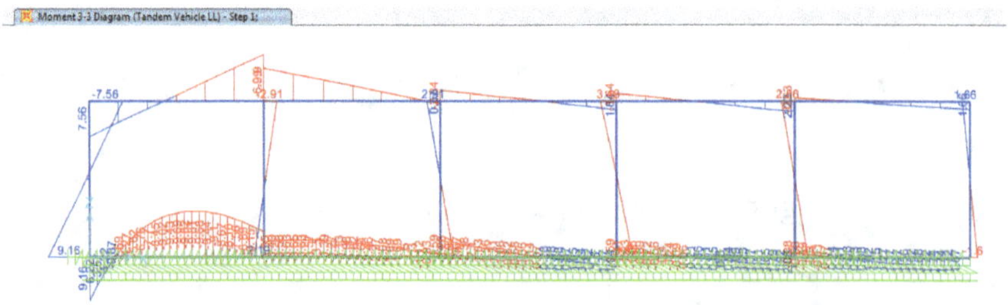

Figure 116. Example 12. BMD for Step No.1

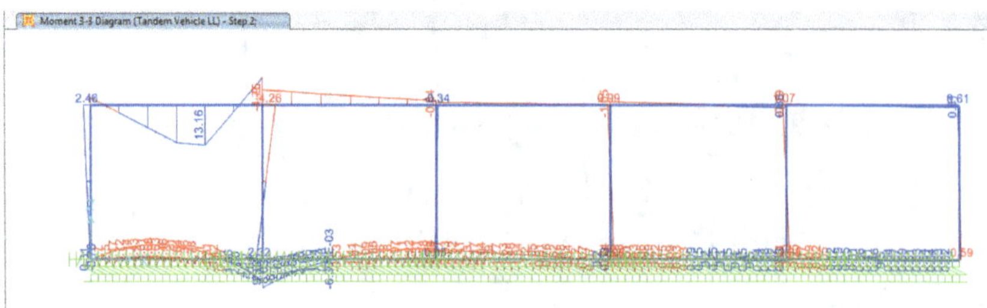

Figure 117. Example 12. BMD for Step No. 2

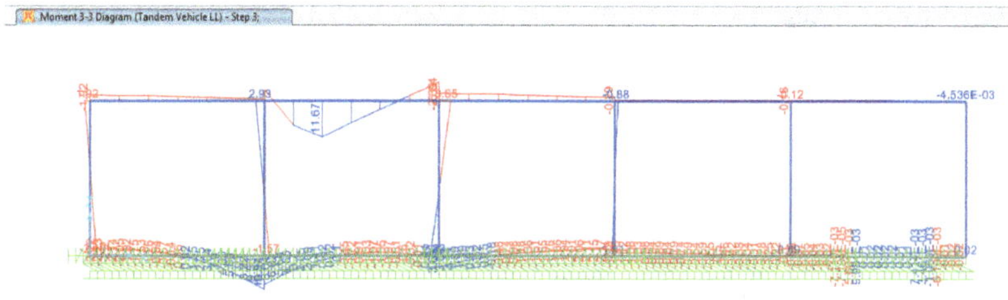

Figure 118. Example 12. BMD for Step No. 3

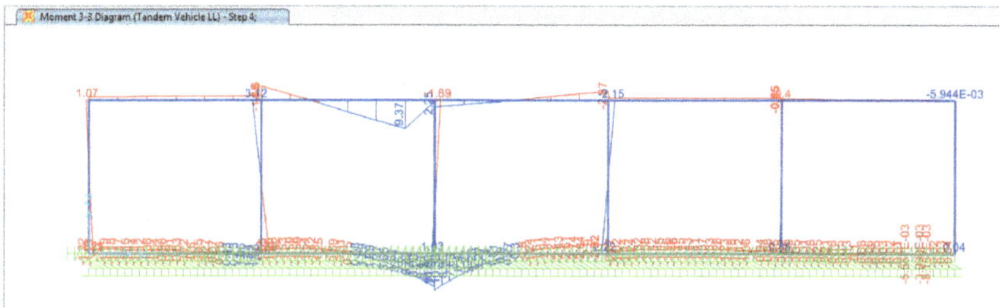

Figure 119. Example 12. BMD for Step No. 4

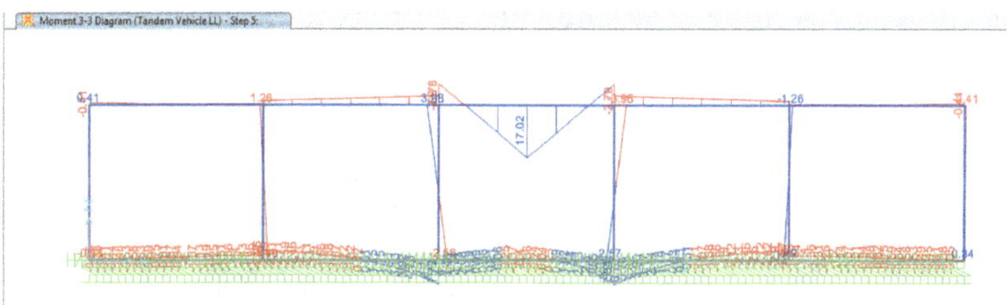

Figure 120. Example 12. BMD for Step No. 5

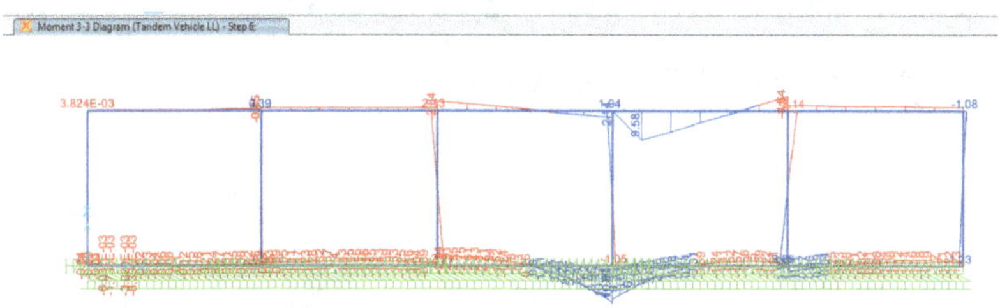

Figure 121. Example 12. BMD for Step No. 6

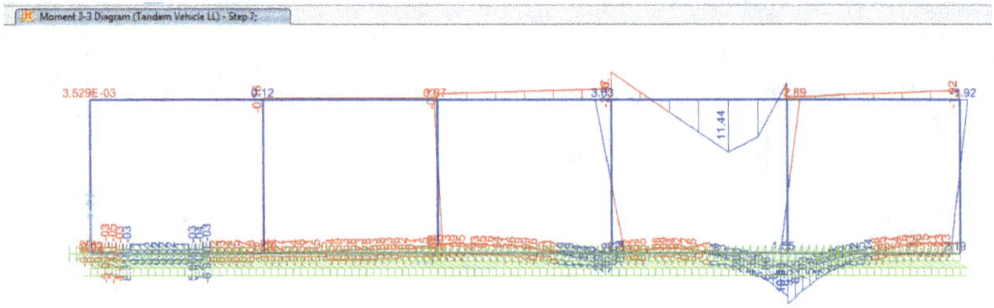

Figure 122. Example 12. BMD for Step No. 7

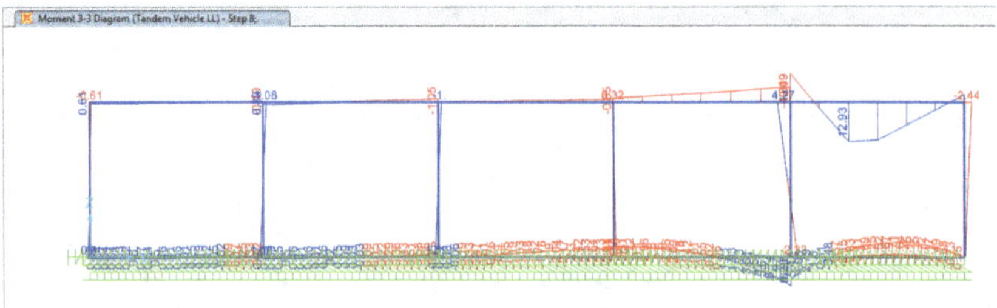

Figure 123. Example 12. BMD for Step No. 8

The tandem envelope case showing the maximum moment value from all cases:

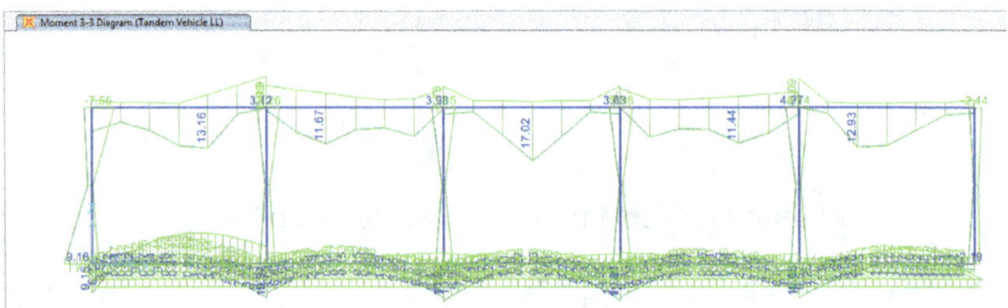

Figure 124. Example 12. Tandem Envelope BMD

Conclusion for Example 12:

The previous Example shows how the software is facilitating the moving load analysis. The load will be assigned one time and the software will study all steps and identify the maximum bending moment for all steps in all locations, similarly, shear and normal forces can be determined. The maximum effect from truck and tandem shall be used for design, for this example, the tandem shows greater moment values.
The moving load has been applied as a concentrated load because the software vehicle axle load cannot be applied as distributed load, but the results will be more conservative.

In the case of load perpendicular to span, the load to be applied as distributed load on the frame elements and the greater effect from both perpendicular and parallel loads to be used for design.

All other loads will be applied as static loads, load combinations to be defined to the software and the straining actions will be used easily for design and checks. Having said, the finite element software became the main tool for the structural design considering the four conditions mentioned previously.

5

Structural Design

The structural design of box culvert is similar to any other reinforced concrete structure. The strength design will be performed and the serviceability and stability conditions to be checked. The design might be done using the software itself or to use the software to perform the structural analysis and complete the design manually or using other tools.

5.1 Material Properties

5.1.1 Modulus of Elasticity

Reference to AASHTO LRFD Article **5.4.2.4**, modulus of elasticity, Ec, may be taken as:

$$E_C = 33{,}000\, K_1 w_C^{1.5} \sqrt{f'_C}$$

Where:

K_1 = correction factor for source of aggregate to be taken as 1.0 unless determined by physical test, and as approved by the authority of jurisdiction

wc = unit weight of concrete (kcf); Refer to AASHTO LRFD **Table 3.5.1-1** or Article **C5.4.2.4**

f'c = specified compressive strength of concrete (ksi)

Reference to AASHTO LRFD Article **5.4.3.2**, the modulus of elasticity, Es, of steel reinforcement shall be assumed as 29,000 ksi for specified minimum yield strengths up to 100 ksi.

5.1.2 Poisson's Ratio

Reference to AASHTO LRFD Article **5.4.2.5**, Concrete poisson's ratio, may be assumed as 0.2. However, for components expected to be subject to cracking, the effect of Poisson's ratio may be neglected.

5.1.3 Modulus of Rupture

Reference to AASHTO LRFD Article **5.4.2.6**,
For normal-weight concrete:

- Except as specified below: $0.24\sqrt{f'_c}$

-When used to calculate the cracking moment of a member: $0.20\sqrt{f'_c}$

5.1.4 Reinforcement Steel

Refer to AASHTO LRFD Article **5.4.3.**

5.2 Limit State Design Method

Reference to AASHTO LRFD Articles **1.3.2.1** and **3.4.1**, the total factored force effect shall be taken as:

$$Q = \sum \eta_i \gamma_i Q_i \leq \phi R_n$$

Where:

For loads for which a maximum value of γ_i is appropriate:

$$\eta_i = \eta_D \eta_R \eta_I \geq 0.95$$

For loads for which a minimum value of γ_i is appropriate:

$$\eta_i = \frac{1}{\eta_D \eta_R \eta_I} \leq 1.0$$

Where:

η_i = load modifier: a factor relating to ductility, redundancy, and operational classification

η_D = a factor relating to ductility

η_R = a factor relating to redundancy

η_I = a factor relating to operational classification

As per AASHTO LRFD Article **12.5.4**, Use a value of 1.0 for all load modifiers (η) for box culvert design, except for earth EV and EH loads, where η_R = 1.05 is used due to the lack of redundancy.

Load Modifiers for Box Culvert Design	
Ductility, η_D	1.0
Redundancy, η_R	1.0 or 1.05
Importance, η_I	1.0
$\eta_i = \eta_D \eta_R \eta_I$	1.0 or 1.05
$\eta_i = \dfrac{1}{\eta_D \eta_R \eta_I}$	1.0 or (1/1.05)

Q_i = force effects from loads specified in AASHTO LRFD

γ_i = load factors specified in AASHTO LRFD **Tables 3.4.1-1** and **3.4.1-2**

R_n = nominal resistance

ϕ = resistance factor: a statistically based multiplier applied to nominal resistance

As per AASHTO LRFD **Table 12.5.5-1**, Use a value of ϕ as follow:

	ϕ	
Structure Type	**Flexure**	**Shear**
Cast in situ	0.90	0.85
Precast	1.00	0.90

As per AASHTO LRFD Article **1.3.2.4,** Strength limit state shall be considered for strength and stability, per Article **1.3.2.2,** the service limit state shall be considered for stress, deformation, and crack width under regular service.

And per Article C**12.5.3**, Culverts as buried structures not to be controlled by fatigue.

5.3 Load Factor and Load Combinations

As Per AASHTO LRFD **Tables 3.4.1-1 and 3.4.1-2,** Load Factors as follows:

Type of Load	**Strength (I) Load Factor**		**Service (I) Load Factor**
	Maximum	**Minimum**	
DC	1.25	0.90	1.00
DW	1.50	0.65	1.00
EV	1.30	0.90	1.00
EH (Barrel)	1.35	0.90*	1.00
EH (wings)	1.50	N/A	1.00
ES	1.50	0.75	1.00
LS	1.75	0	1.00
LL+IM	1.75	0	1.00
WA	1.00	0	1.00

*As per AASHTO LRFD **3.11.7**, a 50% reduction in load may be used in lieu of the minimum load factor but need not to be combined with the minimum load factor specified in Table **3.4.1-2**.

As per AASHTO LRFD Article **C12.11.2.1**, the load combinations might be arranged as follows:

Strength Limit State:
Ia. Maximum vertical load and maximum horizontal load:
1.25DC +1.5DW + (1.30*1.05)EV + 1.75(LL+IM) + (1.35*1.05)EHmax + 1.5ES + 1.75LS
Ib. Maximum vertical load and minimum horizontal load:
1.25DC + 1.5DW + (1.30*1.05)EV + 1.75(LL+IM) + 1.00WA + (0.9/1.05)EHmin + 0.75ES
Ic. Minimum vertical load and maximum horizontal load:
0.90DC + (0.90/1.05)EV + (1.35*1.05)EHmax + 1.75LS

Service Limit State:
Ia. Maximum vertical load and maximum horizontal load:
1.00DC + 1.00DW + 1.00EV + 1.00(LL+IM) + 1.00EHmax + 1.00LS +1.00ES
Ib. Maximum vertical load and minimum horizontal load:

1.00DC + 1.00DW +1.00EV + 1.0(LL+IM) + 1.00WA + 1.00EHmin +1.00ES

Ic. Minimum vertical load and maximum horizontal load:

1.00DC + 1.00EV + 1.00EHmax + 1.00LS

5.4 Strength limit state

5.4.1 Flexural Strength

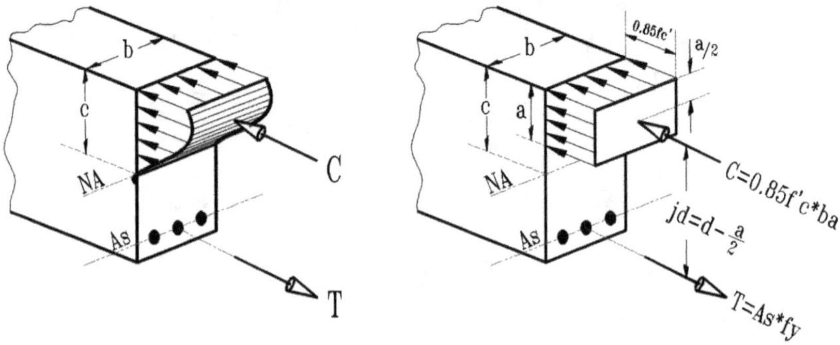

Figure 125. Flexural stresses

Reference to AASHTO LRFD Articles **5.7.2.2, 5.7.3.2, C5.5.4.2.1** and **12.5.5**

Mr = ϕ Mn

$$M_n = A_s f_y \left(d - \frac{a}{2}\right) \quad \& \quad a = \frac{A_s f_y}{0.85 f'_c b}$$

Reinforcement ratio:

$$\rho = \frac{0.85 f'_c}{f_y}\left(1 - \sqrt{1 - \frac{2R_u}{0.85 f'_c}}\right) \quad \& \quad R_u = \frac{M_u}{\phi b d^2}$$

$$A_s = \rho b d$$

Where:
As = required steel area (in2)
b = strip width for design, usually 12 in.
d = the effective depth from the extreme compression fiber to the centroid of the tensile reinforcement (Note: thickness of monolithic wearing or protective surface shall be excluded at the compressive face of the section where applicable.
ρ = required steel ratio (a ratio of steel to concrete areas of a section)
Mu = factored moment (k-in)

ϕ = strength reduction factor for flexure

Design Critical Sections

The following Figure shows the critical sections for the design of flexure which differ in the case of using haunches in slab-wall connections. However, the designer may simplify the design by decreasing the number of sections due to using easier reinforcement details as explained in reinforcement chapter in this manual.

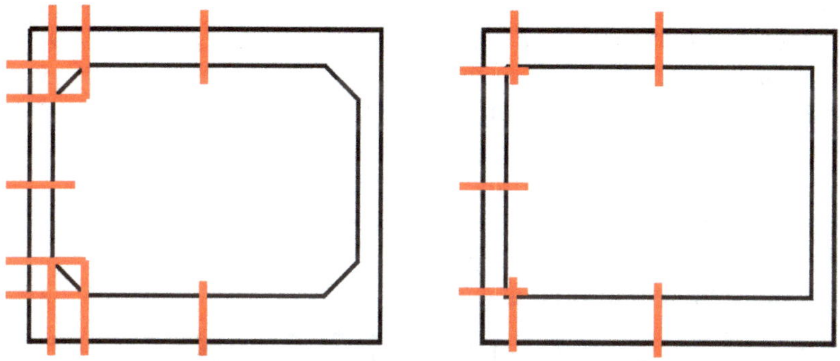

Figure 126. Critical Sections for Flexure Design

5.4.2 Combined Axial and Flexural Loads

Reference to AASHTO LRFD Articles **5.7.4.5,** Wall members subjected to both axial and flexural loads shall be designed considering the interaction between axial and flexural (Interaction diagrams may be used). To construct the interaction diagram, the following steps shall be followed:

1) Determine the maximum factored axial resistance:
$\phi P_n = 0.8\ (\phi P_o)$
$\phi P_o = \phi\ \{0.85f'_c\ (A_g - A_{st}) + A_{st}f_y\}$
Where:
A_g = gross area of a cross-section (in^2.)
A_{st} = total area of steel reinforcement (in^2.)
ϕ = 0.75 for axial compression with tied stirrup

2) Determine the pure bending capacity:
$\phi M_o = 0.75\ M_n$
$\phi M_n = 0.90\ M_n$
If the following equation is satisfied:

$$\frac{A_s - A'_s}{bd} \geq 0.85\beta_1\left(\frac{f'_c d'}{f'_y d}\right)\left(\frac{87}{87 - f_y}\right)$$

Thus, Use the following equation:
$M_n = \{[(A_s - A'_s)\ f_y\ (d - (a/2)] + [A'_s\ f_y\ (d - d')]\}$
Otherwise, use the following equation:

$$M_n = A_s f_y\left(d - \frac{a}{2}\right)$$

3) Determine the balanced point (ϕP_b , ϕM_b):
$\phi P_b = \phi\ \{0.85f'_c\ (b)(a_b) + A'_s\ f'_s - A_s\ f_y\}$
$\phi M_b = \phi\ \{[0.85f'_c\ (b)(a_b)(d - d'' - (a_b/2)] + [A'_s\ f'_s\ (d - d' - d'') + A_s\ f_y\ d'']\}$

Where:

$$a_b = \frac{87}{(87 + f_y)}\beta_1 d$$

$$f'_s = 87\left[1-\left(\frac{d'}{d}\right)\left(\frac{87+f_y}{87}\right)\right] \le f_y$$

A_s = total area of tensile reinforcement (in^2.)
A'_s = total area of compressive reinforcement (in^2.)
d' = distance from concrete compressive surface to the centerline of compressive steel reinforcement (in.)
d" = distance from centerline of tensile reinforcement to the centroid of gross section of member (in.)
$\phi = 0.75$

Note: Interaction diagram might be linearly simplified in case of $\phi P_b > 0.1\ f'_c A_g$

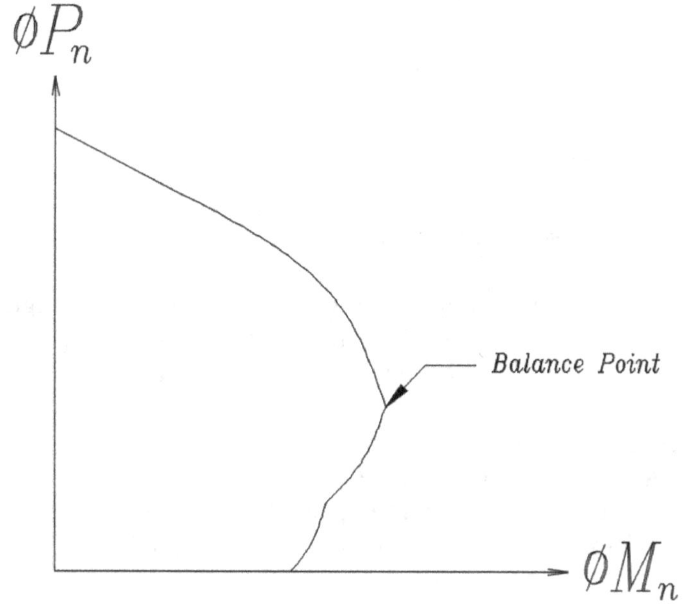

Figure 127. Interaction Diagram

5.4.3 Maximum and Minimum Tensile Steel Reinforcement

5.4.3.1 Minimum Tensile Reinforcement

For Cast-in-place Culverts:
Refer to AASHTO LRFD Article **12.11.4.3.1:**
The amount of tensile reinforcement shall be adequate to develop a factored flexural resistance, $M_r = \phi M_n$. For monolithic or non-composite section, M_r is equal to the lesser of:

1) 1.33 $M_{strength}$
2) $M_{cr} = \gamma 3\ \gamma 1\ S\ fr$ (k-in.)

Where:
S = section modulus for the extreme fiber of the composite section where tensile stress is caused by externally applied loads ($S = bh^2/6$ in.^{3})
$\gamma 3$ = ratio of specified minimum yield strength to ultimate tensile strength of the reinforcement
= 0.67 for A615, Grade 60 reinforcement
= 0.75 for A706, Grade 60 reinforcement
$\gamma 1$ = flexural cracking variability factor
= 1.2 for precast segmental structures
= 1.6 for all other concrete structures
$M_{strength}$ = factored moment required by the applicable strength load combination specified in AASHTO LRFD **Table 3.4.1-1**
fr = modulus of rupture of concrete as specified in section **5.1.3**.

For Precast Culverts:
Refer to AASHTO LRFD Article **12.11.4.3.2:**
1) All box culvert cross-sections subjected to flexural tension, the minimum reinforcement area shall be not less than 0.002 *b*d

2) For top slabs of box culverts with fill depth less than 2.0 ft, the bottom longitudinal reinforcement area shall be the greater of the distribution reinforcement required per AASHTO LRFD Article **9.7.3.2** (**5.6.2** in this manual) or 0.002 *b*d

3) For all other longitudinal reinforcement, the minimum longitudinal reinforcement area shall not be less than 0.03 in.^{2}/ft at each face.

4) Where the fabricated length exceeds 16.0 ft, the minimum reinforcement shall also meet the requirements of AASHTO LRFD Article **5.10.8** (5.6.1 in this manual)

5.4.3.2 Maximum Tensile Reinforcement

As per AASHTO LRFD Article **5.7.2,** the maximum amount of tensile reinforcement shall be such that:

$$\frac{c}{d} = 0.375 \quad \& \quad c = \frac{a}{\beta_1} = \frac{A_S f_y}{0.85 f_c^{'} b \beta_1}$$

Where:
d = Thickness - cover (in)
β1 = ratio of the depth of the equivalent uniformly stressed compression as per AASHTO LRFD Article **5.7.2.2**:

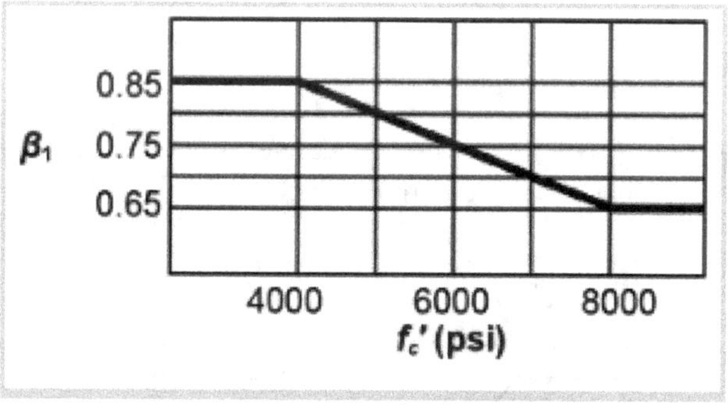

Figure 128. β1chart

For f'c≤ 4.0ksi. β1 = 0.85

For f'c >4.0ksi. $\beta 1 = 0.85 - 0.05\, fc' \left(\frac{f_c^{'} - 4000}{1000} \right)$ & 0.65 ≤

β1 ≤ 0.85

5.4.4 Shear Strength

Maximum design shear should be checked at a distance d_v from the stream face of support or the tip of the haunch where d_v is the effective shear depth as determined in AASHTO LRFD Article **5.8.2.9,** shall be taken as the greater of (in):

$$\left(d - \frac{a}{2}\right) \quad \& \quad a = \frac{A_s f_y}{0.85 f_c' b},$$

(0.72h)
And (0.9 de)
Where:
de = effective depth from extreme compression fiber to the centroid of the tensile force in the tensile reinforcement (in.)
As = area of reinforcing steel on the flexural tension face

Shear Design Critical Sections

The following Figure shows the critical sections for shear design for the two cases, with or without haunches:

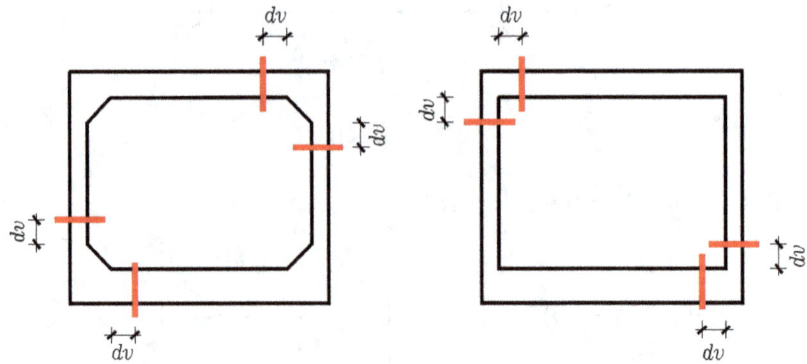

Figure 129. Critical Sections for Shear Design

Factored shear resistance, ϕVn, shall be considered without the presence of shear reinforcement is not taken less than factored shear, Vu. Reference to AASHTO LRFD Article **5.8.2.1**, the factored shear resistance, Vr shall be taken as:

$$V_r = \phi V_n$$

Where:

V_n = nominal shear resistance specified in AASHTO LRFD Article **5.8.3.3** (kip)

ϕ = resistance factor

When the shear capacity of slabs and walls specified in the previous equation is less than factored shear, increase thickness of the section. For headwalls and edge beams, strength of shear reinforcement, in addition to concrete shear strength, shall be considered. Therefore, the required area of shear reinforcement shall be computed as follows:

$$A_v = \frac{V_s(s)}{f_y d}$$

$$V_s = \frac{V_u}{\phi} - V_c$$

Where:
Av = required area of shear reinforcement (in^2)
Vs = shear force to be resisted by shear reinforcement
Vc = nominal shear strength provided by concrete
s = spacing of shear reinforcement steel (in.)

5.4.4.1 Wall Shear

Reference to AASHTO LRFD Article **5.8.3.3,** concrete shear capacity is the least of:

$$\phi V_c = \phi * 0.0316 \beta \sqrt{f'_c} b_v d_v$$

And,
$\phi V_c = \phi * 0.25 * f'_c * b_v * d_v$

Reference to AASHTO LRFD Article **5.8.3.4.1,** for member sizes less than 16 in. and it is not subjected to axial tension, the Simplified Procedure will be followed and the value of β may be taken as the maximum of **2.0**.

As per AASHTO LRFD Article **5.8.3.4.2**, for member sizes not less than 16 in., β should be calculated using the General Procedure as follows:

$$\beta = \frac{4.8}{1+750\varepsilon_s} \cdot \frac{51}{39+s_{xe}}$$

$$\varepsilon_s = \frac{\left(\frac{|M_u|}{d_v} + 0.5N_u + |V_u|\right)}{E_s A_s}$$

$$s_{xe} = s_x \frac{1.38}{a_g + 0.63}$$

12.0 in. $\leq s_{xe} \leq$ 80.0 in.

Where:
Mu = factored moment, not to be taken less than Vu*dv
Nu = factored axial force (negative if compressive)
a_g = maximum aggregate size = 0.75 in.

5.4.4.2 Slab Shear

The Nominal shear strength should be determined as follows:
Reference to AASHTO LRFD Article **5.8.3.3,** for all walls and slabs with fill ≤ 2 ft.

The least of:

$$\phi V_c = \phi * 0.0316\beta\sqrt{f'_c}\, b_v d_v$$

And,
$\phi V_c = \phi * 0.25 * f'_c * b_v * d_v$

Reference to AASHTO LRFD Article **5.14.5.3,** for slabs with earth fill > 2 ft.

$$V_c = \left(0.0676\lambda\sqrt{f'_c} + 4.6\frac{A_s}{b\,d_e}\frac{V_u d_e}{M_u}\right) b\,d_e \leq 0.126\lambda\sqrt{f'_c}\,b\,d_e$$

$$\frac{V_u d_e}{M_u} \leq 1.0$$

For single-cell box culverts only, Vc for slabs monolithic with walls need not be taken to be less than $0.0948\sqrt{f'_c}\,b\,d_e$

Where:
Vu = factored shear
Mu = factored moment occurring simultaneously with Vu at the section considered
As = area of reinforcing steel in the design width (in^2.)

5.4.4.3 Headwall and Edge Beams Shear

Reference to AASHTO LRFD Articles **5.8.2.4 & 5.8.2.5,** a minimum steel area of shear reinforcement (Av) should be provided in flexural members when factored shear exceeds one-half of concrete factored shear.

If $V_u > \frac{1}{2}\phi V_c$

Thus, $A_v \geq 0.0316\sqrt{f'_c}\frac{b_v s}{f_y}$

Where:
Vc = nominal shear resistance provided by concrete section only
ϕ = 0.9 = strength reduction factor for shear
Av = required steel area of shear reinforcement (in^2.)
b = width of section (in.)
s = spacing of shear reinforcement steel (in.)

5.4.5 Slenderness Effect

It is recommended that; for all interior walls and for exterior walls keyed into rock, slenderness effects shall be considered. For exterior walls supported by bottom slab, if the flexure design is adequate, the combined axial and flexure check is not required. In case of considering the slenderness effect, the moment shall be multiplied by moment magnification factor.

Culvert members are considered to be braced against side-sway. Reference to AASHTO LRFD Articles **5.7.4.3,** for members braced against side sway, the effects of slenderness may be neglected if the following equation is satisfied:

$$\frac{K\,l_u}{r} < 34 - \left(12\frac{M_1}{M_2}\right)$$

The previous equation might be used for reinforcing steel design. However, the following equation may be practical for sizing walls:

$$\frac{K\,l_u}{r} < 34$$

Where:
K = 0.65 for interior walls with bottom slab
= 1.0 for exterior walls on rock
= 0.80 for interior walls on rock
lu = unsupported length (clear wall height)
r = radius of gyration and may be assumed as 0.3 times member thickness
M1 = smaller end moment of a wall member
M2 = larger end moment of a wall member
M1/M2 = positive value for single curvature and negative for double curvature

Moment Magnification

Reference to AASHTO LRFD Articles **5.7.4.3,** the simplified procedure in Article **4.5.3.2.2b** is only applicable for walls with K lu/r less than 100. A magnified factored moment, Mm, shall be computed as follows:

$$M_c = \delta_b M_{2b} + \delta_s M_{2s}$$

Since the side-sway is neglected in culverts, the side-sway portion is zero. Therefore, the equation will be modified as follows:

$$M_c = \delta_b M_{2b}$$

$$\delta_b = \frac{C_m}{1 - \frac{P_u}{\phi_k P_e}} \geq 1.0$$

$$C_m = 0.6 + 0.4\left(\frac{M_1}{M_2}\right)$$

$$P_e = \frac{\pi^2 E I}{(K\ l_u)^2}$$

$$E I = \frac{\frac{E_c I_g}{2.5}}{1 + \beta_d}$$

For internal walls, the moment resulting from an axial load with minimum eccentricity may be calculated as follows:

$$M_e = P_u e$$

Where:
M_c = magnified moment
δ_b = moment magnification factor for a member braced against side sway (preferably less than 2.5)
M = largest moment of the wall member due to factored loads or minimum eccentricity
β_d = ratio of maximum factored dead load moment to maximum factored total load moment (always positive)
E_c = modulus of elasticity of concrete

I_g = moment of inertia of a gross concrete section (one-foot strip)
P_e = Euler buckling load
P_u = factored axial load
ϕ_k = 0.75 for axial compression with tied stirrups
e = minimum eccentricity (in.)
h = wall thickness (in.)

5.5 Serviceability limit state

5.5.1 Crack Control

Concrete Cover

Reference to AASHTO LRFD Article **12.10.4.2.4e,** the provisions of Article **5.12.3** shall apply to minimum concrete cover except:

- If wall thickness is less than 2.5 in., the cover shall not be less than 0.75 in. and
- If wall thickness is not less than 2.5 in., the cover shall not be less than 1.0 in.

Reference to AASHTO LRFD Article **12.11.3**, the provisions of Article **5.7.3.4** shall apply to crack width control in reinforced concrete cast-in-place and precast box culverts. All concrete members of box culverts except wing walls shall be checked for crack control.

The spacing of tensile steel reinforcement shall be limited by the following equation:

$$s \le \frac{700\gamma_e}{\beta_s f_{ss}} - 2d_c$$

Solve for f_{ss} (The allowable reinforcement stress):

$$f_{ss} \le \frac{700\,\gamma_e}{\beta_s(s + 2d_c)} \le 0.60 f_y \,(ksi)$$

$$\beta_s = 1 + \frac{d_c}{0.7(h - d_c)}$$

And as per AASHTO LRFD Article **C12.11.3**, Buried box culverts are subject to high compressive thrust forces compared to most flexural members and this thrust can result in a substantial reduction in the stresses at the service limit state that is often ignored in design. The following Equations are used to consider the effect of thrust on stresses at the service limit state:

Actual stress provided in the steel $f_s = \dfrac{M_s + N_s(d - h/2)}{A_s jid}$

$$j = 0.74 + 0.1\frac{e}{d} \le 0.9$$

$$i = \frac{1}{1 - \dfrac{jd}{e}}$$

$$e = \frac{M_s}{N_s} + \left(d - \frac{h}{2}\right)$$

$$\frac{e}{d} \ge 1.15$$

If ($f_s > f_{ss}$), means not satisfactory:

$$A_{scrack} = \frac{f_s}{f_{ss}} \cdot A_s$$

Where:
s = average spacing of tensile steel reinforcement

γ_e = exposure factor

γ_e = 1.00 for Class 1 exposure condition

γ_e = 0.75 for Class 2 exposure condition (recommended for culverts since they are exposed to water)

dc = thickness of concrete cover for tensile reinforcement (in.)

h = wall or slab thickness. Remove any applicable wearing surfaces when they are on the compression face (in.)

fs = tensile stress in steel reinforcement at the service limit state (ksi)

M_s = Service moment (always positive) (k-in)

N_s = Service axial force (positive for compression) (k)

d = distance from compression face to centroid of tension reinforcement (in.)

Exception:

If e/d < 1.15 then crack control need not be checked for the location under investigation. When e/d is less than 1.15, the rectangular member is presumed to behave like an eccentrically loaded column rather than a flexural member. Because of this, interior walls need not be checked for fills greater than 2 ft.

5.6 Other Design Requirements

5.6.1 Reinforcement for Temperature and Shrinkage

Reference to AASHTO LRFD Article **5.10.8,** temperature and shrinkage reinforcement to ensure that the total reinforcement is not less than the following:
Area of reinforcement per foot, on each face and in each direction, shall satisfy:

$$A_s \geq \frac{1.3bh}{2(b+h)f_y}$$

$0.11 \leq As \leq 0.60$

Where:
As = area of reinforcement in each direction and each face (in.^{2}/ft)
b = least width of component section (in.)
h = least thickness of component section (in.)
fy = specified yield strength of reinforcing bars ≤75 ksi.

5.6.2 Distribution of Steel Reinforcement

Reference to AASHTO LRFD Article **5.14.4.1,** Transverse distribution reinforcement shall be placed in the bottoms of culvert top slabs with fill depth less than or equal 2.0 ft.

Distribution reinforcement is important to allow the load to disperse over a larger area than the tire patch which can be assumed to be achieved by the thick fill itself for more than 2.0 ft. fill thickness. Distribution reinforcement may be taken as the percentage of the main reinforcement required for positive moment. Distribution reinforcement limitation per AASHTO LRFD for longitudinal reinforced concrete construction is:

$$\frac{100}{\sqrt{L}} \leq 50\%$$

Where L = span length (ft)

6

Concrete Dimensions

There are no specific concrete dimensions specified by AASHTO LRFD. However, each city, state organization has minimum dimensions followed, if not, assuming the dimensions is left to the discretion of the designer subject to performing a safe and economic design.

The following MoDOT assumptions are recommended by the Author that may be practical but not a mandatory:

Expansion Joints:

It is recommended to avoid increasing the distance between expansion joints than 50 feet to avoid the expansion/shrinkage cracks during the hydration process and the volumetric changes due to temperature differences.

Walls and Slabs:

The minimum thickness for slabs and walls might be assumed to be 8". However, for top slabs with fill depth less than 1 foot, the minimum slab thickness shall be checked as a mandatory per AASHTO LRFD Article **2.5.2.6.3.**

Apron Slab:

It is recommended to follow the same culvert's base slab thickness for Apron slab. The thickness could be less. However, following same bottom slab thickness in lieu of complicated analysis is better.

Wing Walls:

Reference to AASHTO LRFD Article **11.6.1.4,** Wing walls may either be designed as monolithic with the culvert exterior walls or be separated with an expansion joint and designed to be freestanding. Normally the wing wall is jointed with key construction joint or expansion joint.

- Wing walls has two types, straight or flared with an angle (α) as per the following Figures:

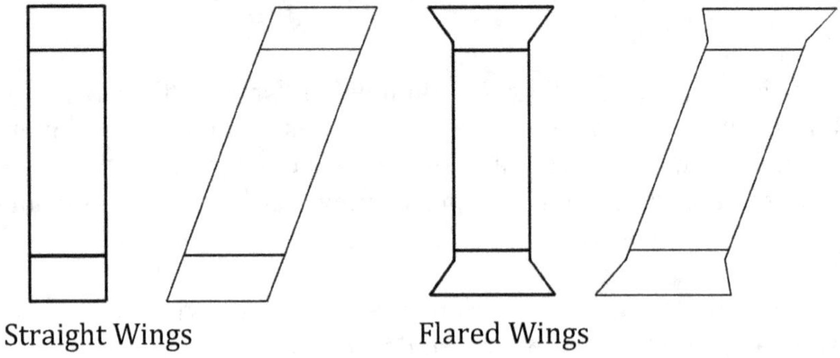

Figure 130. Types of Wing Walls

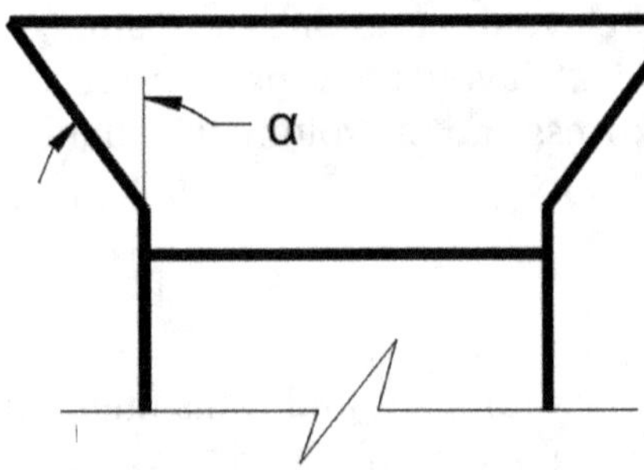

Figure 131. Wing Angle

- The thickness of wing wall might be assumed as same as the adjoining wall
- The slope of wing wall might be 1 (vertical): 2 (horizontal)
- The length of wing wall might be determined as per the following formulas:
  For straight wings:
  $L = 2V / \cos\theta$
  For flared wings:
  $L = 2V / \cos(\theta+\alpha)$
  Where:
  L = wing length
  V = (top slab thickness) + (clear wall height) – 12"
  θ = skew angle
  α = wing angle

- Wing slope might start from a point 12" higher than the top of bottom slab
- Wing wall might be flush with the top of top slab with 3" horizontal distance.

Toe Wall:

12" depth below the bottom slab with uniform or non-uniform thickness. The uniform thickness is recommended to be 10" as minimum.

Headwalls and Edge Beams:

Edge beams dimensions might be initially assumed as 20" width and inverted by 6" above the top slab. And the headwall dimensions shall be assumed as per the height of backfill and the end use.

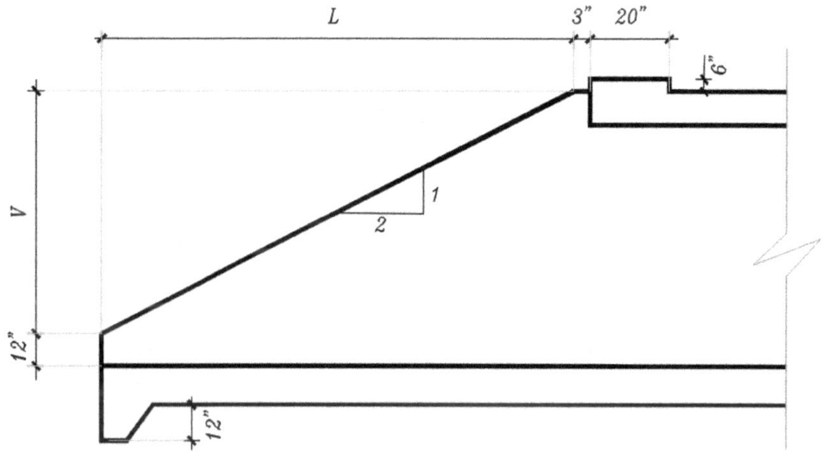

Figure 132. Wing/Toe Walls and Edge Beam Assumed Dimensions

Collar Beam:

Beam dimensions might be assumed as 30" width and 12" depth.

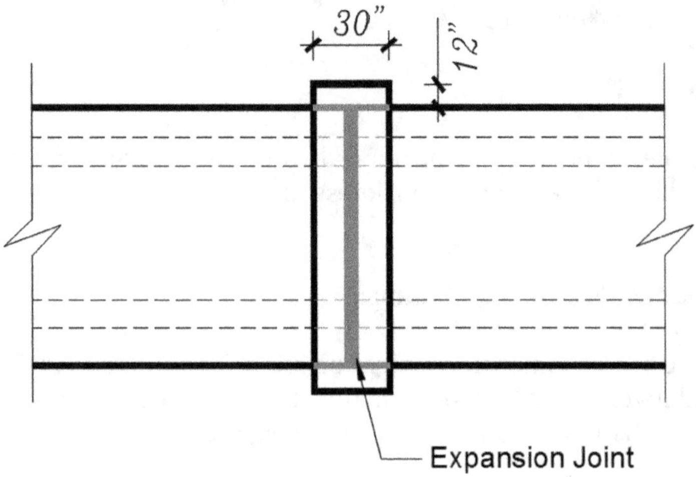

Figure 133. Collar Beam Assumed Dimensions

7

Reinforcement Detailing

Reference to AASHTO LRFD Article **5.11,** for development and splices of reinforcement. The designer shall consider this Article during detailing of steel reinforcing bars.

The following three figures are showing a method of reinforcement steel detailing which might be used. The designer may change the detail considering the sections design and the requirements of the mentioned Article.

The designer shall check the maximum straining actions for every section from the three load combinations Ia, Ib and Ic to identify the worst cases for all locations to choose the required area of reinforcement steel accordingly in full respect for the minimum and maximum reinforcement as per AASHTO LRFD design specifications.

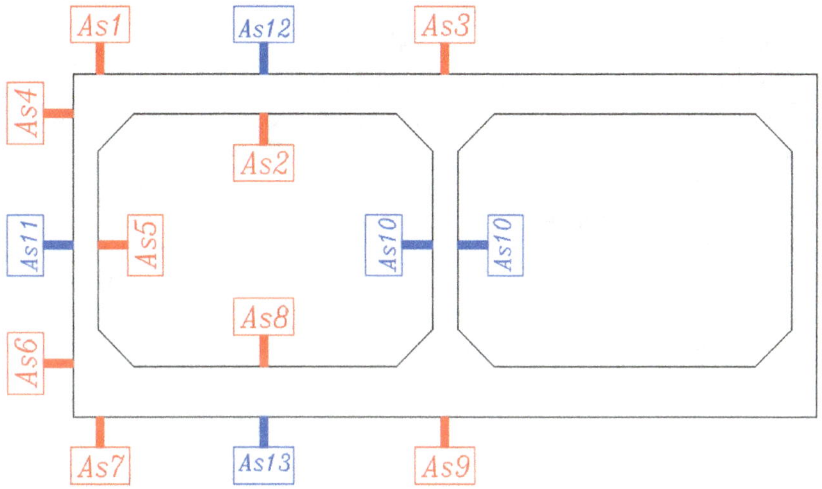

Figure 134. Reinforcement Steel Locations

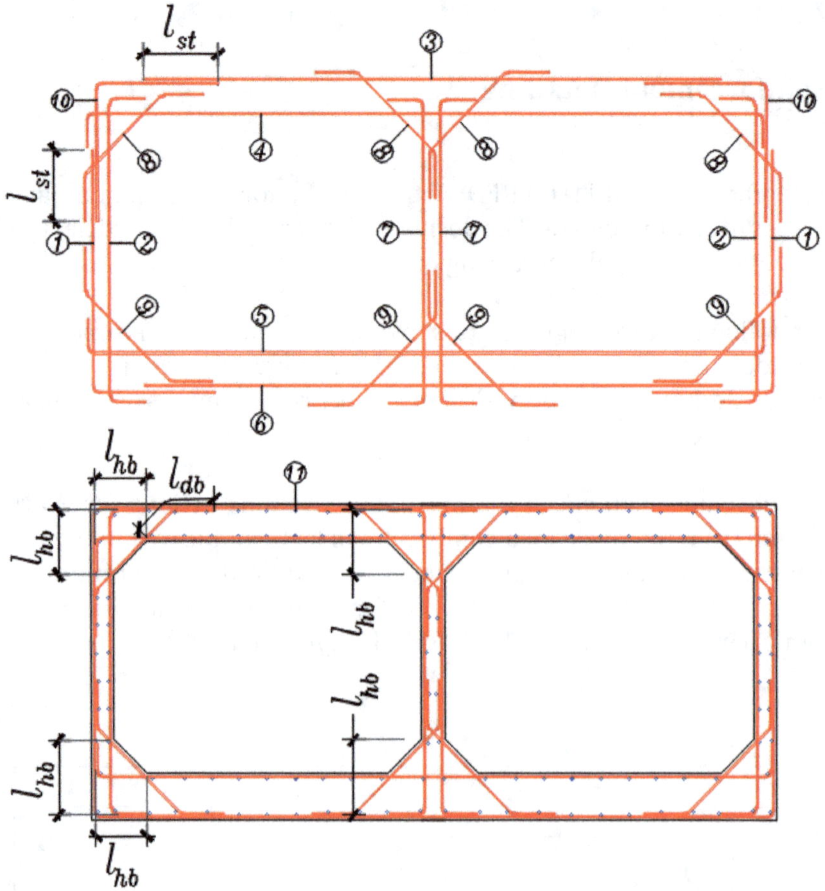

Figure 135. Reinforcement Details

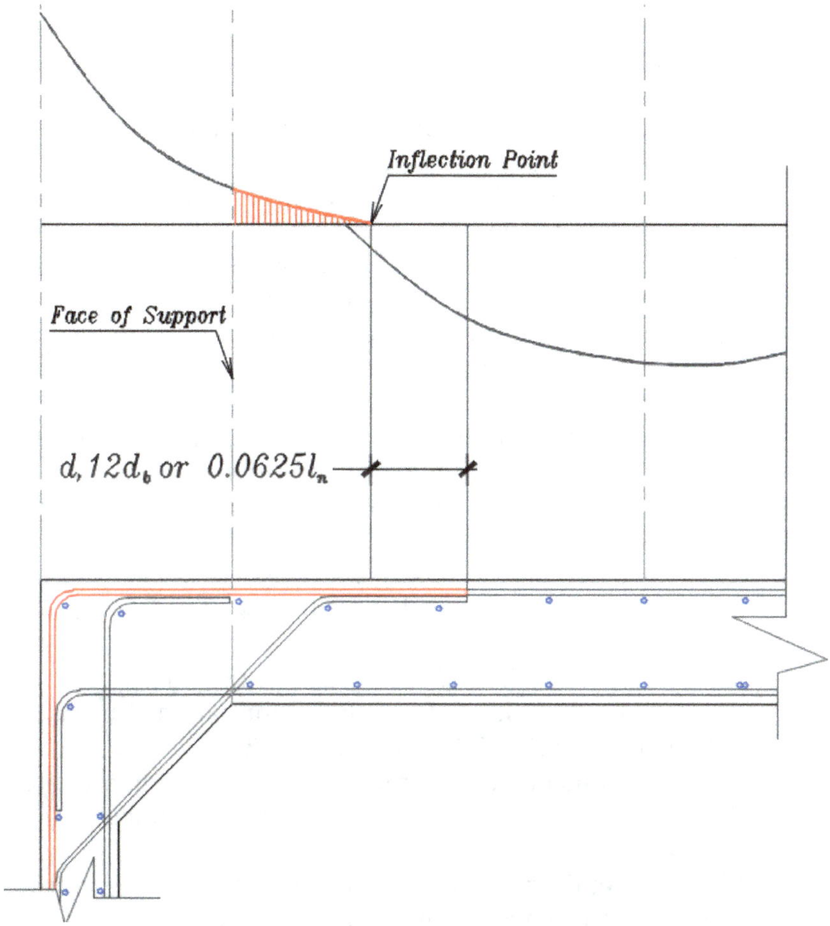

Figure 136. Development of Flexure Reinforcement for Negative Moment

Note that:

- The rebar number 1 covers the negative moment in exterior wall/base connection with area of reinforcement; As6 and As7 and secondary reinforcement As11 (unless As11 covers a negative moment).
- For the point of termination of bara No.1 and 10 see Figure number 136 reference to AASHTO LRFD Article **5.11.1.2.3,** embedment length beyond the point of inflection not less than the effective depth of the member, 12.0 times the nominal diameter of bar, and 0.0625 times the clear span

- The rebar number 2 covers the positive moment of the exterior wall with area of reinforcement; As5
- The rebar number 3 covers the negative moment in top slab-interior wall connection with area of reinforcement; As3 and the secondary reinforcement; As12
- The rebar number 4 covers the positive moment of the top slab with area of reinforcement; As2
- The rebar number 5 covers the positive moment of the bottom slab with area of reinforcement; As8
- The rebar number 6 covers the negative moment of the bottom slab with area of reinforcement; As9 and the secondary reinforcement As13
- The rebar number 7 covers the combined axial and flexural loads for interior walls with area of reinforcement; As10
- The rebar number 8 &9 are for the bottom fibers of haunch section
- The rebar number 10 covers the negative moment in top slab/exterior wall connection with area of reinforcement; As1 and As4
- The splices length L_{st}, refer to AASHTO LRFD Article **5.11.5**
- The hooked development length, L_{hb} ,for bars number 2,4,5 &7, refer to AASHTO LRFD Article **5.11.2.4**
- The development length for deformed bars in compression, L_{db} for bars number 8 &9, refer to AASHTO LRFD Article **5.11.2.2**
- The main reinforcement is shown as linear bars in the culvert cross section as per the previous figures and rebar number 11, appears as dot, and might be considered as secondary, temperature, shrinkage bar or minimum reinforcement in the top & bottom of all sections except the distribution reinforcement in the bottom of slabs with fill less than or equal 2.0 ft. However, some designers may model the whole culvert in 3D model to consider this reinforcement precisely as explained in finite element modeling section.
- The edge beam detail is shown in Figure No.137, unless upstand is required.

Other Details:

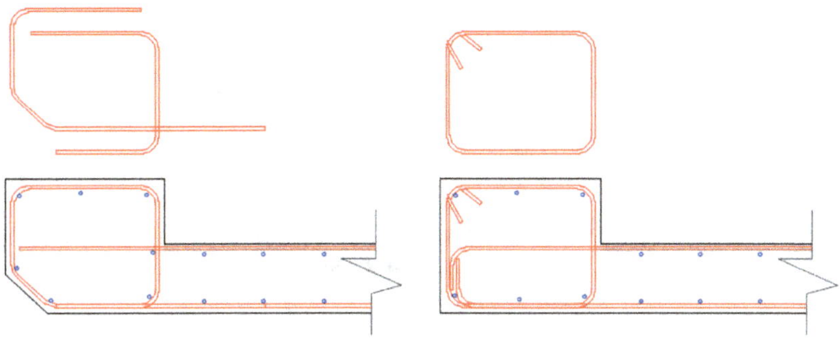

Figure 137. Edge Beam Reinforcement Detail

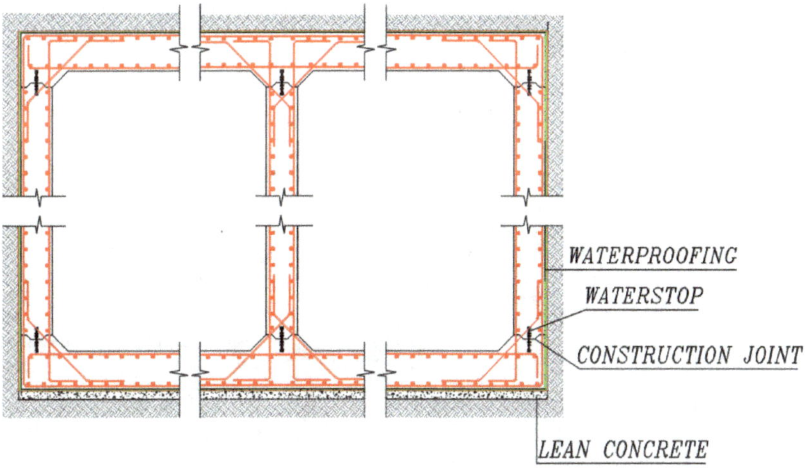

Figure 138. Construction Joint Details Between Walls and Slabs

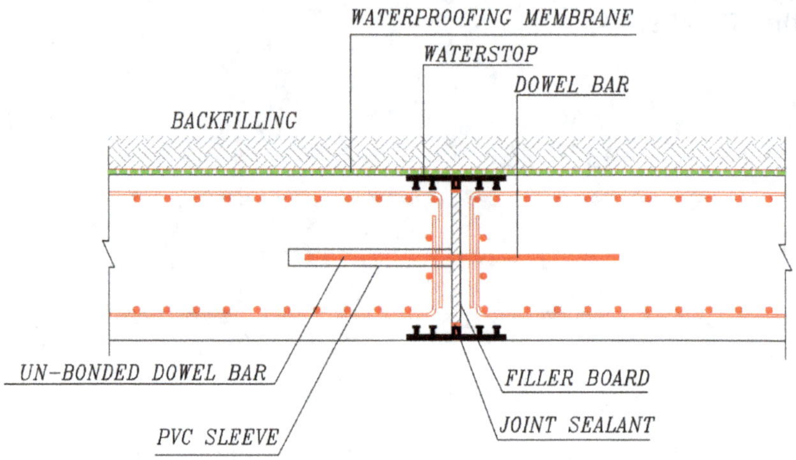

Figure 139. Doweled Expansion Joint Detail between:

- Top Slabs
- Bottom Slabs or,
- Bottom Slab with Apron Slab

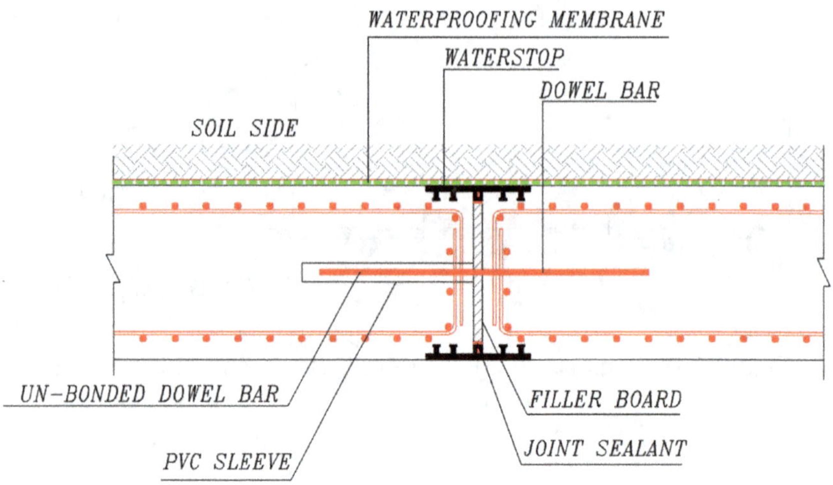

Figure 140. Doweled Expansion Joint Detail between Culvert Walls

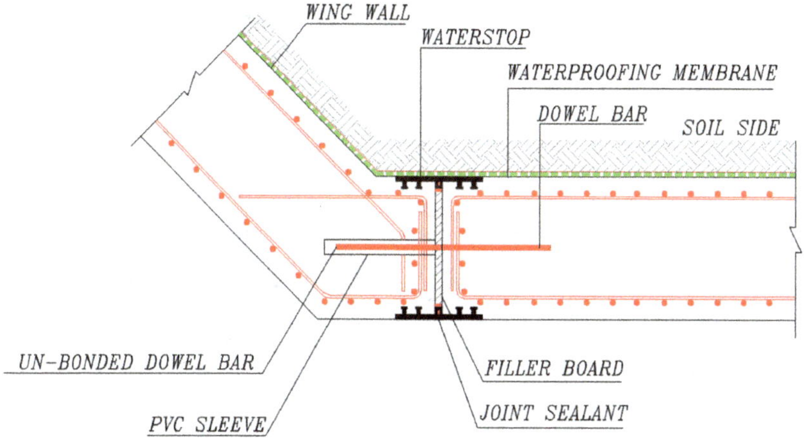

Figure 141. Doweled Expansion Joint Detail between Culvert's Wall and Wing Wall

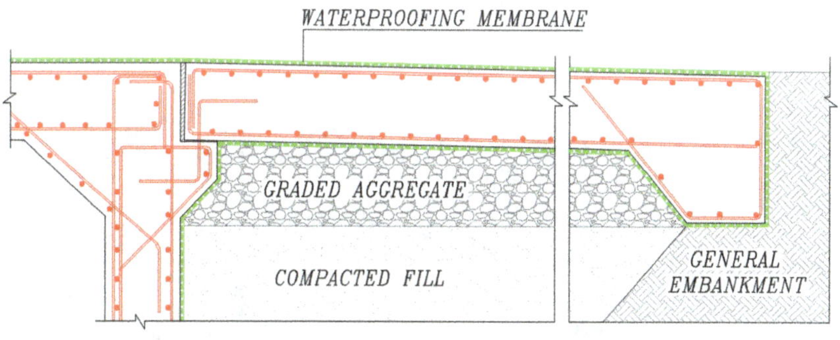

Figure 142. Approach Slab Reinforcement Detail

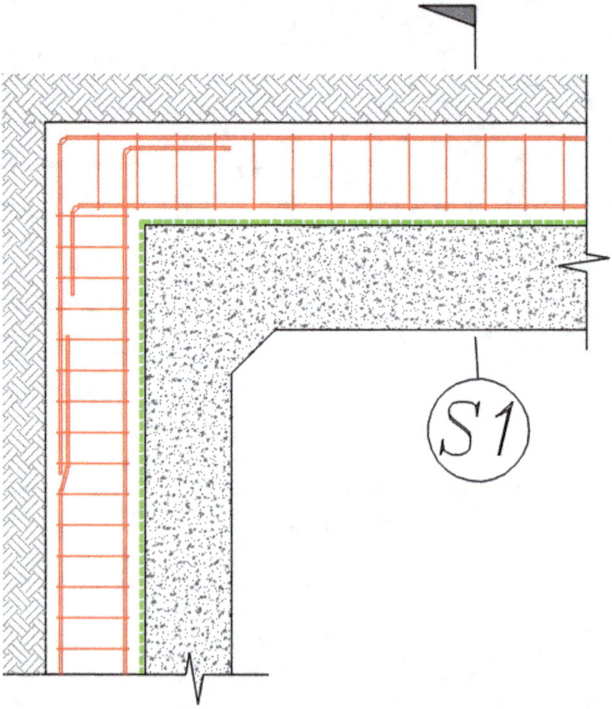

Figure 143. Collar Beam Reinforcement Detail

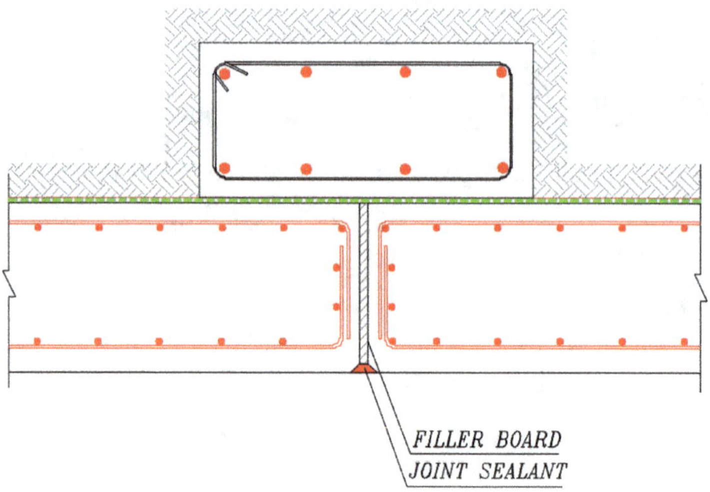

Figure 144. Section (1)

8

Reinforcement Spacing Requirements

8.1 Minimum Spacing of Reinforcing Bars

Reference to AASHTO LRFD Article **5.10.3.1,** the minimum spacing depends on the type of concrete whether it is cast in situ or precast.

Cast in Situ Concrete:
The minimum clear distance between parallel bars in a layer shall not be less than:
• 1.5 times the nominal diameter of the bars,
• 1.5 times the maximum size of the coarse aggregate,
Or
• 1.5 in.

Precast Concrete:
The clear distance between parallel bars in a layer shall not be less than:
• The nominal diameter of the bars,
• 1.33 times the maximum size of the coarse aggregate,
Or
• 1.0 in.

8.2 Maximum Spacing of Reinforcing Bars

Reference to AASHTO LRFD Article **5.10.3.2,** the spacing of the Reinforcement shall not exceed:
• 1.5 times the thickness of the member
Or
• 18.0 in.

9

Complete Examples

9.1 Complete Example 1 (single span precast culvert)

Using the same single cell box culvert in Example 11 within the structural analysis section (FEM) and consider the culvert as precast with 5 ft. fabrication length. The precast suppliers have different cross sections, it is important to generally understand the analysis, design and checking procedure for any dimensions, material properties and project specifications.

The loads were calculated, load cases and load combinations were implemented in the model and the structural analysis was done in the structural analysis section. Same results will be used for this example (follow the analysis results of the Model #2 recommended by the author).

Flexural Design

Figure No. 145 shows the critical sections for flexural design

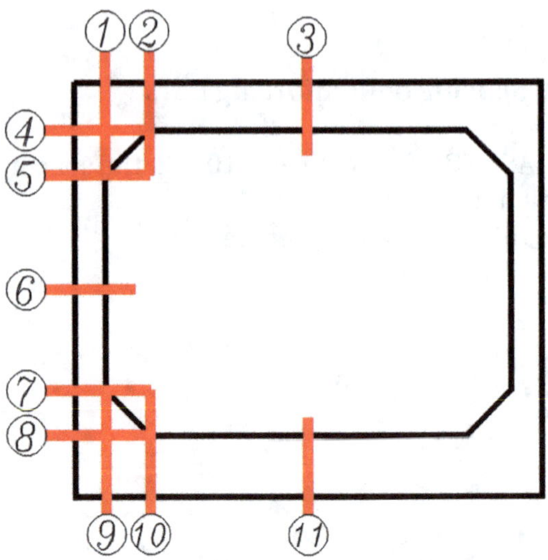

Figure 145. Critical Section Locations for Flexure

The following tables summarize the analysis results which will be used for flexural design:

Bending Moment (Kips.in)

Section No.	h (in.)	Strength (I)			Service (I)		
		Ia	Ib	Ic	Ia	Ib	Ic
1	24	-164.5	-67.2	-87	-83.5	-32.2	-63.3
2	12	-41	158.4	-27.5	52.5	104	7.6
3	12	221.2	308.6	14.8	147.7	199.5	55.6
4	20	-167.8	-88.9	-94	-111	-64.5	-73.7
5	8	-121.1	-82.8	-55.8	-78.5	-56.6	-47.8
6	8	4.34	-70	43	2.6	-42	17.8
7	8	-108.1	-63.6	-64.8	-74.4	-49	-54.8
8	20	-167.8	-61.2	-118.1	-114.5	-47.2	-91.8
9	25	-143.8	-36	-111	-87.5	-12	-88.1
10	13	-49.3	89.8	-35.4	63	132.9	10.8
11	13	239.6	346.6	25.1	165	229.5	74.6

Axial Force (Kips)

Section No.	h (in.)	Strength (I)			Service (I)		
		Ia	Ib	Ic	Ia	Ib	Ic
Top Slab	12	-5.3	-0.7	-4.4	-3.5	-0.9	-2.9
Bottom Slab	13	-6.8	0.3	-6.2	-4.6	-0.17	-4.2
Wall	8	-12.8	-12.8	-4.6	-8.8	-8.8	-5.2

Assume f_y= 60 ksi & E_S= 29,000 ksi
Concrete cover; Reference to AASHTO LRFD Article **5.12.3,** the minimum concrete cover for top slabs used as a driving surface is 2.5 in.

and 1.0 in. for all other members. Use 2.5 in. for top slab and 2 in. for all other members.
ϕ=1.0 (for precast - flexure) & 0.75 for axial compression

Although the members are subjected to combined axial and flexural loads, the flexural design will be mainly done considering the pure flexure loads. The following step is for clarity but not required:
Ag= b*h

Section #	Combo	Mu (K.in)	Pu (K)	φ	b (in)	h (in)	Ag (in^2)	0.10 φ f'c Ag (K)
1	Ia	164.5	5.3	0.75	12	24	288	86.4
1	Ib	67.2	0.7	0.75	12	24	288	86.4
1	Ic	87	4.4	0.75	12	24	288	86.4
2	Ia	41	5.3	0.75	12	12	144	43.2
2	Ib	158.4	0.7	0.75	12	12	144	43.2
2	Ic	27.5	4.4	0.75	12	12	144	43.2
3	Ia	221.4	5.3	0.75	12	12	144	43.2
3	Ib	308.6	0.7	0.75	12	12	144	43.2
3	Ic	14.8	4.4	0.75	12	12	144	43.2
4	Ia	167.8	12.8	0.75	12	20	240	72
4	Ib	88.9	12.8	0.75	12	20	240	72
4	Ic	94	4.6	0.75	12	20	240	72
5	Ia	121.1	12.8	0.75	12	8	96	28.8
5	Ib	82.8	12.8	0.75	12	8	96	28.8
5	Ic	55.8	4.6	0.75	12	8	96	28.8
6	Ia	4.34	12.8	0.75	12	8	96	28.8
6	Ib	70	12.8	0.75	12	8	96	28.8
6	Ic	43	4.6	0.75	12	8	96	28.8
7	Ia	108.1	12.8	0.75	12	8	96	28.8
7	Ib	63.6	12.8	0.75	12	8	96	28.8
7	Ic	64.8	4.6	0.75	12	8	96	28.8
8	Ia	167.8	12.8	0.75	12	20	240	72
8	Ib	61.2	12.8	0.75	12	20	240	72
8	Ic	118.1	4.6	0.75	12	20	240	72
9	Ia	143.8	6.8	0.75	12	25	300	90
9	Ib	36	0.3	0.75	12	25	300	90
9	Ic	111	6.2	0.75	12	25	300	90
10	Ia	49.3	6.8	0.75	12	13	156	46.8
10	Ib	89.8	0.3	0.75	12	13	156	46.8
10	Ic	35.4	6.2	0.75	12	13	156	46.8
11	Ia	239.6	6.8	0.75	12	13	156	46.8
11	Ib	346.6	0.3	0.75	12	13	156	46.8
11	Ic	25.1	6.2	0.75	12	13	156	46.8

The factored axial forces do not exceed the value of (0.1 ϕ f'c Ag), Refer to AASHTO LRFD Article **5.7.4.5,** pure flexure design might be considered. (The previous step is not required by the designer)

Calculate the reinforcement ratio due to pure flexural loads in full respect of the minimum and maximum values as per AASHTO LRFD as follow:

$$\rho = \frac{0.85 f'_c}{f_y}\left(1 - \sqrt{1 - \frac{2R_u}{0.85 f'_c}}\right) \quad \& \quad R_u = \frac{M_u}{\phi b d^2}$$

Refer to AASHTO LRFD Article **12.11.4.3.2**, the minimum reinforcement ratio:
ρ min= 0.002

As per AASHTO LRFD Article **5.7.2,** the maximum reinforcement ratio (ρ max) when:

$$c/d \leq 0.375 \qquad \& \quad c = \frac{a}{\beta_1} = \frac{A_s f_y}{0.85 f'_c b \beta_1}$$

β1 = 0.85 for f'c =4.0ksi.

As=ρ chosen*b*d
ρ chosen is the maximum of ρ and ρ min.

Calculate the values of reinforcement ratio, minimum ratio, section required reinforcement per linear foot and checking the maximum reinforcement ratio conditions as follows:

Section #	Combo	cover (in)	d (in)	ρ	ρ min	ρ chosen	As $in^2/ft.$	c/d
1	Ia	2.5	21.5	0.000496	0.002	0.002	0.516	0.041522
1	Ib	2.5	21.5	0.000202	0.002	0.002	0.516	0.041522
1	Ic	2.5	21.5	0.000262	0.002	0.002	0.516	0.041522
2	Ia	2.5	9.5	0.000635	0.002	0.002	0.228	0.041522
2	Ib	2.5	9.5	0.002492	0.002	0.0025	0.285	0.051903
2	Ic	2.5	9.5	0.000425	0.002	0.002	0.228	0.041522
3	Ia	2.5	9.5	0.003516	0.002	0.00352	0.40128	0.07308
3	Ib	2.5	9.5	0.004967	0.002	0.005	0.57	0.103806
3	Ic	2.5	9.5	0.000228	0.002	0.002	0.228	0.041522
4	Ia	2	18	0.000724	0.002	0.002	0.432	0.041522
4	Ib	2	18	0.000382	0.002	0.002	0.432	0.041522
4	Ic	2	18	0.000404	0.002	0.002	0.432	0.041522
5	Ia	2	6	0.004882	0.002	0.005	0.36	0.103806
5	Ib	2	6	0.00329	0.002	0.0033	0.2376	0.068512
5	Ic	2	6	0.002195	0.002	0.0022	0.1584	0.045675
6	Ia	2	6	0.000168	0.002	0.002	0.144	0.041522
6	Ib	2	6	0.002768	0.002	0.0028	0.2016	0.058131
6	Ic	2	6	0.001684	0.002	0.002	0.144	0.041522
7	Ia	2	6	0.004336	0.002	0.00434	0.31248	0.090104
7	Ib	2	6	0.002509	0.002	0.00251	0.18072	0.052111
7	Ic	2	6	0.002558	0.002	0.0026	0.1872	0.053979
8	Ia	2	18	0.000724	0.002	0.002	0.432	0.041522
8	Ib	2	18	0.000263	0.002	0.002	0.432	0.041522
8	Ic	2	18	0.000509	0.002	0.002	0.432	0.041522
9	Ia	2	23	0.000379	0.002	0.002	0.552	0.041522
9	Ib	2	23	9.46E-05	0.002	0.002	0.552	0.041522
9	Ic	2	23	0.000292	0.002	0.002	0.552	0.041522
10	Ia	2	11	0.000569	0.002	0.002	0.264	0.041522
10	Ib	2	11	0.00104	0.002	0.002	0.264	0.041522
10	Ic	2	11	0.000408	0.002	0.002	0.264	0.041522
11	Ia	2	11	0.00282	0.002	0.00282	0.37224	0.058547
11	Ib	2	11	0.004129	0.002	0.004129	0.54502	0.085723
11	Ic	2	11	0.000289	0.002	0.002	0.264	0.041522

The table shows the maximum value of c/d is 0.103806 which does not exceed 0.375, this means that the reinforcement does not exceed the maximum amount per AASHTO LRFD.

Check of Cracking:

The procedure of checking crack control is as follow:

- Calculating dc = cover + db /2
  Assume dc = cover
- Calculating $\beta_s = 1 + \frac{d_c}{0.7(h - d_c)}$
- Calculating the allowable reinforcement stress:
  $$f_{ss} \leq \frac{700\,\gamma_e}{\beta_s(s + 2d_c)} \leq 0.60 f_y\,(ksi),\ \gamma_e = 0.75$$
  & 0.6 f y= 0.6*60= 36 ksi. (f_{ss} shall not exceed 36 ksi)
- Find the actual stress provided in the steel:
  $$f_s = \frac{M_s + N_s(d - h/2)}{A_s jid}$$
  $$j = 0.74 + 0.1\frac{e}{d} \leq 0.9 \ \ \&\ \ i = \frac{1}{1 - \frac{jd}{e}}$$
  $$e = \frac{M_s}{N_s} + \left(d - \frac{h}{2}\right)$$

Consider that $\frac{e}{d} \geq 1.15$ otherwise, crack check is not required

- Compare the allowable and actual stresses to check whether reinforcement increment is required or not.
- If ($f_s > f_{ss}$), means not satisfactory and reinforcing area shall be modified as follow:
  $$A_{scrack} = \frac{f_s}{f_{ss}} \cdot A_s$$

Apply the equations as per the mentioned procedure using an excel spreadsheet, the results are as follows:

Section #	Combo	cover (in)	d (in)	As $in^2/ft.$	βs	fss (ksi)	fss chosen
1	Ia	2.5	21.5	0.516	1.166113	38.01804	36
1	Ib	2.5	21.5	0.516	1.166113	38.01804	36
1	Ic	2.5	21.5	0.516	1.166113	38.01804	36
2	Ia	2.5	9.5	0.228	1.37594	32.2204	32.22
2	Ib	2.5	9.5	0.285	1.37594	32.2204	32.22
2	Ic	2.5	9.5	0.228	1.37594	32.2204	32.22
3	Ia	2.5	9.5	0.40128	1.37594	32.2204	32.22
3	Ib	2.5	9.5	0.57	1.37594	32.2204	32.22
3	Ic	2.5	9.5	0.228	1.37594	32.2204	32.22
4	Ia	2	18	0.432	1.15873	43.04281	36
4	Ib	2	18	0.432	1.15873	43.04281	36
4	Ic	2	18	0.432	1.15873	43.04281	36
5	Ia	2	6	0.36	1.47619	33.78629	33.79
5	Ib	2	6	0.2376	1.47619	33.78629	33.79
5	Ic	2	6	0.1584	1.47619	33.78629	33.79
6	Ia	2	6	0.144	1.47619	33.78629	33.79
6	Ib	2	6	0.2016	1.47619	33.78629	33.79
6	Ic	2	6	0.144	1.47619	33.78629	33.79
7	Ia	2	6	0.31248	1.47619	33.78629	33.79
7	Ib	2	6	0.18072	1.47619	33.78629	33.79
7	Ic	2	6	0.1872	1.47619	33.78629	33.79
8	Ia	2	18	0.432	1.15873	43.04281	36
8	Ib	2	18	0.432	1.15873	43.04281	36
8	Ic	2	18	0.432	1.15873	43.04281	36
9	Ia	2	23	0.552	1.124224	44.36395	36
9	Ib	2	23	0.552	1.124224	44.36395	36
9	Ic	2	23	0.552	1.124224	44.36395	36
10	Ia	2	11	0.264	1.25974	39.59149	36
10	Ib	2	11	0.264	1.25974	39.59149	36
10	Ic	2	11	0.264	1.25974	39.59149	36
11	Ia	2	11	0.37224	1.25974	39.59149	36
11	Ib	2	11	0.54502	1.25974	39.59149	36
11	Ic	2	11	0.264	1.25974	39.59149	36

Section #	Combo	Ms (k.in)	Ns (k)	e (in)	e/d	j	i
1	Ia	83.5	3.5	33.35714	1.551495	0.89515	2.36384
1	Ib	32.2	0.9	45.27778	2.105943	0.950594	1.82278
1	Ic	63.3	2.9	31.32759	1.457097	0.88571	2.55010
2	Ia	52.5	3.5	18.5	1.947368	0.934737	1.92308
2	Ib	104	0.9	119.0556	12.53216	1.993216	1.18913
2	Ic	7.6	2.9	6.12069	0.644283	0.804428	4.02312
3	Ia	147.7	3.5	45.7	4.810526	1.221053	1.34018
3	Ib	199.5	0.9	225.1667	23.70175	3.110175	1.15104
3	Ic	55.6	2.9	22.67241	2.38657	0.978657	1.69511
4	Ia	111	4.6	32.13043	1.785024	0.918502	2.05999
4	Ib	64.5	0.17	387.4118	21.52288	2.892288	1.15524
4	Ic	73.7	4.2	25.54762	1.419312	0.881931	2.64117
5	Ia	78.5	4.6	19.06522	3.177536	1.057754	1.49899
5	Ib	56.6	0.17	334.9412	55.82353	6.322353	1.12772
5	Ic	47.8	4.2	13.38095	2.230159	0.963016	1.75999
6	Ia	2.6	4.6	2.565217	0.427536	0.782754	1.20359
6	Ib	42	0.17	249.0588	41.5098	4.89098	1.13356
6	Ic	17.8	4.2	6.238095	1.039683	0.843968	5.31225
7	Ia	74.4	4.6	18.17391	3.028986	1.042899	1.52510
7	Ib	49	0.17	290.2353	48.37255	5.577255	1.13032
7	Ic	54.8	4.2	15.04762	2.507937	0.990794	1.65306
8	Ia	114.5	4.6	32.8913	1.827295	0.922729	2.02008
8	Ib	47.2	0.17	285.6471	15.86928	2.326928	1.17183
8	Ic	91.8	4.2	29.85714	1.65873	0.905873	2.20324
9	Ia	87.5	8.8	20.44318	0.888834	0.828883	14.8261
9	Ib	12	8.8	11.86364	0.51581	0.791581	1.87043
9	Ic	88.1	5.2	27.44231	1.193144	0.859314	3.57411
10	Ia	63	8.8	11.65909	1.059917	0.845992	4.95461
10	Ib	132.9	8.8	19.60227	1.782025	0.918202	2.06295
10	Ic	10.8	5.2	6.576923	0.597902	0.79979	2.96155
11	Ia	165	8.8	23.25	2.113636	0.951364	1.81854
11	Ib	229.5	8.8	30.57955	2.779959	1.017996	1.57776
11	Ic	74.6	5.2	18.84615	1.713287	0.911329	2.13638

Section #	Combo	fs (ksi)	fss chosen	Notes	As crack $in^2/ft.$	As final $in^2/ft.$
1	Ia	4.973422	36	OK	----------	0.516
1	Ib	2.119877	36	OK	----------	0.516
1	Ic	3.625664	36	OK	----------	0.516
2	Ia	16.63012	32.22	OK	----------	0.228
2	Ib	16.69708	32.22	OK	----------	0.285
2	Ic	-2.53215	32.22	e/d<1.15	----------	0.228
3	Ia	25.63993	32.22	OK	----------	0.40128
3	Ib	10.45376	32.22	OK	----------	0.57
3	Ic	18.2982	32.22	OK	----------	0.228
4	Ia	10.04554	36	OK	----------	0.432
4	Ib	2.534838	36	OK	----------	0.432
4	Ic	5.923973	36	OK	----------	0.432
5	Ia	25.6072	33.79	OK	----------	0.36
5	Ib	5.601951	33.79	OK	----------	0.2376
5	Ic	34.88882	33.79	$f_s > f_{ss}$	0.16355	0.16355
6	Ia	-14.4965	33.79	e/d<1.15	----------	0.144
6	Ib	6.313452	33.79	OK	----------	0.2016
6	Ic	6.763683	33.79	e/d<1.15	----------	0.144
7	Ia	28.03443	33.79	OK	----------	0.31248
7	Ib	7.218022	33.79	OK	----------	0.18072
7	Ic	34.35474	33.79	$f_s > f_{ss}$	0.19033	0.19033
8	Ia	10.43854	36	OK	----------	0.432
8	Ib	2.290215	36	OK	----------	0.432
8	Ic	8.079989	36	OK	----------	0.432
9	Ia	1.153038	36	e/d<1.15	----------	0.552
9	Ib	-5.55388	36	e/d<1.15	----------	0.552
9	Ic	3.659627	36	OK	----------	0.552
10	Ia	8.428988	36	e/d<1.15	----------	0.264
10	Ib	31.35918	36	OK	----------	0.264
10	Ic	-4.97203	36	e/d<1.15	----------	0.264
11	Ia	28.88159	36	OK	----------	0.37224
11	Ib	27.94567	36	OK	----------	0.54502
11	Ic	17.33309	36	OK	----------	0.264

The final areas of reinforcement after cracking check shall be used. The conclusion of flexural transversal reinforcement areas is as follow:

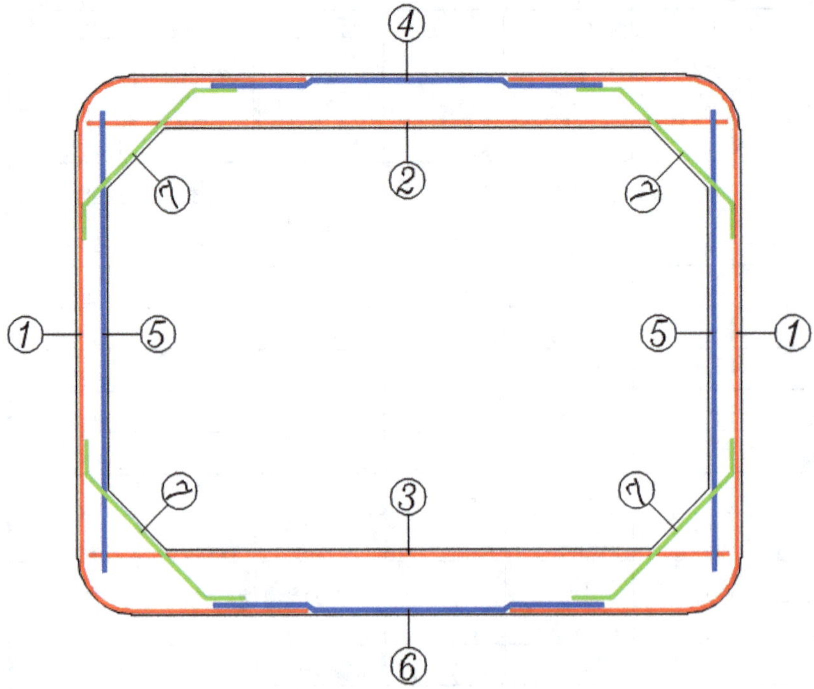

Figure 146. Flexural Reinforcement

- Rebar No. 1 covers the reinforcement for external side sections No. 1, 2,4,5,6, 7,8,9 &10
  The maximum area of reinforcement is 0.552 in^2/ft

- Rebar No. 2 covers the reinforcement for internal side section No. 3
  The area of reinforcement is 0.57 in^2/ft

- Rebar No. 3 covers the reinforcement for internal side section No. 11
  The area of reinforcement is 0.54502 in^2/ft

- Rebar No. 4 shall be minimum reinforcement
  The area of reinforcement is 0.228 in^2/ft

- Rebar No. 5 covers the reinforcement for internal side section No. 6
  The area of reinforcement is 0.144 in^2/ft

- Rebar No. 6 shall be minimum reinforcement
  The area of reinforcement is 0.264 in^2/ft

- Rebar No. 7 covers the reinforcement for internal side sections No. 1 &9 which shall be minimum reinforcement
  The maximum area of reinforcement is 0.552 in^2/ft

As discussed, design of reinforcement shall be done as per the details will be followed by the designer considering the sections design results.

Temperature and Shrinkage Reinforcement

Reference to AASHTO LRFD Article **5.10.8,** area of longitudinal reinforcement per foot, on each face and in each direction, shall satisfy:

$$A_s \geq \frac{1.3bh}{2(b+h)f_y}$$

Section	b (in.)	h (in.)	As (in^2/ft.)
Top slab	12	12	0.065
Top slab corner	12	24	0.087
Wall	12	8	0.052
Bottom Slab	12	13	0.067
Bottom Slab corner	12	25	0.089

Distribution Reinforcement

Since the fill depth above the culvert exceeded 2 ft., the distribution reinforcement (in the bottom of culver's top slab) is not required.

Note: The normal practice for precast culverts is using welded wire fabricated (WWF) reinforcement. The designer will decide about the optimum type whether traditional or WWF but he shall consider all requirements of AASHTO LRFD for any type of reinforcement used by choosing the safe area of reinforcement in full respect to all conditions like development length, splice length, location of bar termination, and minimum & maximum spacing between reinforcing bars.

Design of Shear

Figure No. 147 shows the critical sections for shear as follow:

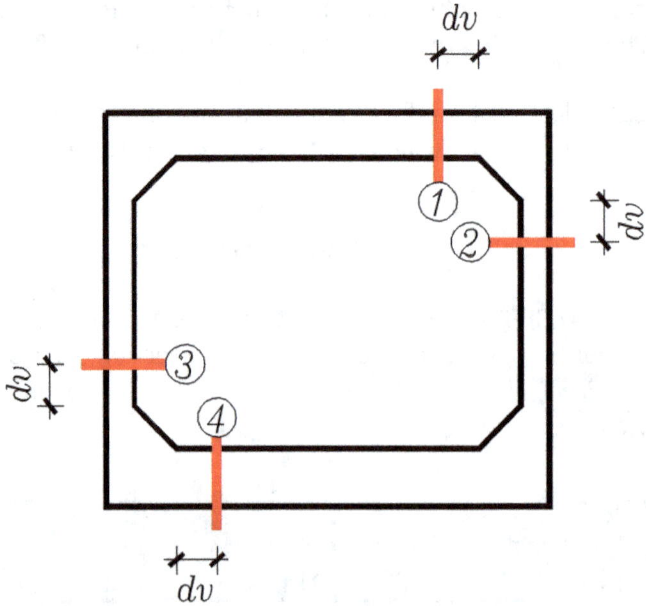

Figure 147. Critical Section Locations for Shear

Note: The designer shall consider the maximum shear value for every slab or wall in distance $\mathbf{d_v}$, whenever the location (right, left, top or bottom). The section locations in the previous Figure are illustrative only.

Calculate $\mathbf{d_v}$

Section No.	Cover (in.)	h (in.)	d (in.)	As (in^2/ft)	a	d - (a/2)	0.72 h	0.9 de	dv (in.)
1	2.5	12	9.5	0.552	0.811765	9.094118	8.64	8.55	9.09412
2	2	8	6	0.552	0.811765	5.594118	5.76	5.4	5.76
3	2	8	6	0.552	0.811765	5.594118	5.76	5.4	5.76
4	2	13	11	0.552	0.811765	10.59412	9.36	9.9	10.5941

Shear Force at distance dv (kips)

Section No.	dv (in.)	Strength (I)		
		Ia	Ib	Ic
1	9.09412	8.10	8.10	2.40
2	5.76	4.27	0.50	3.50
3	5.76	4.80	0.20	4.44
4	10.5941	8.50	8.30	3.20

Check Shear of walls:

Maximum ultimate shear force for walls is 4.80 kips
Reference to AASHTO LRFD Article **5.8.3.3,** concrete shear capacity is the least of:

$$\phi V_c = \phi * 0.0316 \beta \sqrt{f'_c} b_v d_v$$

And,
$\phi V_c = \phi * 0.25 * f'_c * b_v * d_v$
$\phi = 0.9$ (for precast – shear)
Reference to AASHTO LRFD Article **5.8.3.4.1,** wall size is less than 16 in. and it is not subjected to axial tension, consider $\beta = 2.0$.
$\phi V_c = 0.9 * 0.0316 * 2 * \sqrt{4} * 12 * 5.76 = 7.86$ kips.
$\phi V_c = 0.9 * 0.25 * 4 * 12 * 5.76 = 62.21$ kips.
Use $\phi V_n = 7.86$ kips. $> V_u = 4.80$ kips. OK

Check Shear of Top Slab:

Maximum ultimate shear force for top slab is 8.10 kips with maximum associated ultimate moment = 106 kips.in.
Reference to AASHTO LRFD Article **5.14.5.3,** for slabs with earth fill > 2 ft.

$$V_c = \left(0.0676 \lambda \sqrt{f'_c} + 4.6 \frac{A_s}{b\, d_e} \frac{V_u d_e}{M_u} \right) b\, d_e \leq 0.126 \lambda \sqrt{f'_c}\, b\, d_e$$

$$\frac{V_u d_e}{M_u} \leq 1.0$$

$V_u d_e / M_u = (8.10*9.50)/106 = 0.726 < 1$: use 0.726

$\phi V_c = 0.9*((0.0676*\sqrt{4})+(4.6*(0.552/(12*9.50))*0.726))*12*9.50 =$ 15.53 kips.
$0.126\sqrt{f'_c}\, b\, d_e = 0.126*\sqrt{4}*12*9.50 = 28.728$ ksi. > 15.53 kips. OK

For single-cell box culverts, Vc for slabs monolithic with walls need not be taken to be less than $0.0948\sqrt{f'_c}\, b\, d_e$

$\phi V_c = 0.9*0.0948*\sqrt{4}*12*9.50 = 19.45$ kips.
Use $\phi V_c = 19.45$ kips. > $V_u = 8.10$ kips. OK

Check Shear of Bottom Slab:

Maximum ultimate shear force for bottom slab is 8.50 kips with maximum associated ultimate moment = 150 kips.in.
Reference to AASHTO LRFD Article **5.14.5.3,** for slabs with earth fill > 2 ft.

$$V_c = \left(0.0676\lambda\sqrt{f'_c} + 4.6\frac{A_s}{b\, d_e}\frac{V_u d_e}{M_u}\right) b\, d_e \le 0.126\lambda\sqrt{f'_c}\, b\, d_e$$

$$\frac{V_u d_e}{M_u} \le 1.0$$

$V_u d_e / M_u = (8.50*11)/150 = 0.623 < 1$: use 0.623

$\phi V_c = 0.9*((0.0676*\sqrt{4})+(4.6*(0.552/(12*11))*0.623))*12*11 =$ 19.43 kips.
$0.126\sqrt{f'_c}\, b\, d_e = 0.126*\sqrt{4}*12*11 = 33.264$ ksi. > 19.43 kips. OK

For single-cell box culverts only, Vc for slabs monolithic with walls need not be taken to be less than $0.0948\sqrt{f'_c}\, b\, d_e$

$\phi V_c = 0.9*0.0948*\sqrt{4}*12*11 = 22.52$ kips.
Use $\phi V_c = 22.52$ kips. > $V_u = 8.50$ kips. OK
Shear is safe

Design of Inlet/Outlet

Headwall dimensions:
The fill depth is 5.0 feet, assuming the fill depth in the headwall location is 2.0 feet. Therefore, there is headwall required. Assuming the headwall height from the top of culvert's top slab is 6.0 feet to include

a concrete barrier with minimum thickness 7.5". The inlet precast segment will be casted monolithically with the headwall as per the following figure:

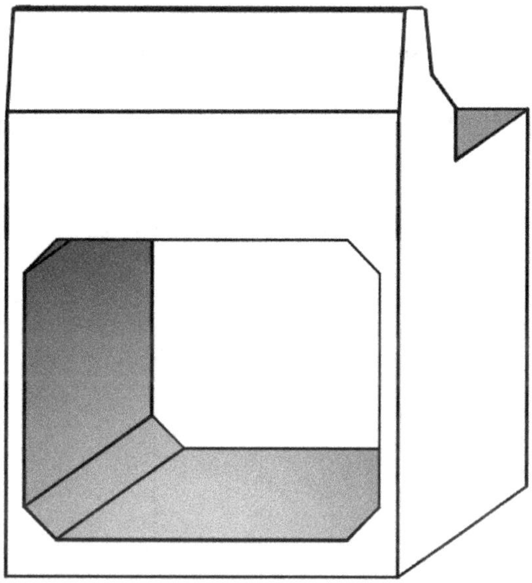

Figure 148. Precast Culver (Inlet Segment)

Wing wall dimensions:

Assume free standing flared wing walls, considering expansion joint between the wing wall-Apron slab and culvert's inlet segment.

V = (top slab thickness) + (clear wall height) – 12"

Note that the 2.0 feet of fill above the culvert in the inlet location might affect the slope. Therefore, consider the end of wing wall 3.0 feet instead of 1.0. Hence, the equation will be as follow:

V = (top slab thickness) + (clear wall height) +24" (filling) – 36" (end height)

V = 12" + (9'*12) + 24" – 36" = 108"

θ = Zero

Assume $\alpha = 30^\circ$

$L = 2V / \cos(\theta+\alpha)$

$L = 2*108 / \cos(30^\circ) = 249.415$ in. = 20.78 feet

Consider L = 21 feet

Apron slab dimensions:

Consider same culvert's bottom slab thickness.

Toe wall dimensions:

Assume one foot minimum width and also depth from the bottom of bottom slab with 45 ° inclination.

The following Figures show the assumed concrete dimensions for the inlet:

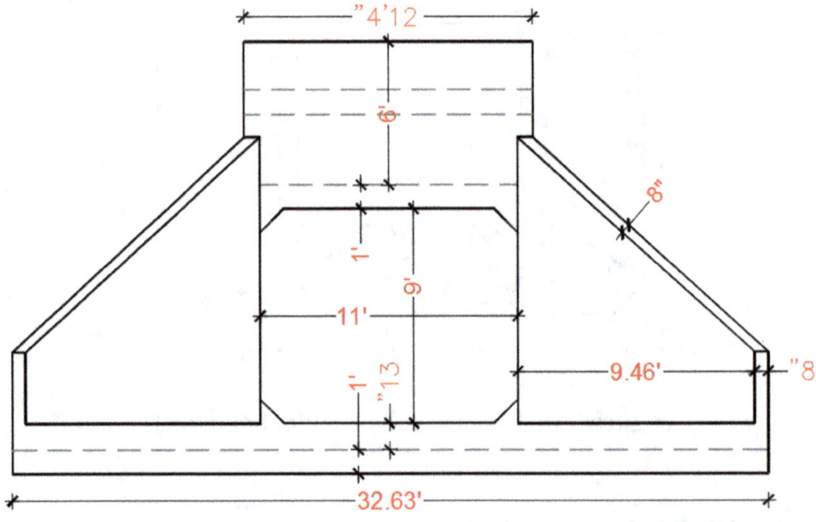

Figure 149. View (1)

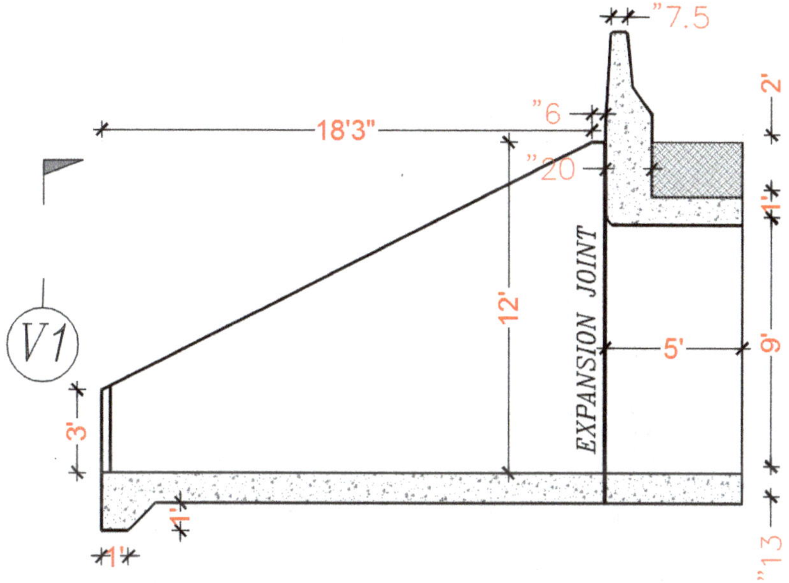

Figure 150. Section (1)

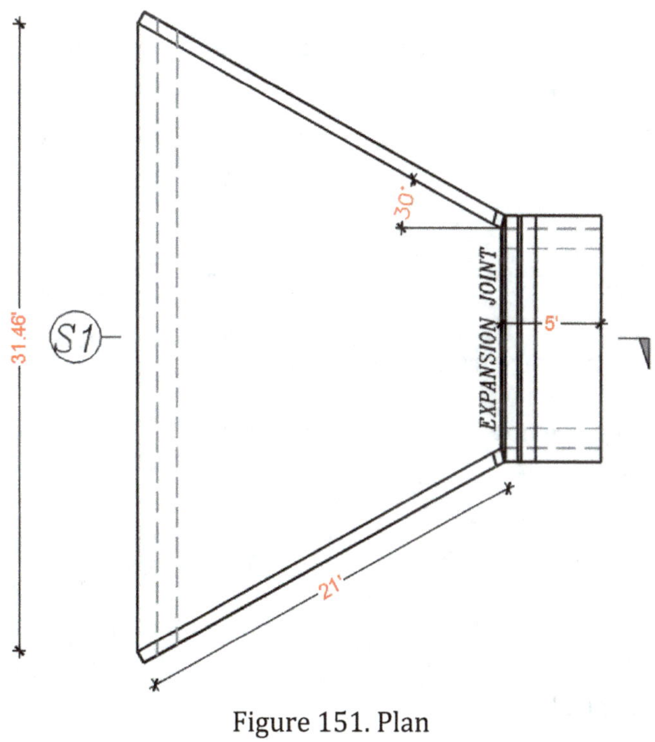

Figure 151. Plan

Design of Wing Wall

The wing walls might be designed as a cantilever wall supported by the apron slab. The free body diagram is as follows:

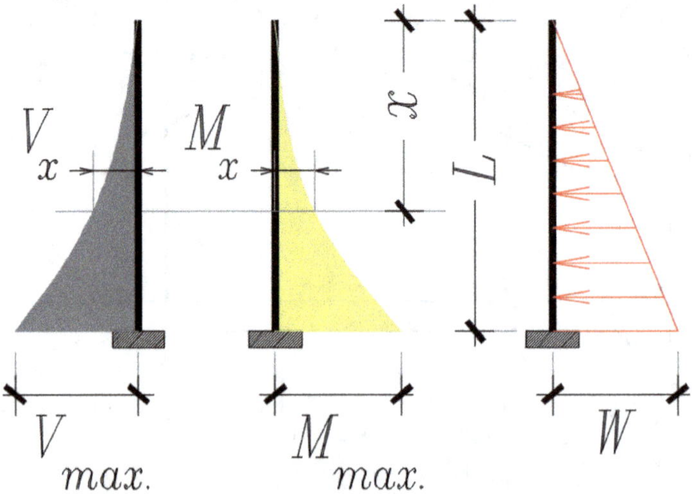

Figure 152. Free Body Diagram for Wing Wall

$W = \gamma_{soil} * L * k_a$

$V_{max.} = \frac{WL}{2}$ & $V_x = \frac{Wx^2}{2L}$

$M_{max.} = \frac{WL^2}{6}$ & $M_x = \frac{Wx^3}{6L}$

Where x is any space from the free end.

Applying the previous equations to the wing wall to get the design moment and shear:
At the bottom of wall strip:
W= Pb = k γs z
z= L (variable)
Wu= Pu = 1.5 Pb
Mu = Pu $z^2/6$

At the top of wall strip:
Pt = Zero

Reference to AASHTO LRFD **3.11.5.3,** ka to be considered and ignore the passive pressure due to water.

Assume k=0.5, the maximum moment values for every linear foot in the very bottom of the wing wall will be as follows:

Z (ft)	γ (kcf)	k	P (kips/ft)	Pu (kips/ft)	Mu (bott) (k.f/ft)	Mu (k.in/ft)
12.00	0.12	0.5	0.72	1.08	25.92	311.04
11.56	0.12	0.5	0.6936	1.0404	23.17207	278.0648
11.12	0.12	0.5	0.6672	1.0008	20.62555	247.5066
10.70	0.12	0.5	0.642	0.963	18.37565	220.5077
10.24	0.12	0.5	0.6144	0.9216	16.10613	193.2735
9.80	0.12	0.5	0.588	0.882	14.11788	169.4146
9.40	0.12	0.5	0.564	0.846	12.45876	149.5051
8.93	0.12	0.5	0.5358	0.8037	10.68183	128.182
8.50	0.12	0.5	0.51	0.765	9.211875	110.5425
8.05	0.12	0.5	0.483	0.7245	7.824902	93.89882
7.61	0.12	0.5	0.4566	0.6849	6.610666	79.32799
7.17	0.12	0.5	0.4302	0.6453	5.529027	66.34833
6.73	0.12	0.5	0.4038	0.6057	4.572318	54.86782
6.30	0.12	0.5	0.378	0.567	3.750705	45.00846
5.85	0.12	0.5	0.351	0.5265	3.003024	36.03629
5.41	0.12	0.5	0.3246	0.4869	2.375106	28.50128
5.00	0.12	0.5	0.3	0.45	1.875	22.5
4.54	0.12	0.5	0.2724	0.4086	1.40365	16.8438
4.10	0.12	0.5	0.246	0.369	1.033815	12.40578
3.66	0.12	0.5	0.2196	0.3294	0.735418	8.825021
3.22	0.12	0.5	0.1932	0.2898	0.500794	6.009525

Calculating the reinforcement area and checking minimum and maximum reinforcement ratios:

Z (ft)	φ	b (in.)	h (in.)	Ag (in^2)	Cover (in.)	d (in.)	ρ
12.00	1	12	8	96	2	6	0.0136421
11.56	1	12	8	96	2	6	0.0119980
11.12	1	12	8	96	2	6	0.0105266
10.70	1	12	8	96	2	6	0.0092646
10.24	1	12	8	96	2	6	0.0080247
9.80	1	12	8	96	2	6	0.0069640
9.40	1	12	8	96	2	6	0.0060958
8.93	1	12	8	96	2	6	0.0051823
8.50	1	12	8	96	2	6	0.0044386
8.05	1	12	8	96	2	6	0.0037465
7.61	1	12	8	96	2	6	0.0031479
7.17	1	12	8	96	2	6	0.0026203
6.73	1	12	8	96	2	6	0.0021579
6.30	1	12	8	96	2	6	0.0017639
5.85	1	12	8	96	2	6	0.0014078
5.41	1	12	8	96	2	6	0.0011105
5.00	1	12	8	96	2	6	0.0008748
4.54	1	12	8	96	2	6	0.0006536
4.10	1	12	8	96	2	6	0.0004807
3.66	1	12	8	96	2	6	0.0003415
3.22	1	12	8	96	2	6	0.0002323

Z (ft)	ρ min	ρ chosen	As (in^2)	c	c/d
12.00	0.002	0.014	1.008	1.7439	0.2907
11.56	0.002	0.012	0.864	1.4948	0.2491
11.12	0.002	0.01	0.72	1.2457	0.2076
10.70	0.002	0.0093	0.6696	1.1585	0.1931
10.24	0.002	0.008	0.576	0.9965	0.1661
9.80	0.002	0.006	0.432	0.7474	0.1246
9.40	0.002	0.007	0.504	0.8720	0.1453
8.93	0.002	0.0052	0.3744	0.6478	0.1080
8.50	0.002	0.0044	0.3168	0.5481	0.0913
8.05	0.002	0.0037	0.2664	0.4609	0.0768
7.61	0.002	0.0031	0.2232	0.3862	0.0644
7.17	0.002	0.0026	0.1872	0.3239	0.0540
6.73	0.002	0.00216	0.1555	0.2691	0.0448
6.30	0.002	0.002	0.144	0.2491	0.0415
5.85	0.002	0.002	0.144	0.2491	0.0415
5.41	0.002	0.002	0.144	0.2491	0.0415
5.00	0.002	0.002	0.144	0.2491	0.0415
4.54	0.002	0.002	0.144	0.2491	0.0415
4.10	0.002	0.002	0.144	0.2491	0.0415
3.66	0.002	0.002	0.144	0.2491	0.0415
3.22	0.002	0.002	0.144	0.2491	0.0415

The c/d values do not exceed 0.375. Hence, the ratios are not exceeding the maximum acceptable values.

Check of Wing Wall Cracking:
The cracking check for wing walls is not required as mentioned previously. However, the following crack calculations are done for extra safety.
The un-factored axial force (Ns) is considered as the weight of the concrete of every strip
= Strip width * strip height * wall thickness * γ concrete

Z (ft)	βs	fss	fss chosen	Ms (k.in)	Ns kips
12.00	1.476	33.786	36	207.36	1.20
11.56	1.476	33.786	36	185.38	1.16
11.12	1.476	33.786	36	165.00	1.11
10.70	1.476	33.786	36	147.01	1.07
10.24	1.476	33.786	36	128.85	1.02
9.80	1.476	33.786	36	112.94	0.98
9.40	1.476	33.786	36	99.67	0.94
8.93	1.476	33.786	36	85.45	0.89
8.50	1.476	33.786	36	73.70	0.85
8.05	1.476	33.786	36	62.60	0.81
7.61	1.476	33.786	36	52.89	0.76
7.17	1.476	33.786	36	44.23	0.72
6.73	1.476	33.786	36	36.58	0.67
6.30	1.476	33.786	36	30.01	0.63
5.85	1.476	33.786	36	24.02	0.59
5.41	1.476	33.786	36	19.00	0.54
5.00	1.476	33.786	36	15.00	0.50
4.54	1.476	33.786	36	11.23	0.45
4.10	1.476	33.786	36	8.27	0.41
3.66	1.476	33.786	36	5.88	0.37
3.22	1.476	33.786	36	4.01	0.32

Z (ft)	e	e/d	j	i	fs	Notes
12.00	174.714	29.119	3.652	1.143	8.306	OK
11.56	162.280	27.047	3.445	1.146	9.172	OK
11.12	150.311	25.052	3.245	1.149	10.383	OK
10.70	139.319	23.220	3.062	1.152	10.525	OK
10.24	127.766	21.294	2.869	1.156	11.421	OK
9.80	117.190	19.532	2.693	1.160	14.191	OK
9.40	107.979	17.997	2.540	1.164	11.357	OK
8.93	97.646	16.274	2.367	1.170	14.018	OK
8.50	88.657	14.776	2.218	1.177	15.202	OK
8.05	79.724	13.287	2.069	1.184	16.395	OK
7.61	71.460	11.910	1.931	1.194	17.628	OK
7.17	63.660	10.610	1.801	1.204	18.743	OK
6.73	56.324	9.387	1.679	1.218	19.881	OK
6.30	49.604	8.267	1.567	1.234	18.720	OK
5.85	43.046	7.174	1.457	1.255	15.944	OK
5.41	37.104	6.184	1.358	1.281	13.353	OK
5.00	31.985	5.331	1.273	1.314	11.073	OK
4.54	26.722	4.454	1.185	1.363	8.697	OK
4.10	22.162	3.694	1.109	1.429	6.636	OK
3.66	18.067	3.011	1.041	1.528	4.812	OK
3.22	14.436	2.406	0.981	1.688	3.252	OK

Check of Wing Wall Shear:

Calculate d_v

Section No.	Cover (in.)	h (in.)	d (in.)	As (in²/ft)	a	d - (a/2)	0.72 h	0.9 de	dv (in.)
Wing	2	8	6	1.008	1.482	5.2588	5.76	5.4	5.76

Calculating the maximum ultimate shear force for wing walls:

$V_x = \frac{Wx^2}{2L}$

x= 12 – (5.76/12)= 11.52 ft.

W = 1.08 kips.

$V_x = \frac{Wx^2}{2L} = 5.97$ kips

Reference to AASHTO LRFD Article **5.8.3.3,** concrete shear capacity is the least of:

$$\phi V_c = \phi * 0.0316\beta\sqrt{f'_c} b_v d_v$$

And,

$\phi V_c = \phi * 0.25 * f'_c * b_v * d_v$

$\phi = 0.9$ (for precast – shear)

Reference to AASHTO LRFD Article **5.8.3.4.1,** wall size is less than 16 in. and it is not subjected to axial tension, consider $\beta = 2.0$.

$\phi V_c = 0.9 * 0.0316*2* \sqrt{4} * 12 * 5.76 = 7.86$ kips.

$\phi V_c = 0.9 * 0.25* 4 * 12 * 5.76 = 62.21$ kips.

Use $\phi V_n = 7.86$ kips. > $V_u = 5.97$ kips.   OK

Wing wall shear is safe.

Apron Slab Design:

Apron slab is loaded with water load and supported directly by soil, it might experience minimum moments except the section in the connection with the wing wall. Since the connection between the wing wall and apron slab is rigid, the same wing wall support moment will be transferred to apron slab for equilibrium. Therefore, the maximum moment acts on apron slab may be considered as 311.04 kips.in.

Considering the same thickness and reinforcement for culvert's bottom slab, checking the maximum design moment of bottom slab which was 346.60 kips.in, and comparing with the value 311.04 kips.in, the bottom slab section and reinforcement will be adequate for apron slab.

Verification:

The previous assumption is the easiest and fastest for the designer from the point of view of the author. In the following, the correctness and safety of this method will be verified by making a three-dimensional finite element model using SAP 2000 software, applying all expected loads and load combinations, and exploring the results. This

model is complicated and time consuming which is not required by the designer but this is used in this manual for the sake of clarity only. Material properties and concrete dimensions have been applied to the model. The wing wall earth loads have been applied to every strip as done in the manual design and the self-weight of the structure is taken in consideration which was ignored in the manual design. And the water load has been applied to the apron slab which ignored in the wing wall. Furthermore, the soil has been represented by springs.
(WA) On Apron Slab:

WA for both wall and base = 0.56 / 1.0 = 0.56 ksf.
(DC) Self-weight for both wing wall & apron slab:
To be calculated automatically by the software.

Load Combinations:

Strength Limit State:
Ia. 1.25DC + 1.50EH
I.b 1.25DC + 1.00WA + 1.50EH
I.c 0.90DC + 1.50EH

Service Limit State:
I.a 1.00DC + 1.00EH
I.b 1.00DC + 1.00WA + 1.00EH

The following Figure shows the 3D model in extruded view:

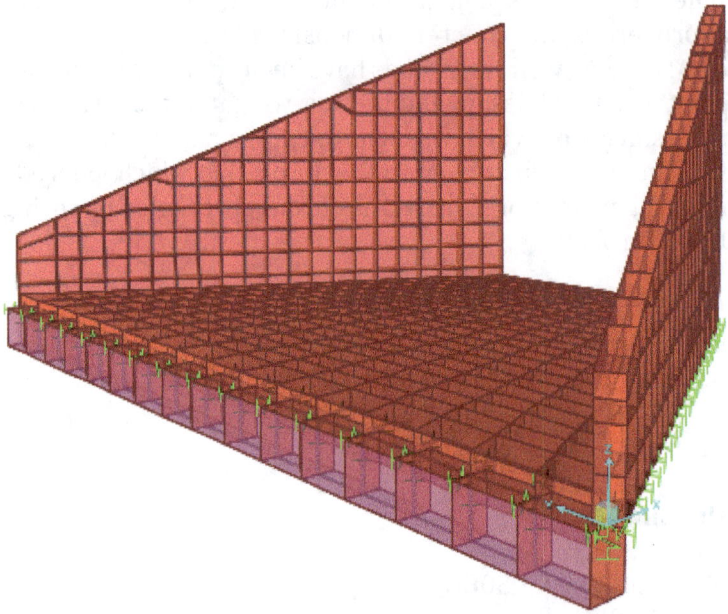

Figure 153. FEM for Wing Wall and Apron Slab

Outputs:

The maximum wing wall & apron slab moment value from the three strength limit state combos in the connection between wing wall & apron slab resulted from the combination (I.b) which is 24.4 k.in/in, equals to 292.8 k.in/ft. this is less than the maximum value from the manual design which was 311.04 k.in/ft. as per the contour range in the following Figure the highest values are in the connection between wing wall & apron slab. Therefore, the previous assumption was correct and can be followed safely.

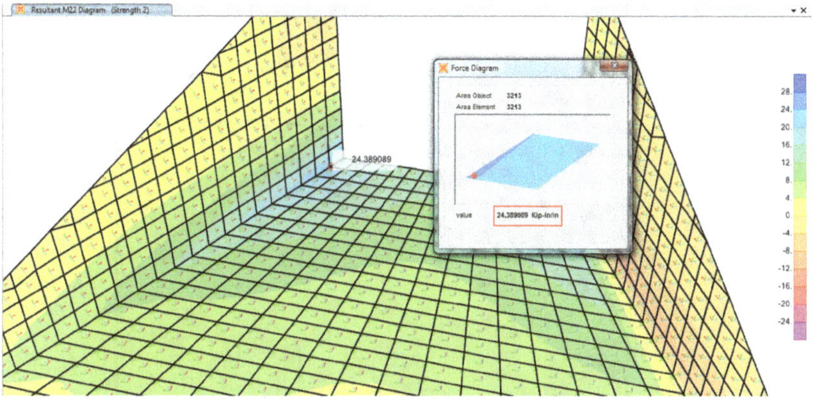

Figure 154. SAP 2000 M22, Strength I.b Combinaiton

Wing wall and apron slab reinforcement:

Reference to AASHTO LRFD Article **5.10.3.2,** the spacing of the Reinforcement shall not exceed:

- 1.5 times the thickness of the member = 12 in.

Or

- 18.0 in.

Consider maximum spacing between reinforcing bars is 12 in. The reinforcement values will differ from location to the other as per the following Figure:

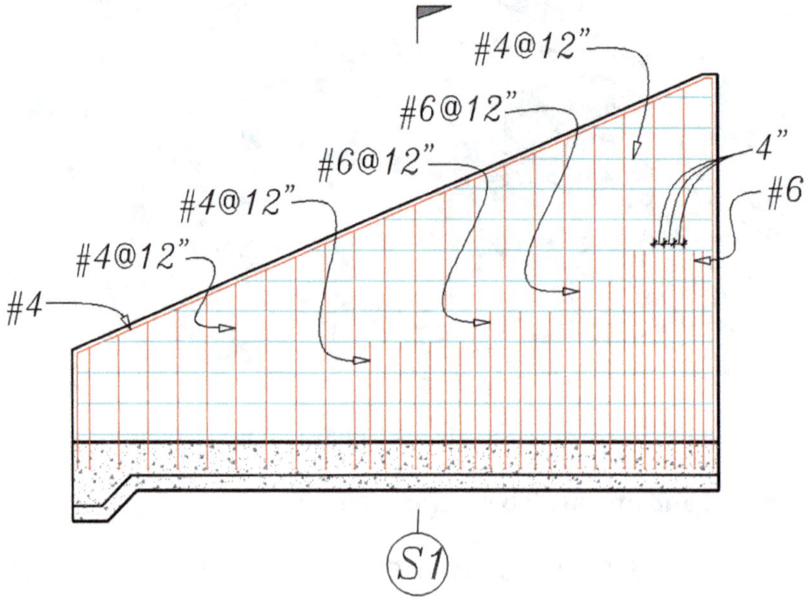

Figure 155. Wing Wall Reinforcement

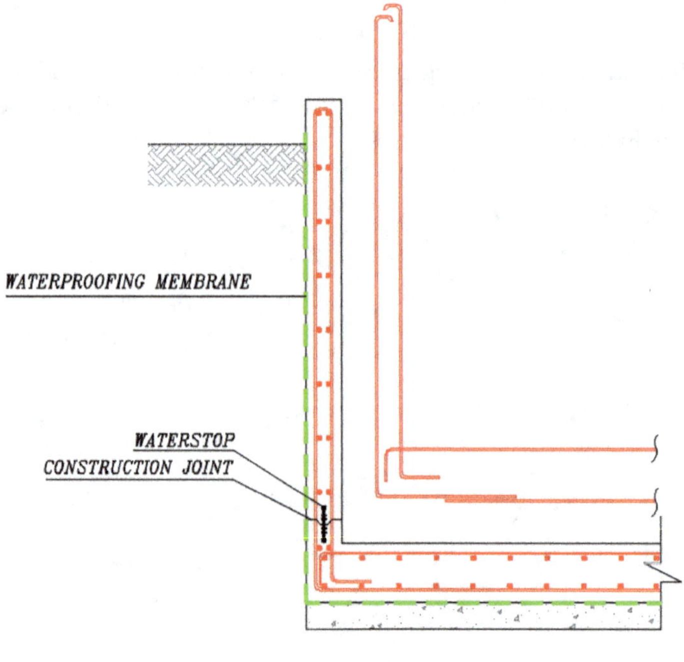

Figure 156. Section (1)

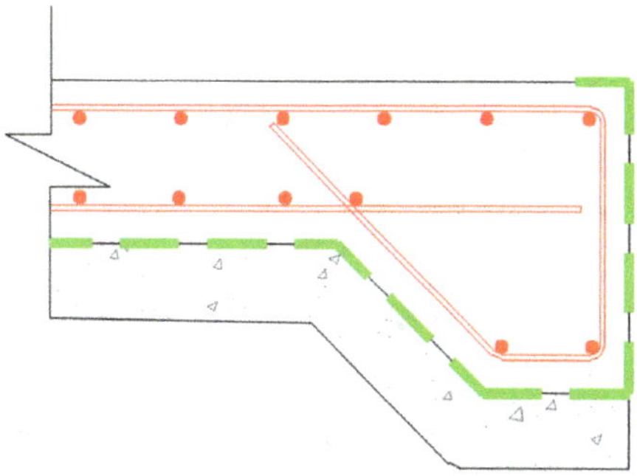

Figure 157. Toe Wall Detail in Apron Slab Edge

The maximum area of main reinforcement for the bottom slab was 0.552 in^2 and the maximum for the wall was 1.008 in^2 in the highest wing wall location.

Consider the reinforcement of apron slab as per the following figure:

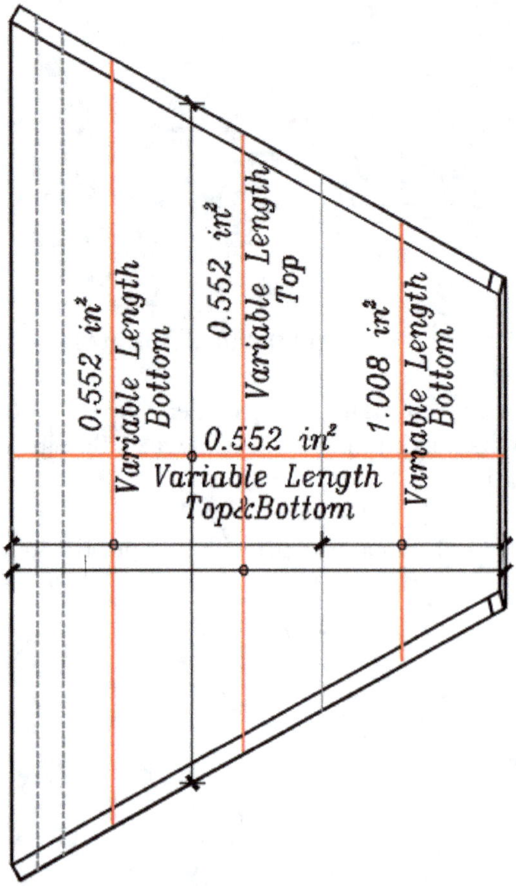

Figure 158. Apron Slab Reinforcement

Design of Headwall:

The headwall normally supports the load of backfilling. However, vehicular collision forces are applicable for headwalls and railings as per AASHTO LRFD Article **C12.6.1.**

If the headwall or railing is vulnerable to vehicular collision when located within a distance of 30.0 ft. to the edge of roadway, the designer shall consider that during headwall/railing design according to either AASHTO LRFD Article **3.6.5.1** (When structural resistance is provided), or AASHTO LRFD Article **2.3.2.2.1** (appropriate in case of redirecting or absorbing the collision load).

Furthermore, the culvert's inlet segment shall be studied due to the effect of transferring collision loads from barrier or railing. In this case, the Author recommends to perform three dimensional finite element analysis to the inlet segment with the barrier for accuracy and integrity.

For this example, there is no vehicular collision load considered, and the filling depth behind the headwall is low. Therefore, the headwall shall be designed due to the soil lateral load as explained previously.

Headwall Applicable Loads (ksf.):

Consider the lateral earth pressure and ignore the live load effect.
EHbottom max. = 0.12 * 2 * 0.5 *1 = 0.12 ksf
EH @2 ft. height from bottom = Zero

The headwall section provided with minimum reinforcement is more than enough to carry out this minor load and the culvert design might not be affected.

Important Note:

Each supplier or fabricator of precast culverts has his own details which include the different barrel types, joints, connections, etc. These details differ according to each supplier's system and may be unconventional. The supplier must perform the proper design of his own system and obtain the necessary certificates and approvals, as well as conduct sufficient practical tests to adopt this system. For example; some precast barrel or wing wall segment joints may cured using mechanical or doweled connections, i.e. some of segment joint connection methods are tapered tie connection, connection plates, doweled connection and others. Another example, the precast culvert may be four sided, three sided, or clam shell culvert. The previous example explains the four-sided box culvert. Having said the market is full of different suppliers with different systems, as long as the designer understands the concept, he can familiarize himself with the other methodologies if he comes into contact with them in his practical life.

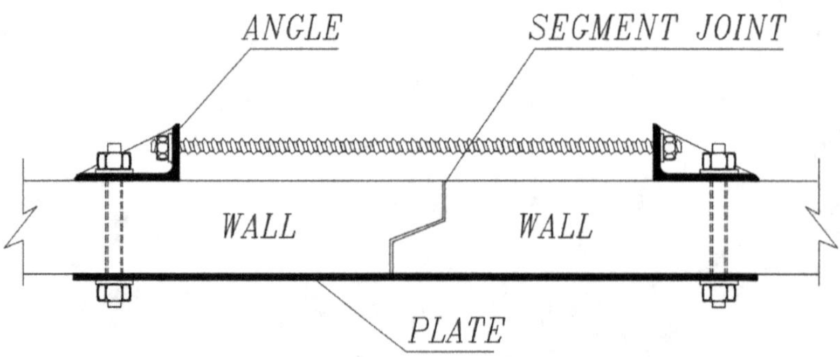

Figure 159. Tapered Tie Connection

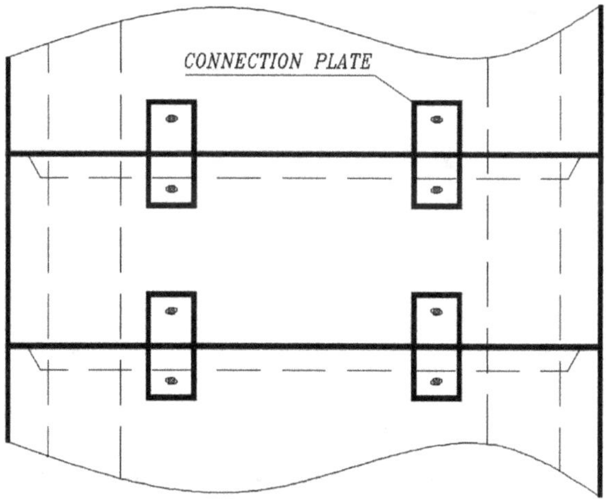

Figure 160. Connection Plates

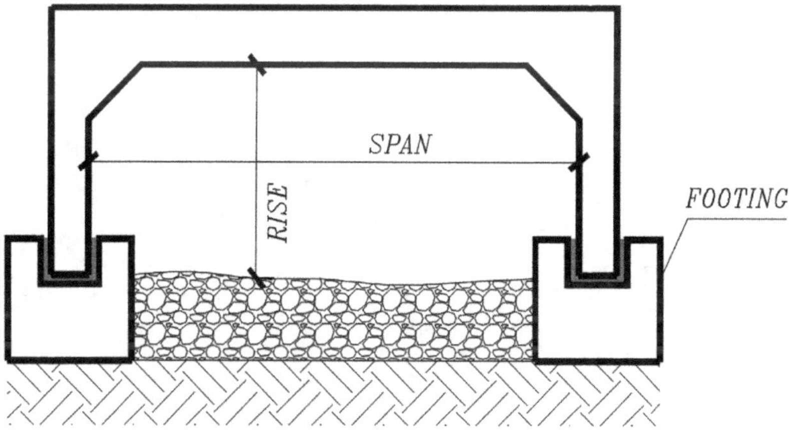

Figure 161. Three side Culvert

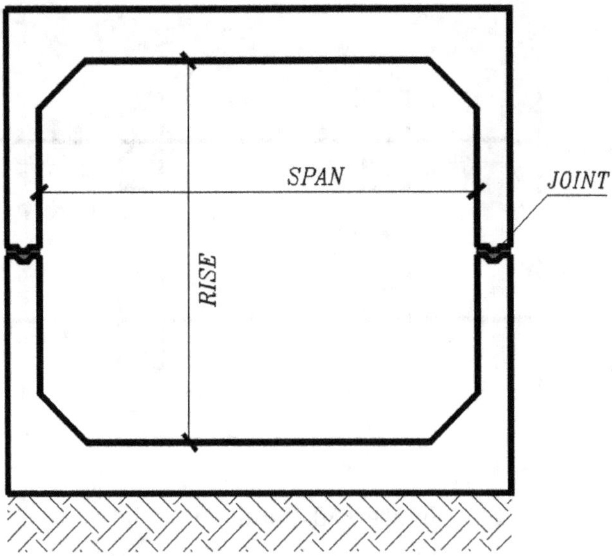

Figure 162. Clam Shell Culvert

9.2 Complete Example 2 (Multi span cast in-situ culvert)

Completing the Example No.12 by using the same model (vehicular live load) and add all other applicable loads. Then, apply load combinations for strength and serviceability, and follow the procedure of design and checking the culvert accordingly.

Load calculation:

(DC):

Will be calculated automatically be the software as per the material properties and section dimensions assigned.

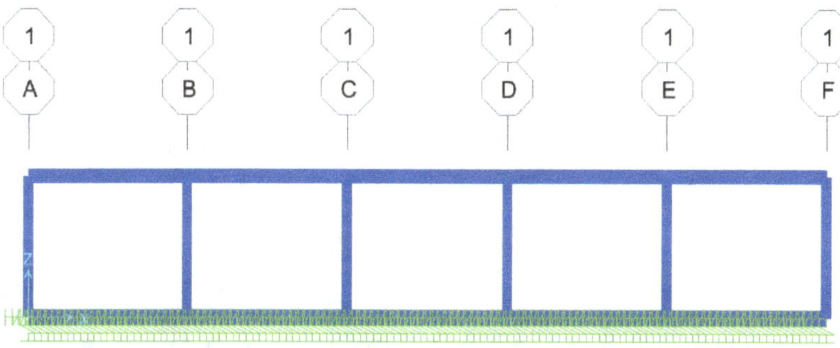

Figure 163. Section Dimensions

(DW):

The future wearing surface load might be neglected as there is backfilling above the culvert top slab.

(WA):

Assume that the culvert is flowing full

WA for both wall lateral load and base vertical load

WA = γ water *R *1 ft = (62.4/1000) *9 *1.0 = 0.56 klf.

The water loads have been applied to the software as per the following Figure. Note that the interior walls resist lateral water pressure from both sides which results to a zero load but the designer might add an additional load case by applying the load from one direction to consider clogging of any cell during the operation due to maintenance or any other reason and consider the resulting biaxial reinforcement in both faces, this leads to a conservative design anticipating the worst case scenarios. The load combinations Strength Ib and

Service Ib shall be applied in both water load cases to check the maximum effect in all sections.

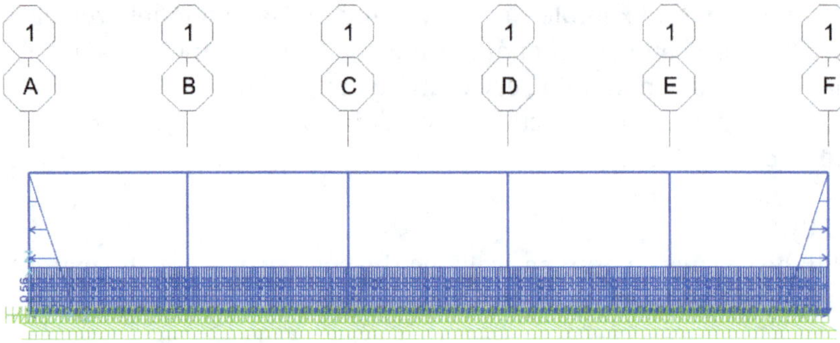

Figure 164. Water Loads Case.1

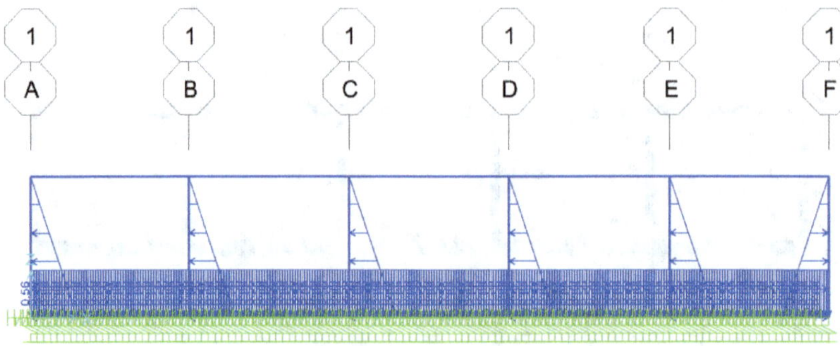

Figure 165. Water Loads Case.2

(LL):
Calculated and applied in the software. See Example No.12

(EH):
(At centerline)
Asssume paving thickness =12 in.
EHtop max. = γ soil *(H+0.5Ts/t) *ko *1 ft
= 0.12 *(0.5+ (0.5*1.0)) *0.5 * 1ft = 0.06 klf.
EHtop min. = 0.5 *γ soil *(H+0.5Ts/t) *ko *1 ft = 0.03 klf.
EHbottom max. = γ soil *(H+Ts/t+R+0.5Ts/b) *ko *1 ft
= 0.12*(0.5+1.0+9+(13/12*2)) *0.5 * 1ft = 0.66 klf.
EHbottom min. = 0.5 * γ soil *(H+Ts/t+R+0.5Ts/b) *ko *1 ft = 0.33 klf.

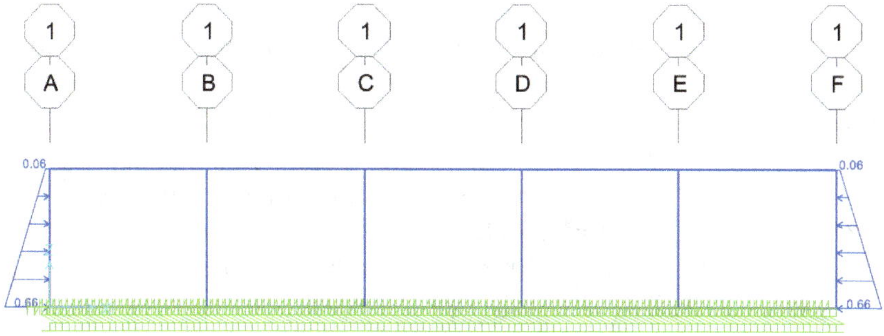

Figure 166. EHmax Loads

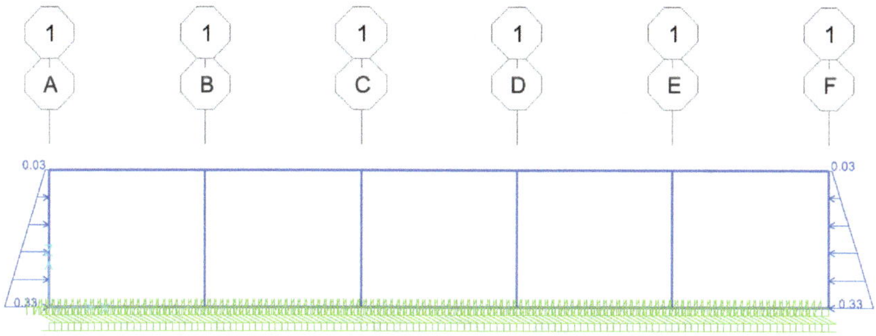

Figure 167. EHmin Loads

(EV):

H= 0.5 ft.

$$F\,e = 1 + 0.20\frac{H}{B\,C} = 1 + 0.20\frac{0.5}{59} = 1.00 < 1.15 \text{ OK}$$

WEv = F e γs H * 1 ft = 1.00 *(120/1000) * 0.5 = 0.06 klf.

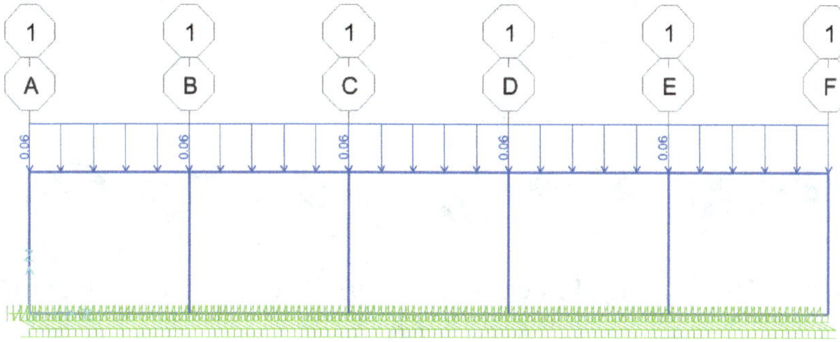

Figure 168. EV Loads

(ES):

Since DW is not considered, earth surcharge load might be neglected.

(LS):

Culvert is not skewed

Distance form top of pavement to bottom of box culvert = 1.5+ (12/12) + 9 + (13/12) =12.58 ft.

Using the table for skew ≤ 30° and linear interpolation:

$$heq = 2 + \frac{20-12.58}{20-10} * (3-2) = 2.74 \text{ ft}$$

Δp = k γs heq

Δp =0.5*0.120*2.74 * 1 ft = 0.16 klf.

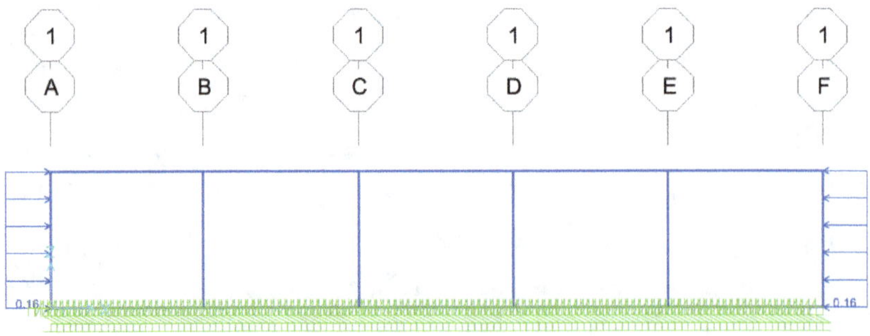

Figure 169. LS Loads

Structural Analysis:

After applying the loads, load combinations, and running the model, the output for all combinations to be taken for design and check. The following Figures show the outputs for the Strength Ia combination as example:

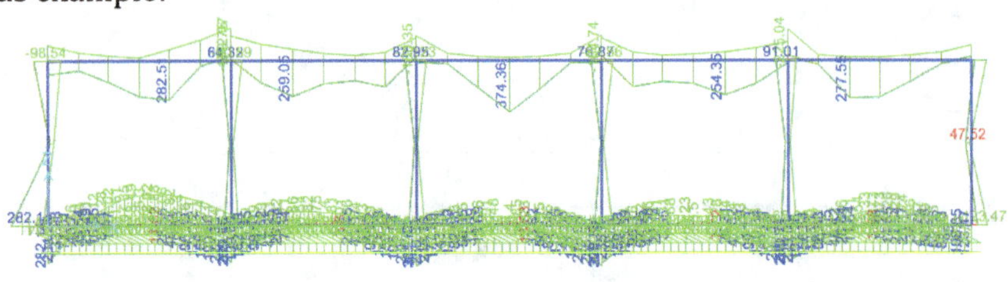

Figure 170. Bending Moment Diagram for Strength Ia Combination (K.in)

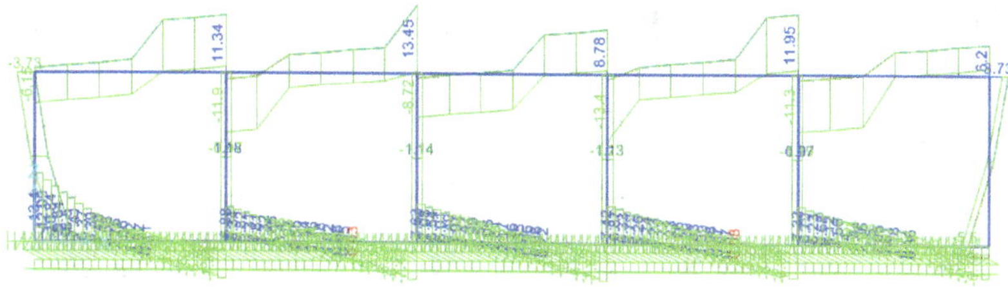

Figure 171. Shear Force Diagram for Strength Ia Combination (Kips)

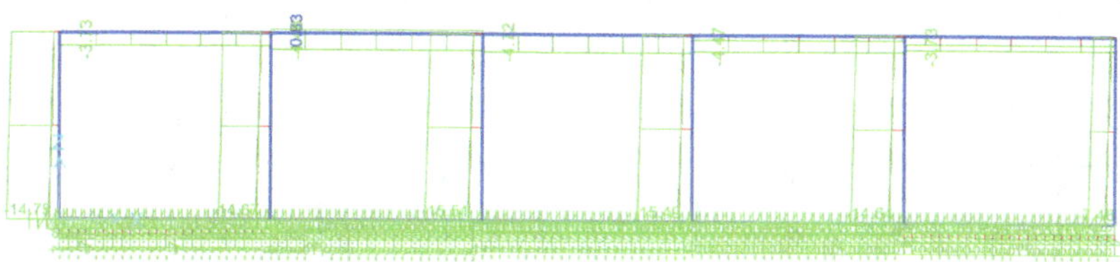

Figure 172. Axial Force Diagram for Strength Ia Combination (Kips)

Flexural Design

The analysis results for flexural design are shown in a tabulated way considering the maximum straining actions for all section as follows:

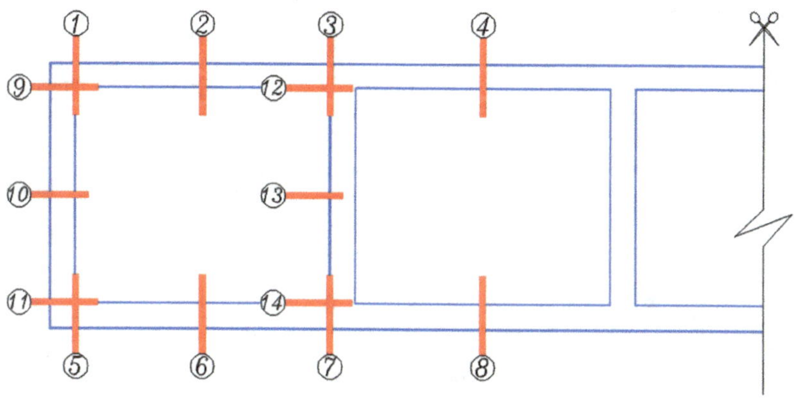

Figure 173. Critical Section for Flexural Design

Bending Moment (Kips.in)

Sec. No.	h (in.)	Strength (I)				Service (I)			
		Ia	Ib	Ib*	Ic	Ia	Ib	Ib*	Ic
1	12	-111.77 98.54	148.38 -61.94	169.6 -40.7	-60.88	-68.25	77.9	99.11	-38.73
2	12	281.44 -77.13	248.13 -74.8	290.4 -67.04	2.1	163.2	162.8	170.8	8.76
3	12	-242.1	-264.22	-265.6	-27.3	-148.3	162.3	-163.6	-1.78
4	12	374.4	377.05	377.1	15.22	217.7	219.6	219.6	14.12
5	13	-282.14	-173.9	-196	-84.67	-171.5	-90.16	-112.2	-61.63
6	13	228	259	250.7	10.1	137.5	163.3	153.2	20
7	13	-301.1	-336.6	-279.3	-36.9	-189.4	-219.4	-180.1	-39.7
8	13	96.9	104.55	89.8	21.2	60.44	70.3	41.4	22.4
9	8	-98.54 111.77	148.38 -61.94	169.6 -40.7	-60.9	-68.25	77.9	99.11	-38.73
10	8	-49.8	-45.11	-46.3	46.9	-30.11	-28.5	-28.7	28.44
11	8	-282.14	-173.09 64.51	-196 42.42	-84.7	-171.6	-90.16	-112.3	-61.63
12	8	91	112.76	96.9	0.8	53.1	72.6	56.7	1.78
13	8	19.76	40.31	23.4	1.6	13	27.5	13.5	0.63
14	8	65.1	134.55	64.6	2.3	38	107.3	37.4	2.7

*considering two cases of loading due to two probabilities of water load (WA)

Note:

- Due to the different moving vehicular live load steps, there are two moment values with different signs in some sections.
- Sections 12 to 14 values are always positive as the interior wall maximum straining actions will be considered in both wall faces.

Axial Force (Kips)

Section No.	h (in.)	Strength (I)				Service (I)			
		Ia	Ib	Ib*	Ic	Ia	Ib	Ib*	Ic
Outer Top Slab	12	3.73	3.05	3.41	3.06	2.33	1.7	2.04	1.92
Inner Top Slab	12	4.72	4.25	4.0	3.05	2.74	2.5	2.61	1.9
Outer wall	8	14.75	14.24	14.1	2.31	9	8.72	8.56	2.3
Inner wall	8	15.51	15.51	15.5	3.15	9.8	9.93	9.92	3.5
Outer Bottom Slab	13	7.83	3.96	1.5	4.9	4.96	1.31	1.04	3.3
Inner Bottom Slab	13	8.54	4.55	2.13	4.8	5.36	2.03	1.4	3.24

*considering two cases of loading due to two probabilities of water load (WA)

Assume f_y= 60 ksi & E_s= 29,000 ksi

Concrete cover; Reference to AASHTO LRFD Article **5.12.3,** consider the concrete cover as follow:

Bottom slab: 3 in. from bottom and 2 in. from top

Top slab: 2 in. from both bottom and top

Walls: 2 in. from both bottom and top

ϕ=0.9 (for cast in-situ - flexure) & 0.75 (for axial compression)

The design for all members except the interior walls will be done based on the pure flexural loads and the interior walls shall be designed considering the combined axial and flexural loads.

Calculate the reinforcement ratio due to pure flexural loads for sections 1 to 11:

$$\rho = \frac{0.85 f_c'}{f_y}\left(1-\sqrt{1-\frac{2R_u}{0.85 f_c'}}\right) \quad \& \quad R_u = \frac{M_u}{\phi b d^2}$$

Section #	Combo	Mu (K.in)	φ	b (in)	d (in)	ρ	As (in^2)
1	Ia	111.77	0.9	12	10	0.00175	0.2102
1	Ia--	98.54	0.9	12	10	0.00154	0.1850
1	Ib	148.4	0.9	12	10	0.00234	0.2806
1	Ib--	61.94	0.9	12	10	0.00096	0.1157
1	Ib*	169.6	0.9	12	10	0.00268	0.3217
1	Ib*--	40.7	0.9	12	10	0.00063	0.0758
1	Ic	60.88	0.9	12	10	0.00095	0.1137
2	Ia	281.44	0.9	12	10	0.00452	0.5429
2	Ia--	77.13	0.9	12	10	0.00120	0.1444
2	Ib	248.13	0.9	12	10	0.00397	0.4762
2	Ib--	74.8	0.9	12	10	0.00117	0.1400
2	Ib*	290.4	0.9	12	10	0.00467	0.5609
2	Ib*--	67.04	0.9	12	10	0.00104	0.1253
2	Ic	2.1	0.9	12	10	0.00003	0.0039
3	Ia	242.1	0.9	12	10	0.00387	0.4642
3	Ib	264.22	0.9	12	10	0.00424	0.5083
3	Ib*	265.6	0.9	12	10	0.00426	0.5111
3	Ic	27.3	0.9	12	10	0.00042	0.0507
4	Ia	374.4	0.9	12	10	0.00611	0.7328
4	Ib	377.05	0.9	12	10	0.00615	0.7383
4	Ib*	377.1	0.9	12	10	0.00615	0.7384
4	Ic	15.22	0.9	12	10	0.00024	0.0282
5	Ia	282.14	0.9	12	10	0.00454	0.5443
5	Ib	173.9	0.9	12	10	0.00275	0.3300
5	Ib*	196	0.9	12	10	0.00311	0.3732
5	Ic	84.67	0.9	12	10	0.00132	0.1586
6	Ia	228	0.9	12	10	0.00364	0.4362
6	Ib	259	0.9	12	10	0.00415	0.4979
6	Ib*	250.7	0.9	12	10	0.00401	0.4813
6	Ic	10.1	0.9	12	10	0.00016	0.0187
7	Ia	301.1	0.9	12	10	0.00485	0.5825
7	Ib	336.6	0.9	12	10	0.00546	0.6549
7	Ib*	279.3	0.9	12	10	0.00449	0.5385

7	Ic	36.9	0.9	12	10	0.00057	0.0687
8	Ia	96.9	0.9	12	10	0.00152	0.1819
8	Ib	104.55	0.9	12	10	0.00164	0.1964
8	Ib*	89.8	0.9	12	10	0.00140	0.1684
8	Ic	21.2	0.9	12	10	0.00033	0.0394
9	Ia	98.54	0.9	12	6	0.00439	0.3164
9	Ia--	111.77	0.9	12	6	0.00501	0.3609
9	Ib	148.38	0.9	12	6	0.00676	0.4870
9	Ib--	61.94	0.9	12	6	0.00272	0.1959
9	Ib*	169.6	0.9	12	6	0.00781	0.5622
9	Ib*--	40.7	0.9	12	6	0.00177	0.1276
9	Ic	60.9	0.9	12	6	0.00267	0.1925
10	Ia	49.8	0.9	12	6	0.00218	0.1567
10	Ib	45.11	0.9	12	6	0.00197	0.1417
10	Ib*	46.3	0.9	12	6	0.00202	0.1455
10	Ic	46.9	0.9	12	6	0.00205	0.1474
11	Ia	282.14	0.9	12	6	0.01377	0.9912
11	Ib	173.1	0.9	12	6	0.00798	0.5747
11	Ib--	64.51	0.9	12	6	0.00284	0.2042
11	Ib*	196	0.9	12	6	0.00914	0.6580
11	Ib*--	42.42	0.9	12	6	0.00185	0.1331
11	Ic	84.7	0.9	12	6	0.00376	0.2704

(Ib--) for the second moment value

To design the combined axial and flexural loads for interior wall sections 12 to 14, using the interaction diagrams L4-60.6 from ACI handbook SP-17(14) volume 3 (design aids):

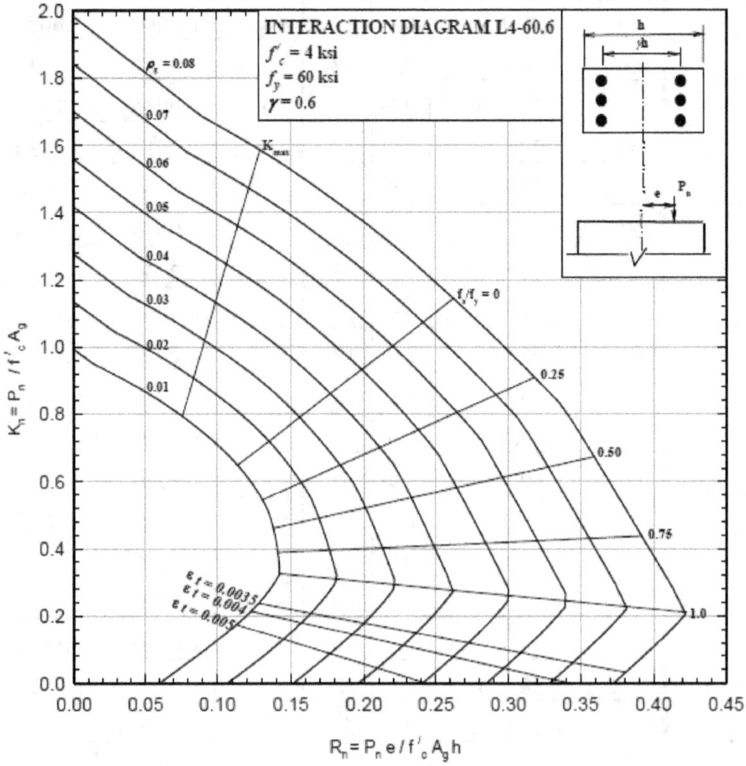

Figure 174. ACI Handbook Interaction Diagram

$Kn = Pn / f'c\ Ag$
$Rn = Pn\ e / f'c\ Ag\ h = Mn / f'c\ Ag\ h$
$Pu = \phi Pn$
$Mu = \phi Mn$

Value of ϕ:
Reference to AASHTO LRFD Article **5.5.4.2,** Value of ϕ for transition zone:

$$0.75 \le \emptyset = 0.75 + \frac{\varepsilon_t - \varepsilon_{cl}}{\varepsilon_{tl} - \varepsilon_{cl}} \le 0.9$$

Reference to AASHTO LRFD Table **C5.7.2.1-1:**
Values of ε_{cl} & ε_{tl} for yield strength 60 ksi are 0.002 and 0.005 respectively
Reference to AASHTO LRFD Article **5.7.2.1:**

$$\varepsilon_t = \frac{0.003(d - c)}{c}$$

By applying the previous equations, εt exceeds 0.005. Use ϕ=0.9

Calculating the values Kn & Rn and getting the reinforcement ratio due to combined axial and flexural loads from interaction diagrams as follows:

Section #	Combo	Pu (K)	Mu (K.in)	φ	h (in)	Ag (in^2)	Kn	Rn	ρ Combined
12	Ia	15.51	91	0.9	8	96	0.0499	0.0366	0.01
12	Ib	15.51	112.76	0.9	8	96	0.0499	0.0453	0.01
12	Ib*	15.5	96.9	0.9	8	96	0.0498	0.0389	0.01
12	Ic	3.15	0.8	0.9	8	96	0.0101	0.0003	0.01
13	Ia	15.51	19.76	0.9	8	96	0.0499	0.0079	0.01
13	Ib	15.51	40.31	0.9	8	96	0.0499	0.0162	0.01
13	Ib*	15.5	23.4	0.9	8	96	0.0498	0.0094	0.01
13	Ic	3.15	1.6	0.9	8	96	0.0101	0.0006	0.01
14	Ia	15.51	65.1	0.9	8	96	0.0499	0.0262	0.01
14	Ib	15.51	134.55	0.9	8	96	0.0499	0.0541	0.01
14	Ib*	15.5	64.6	0.9	8	96	0.0498	0.0260	0.01
14	Ic	3.15	2.3	0.9	8	96	0.0101	0.0009	0.01

All biaxial section reinforcement ratios are below the minimum value. Therefore, the minimum value ρ=0.01 shall be used

Minimum reinforcement values as per AASHTO LRFD as follows:

Refer to AASHTO LRFD Article **12.11.4.3.1:**

($M_r = \phi M_n$) shall be greater or equal to the lesser of:

1) 1.33 $M_{strength}$
2) $M_{cr} = \gamma 3 \ \gamma 1 \ S \ f_r$ (k-in.)

$$M_n = A_s f_y \left(d - \frac{a}{2}\right) \quad \& \quad a = \frac{A_s f_y}{0.85 f'_c b}$$

$\phi = 0.9$
$S = bh^2/6$ in.^{3}
$\gamma 1 = 1.6$
Using A615, Grade 60 reinforcement; $\gamma 3 = 0.67$

Normal weight concrete, fr is used to calculate the cracking moment:

$$fr = 0.20\sqrt{f_c^{'}}$$

As=ρ chosen*b*d

ρ chosen is the maximum of ρ and ρ min.

Checking the minimum and maximum limits of reinforcement for sections 1 to 11 as follows:

Section #	Combo	S (in^3)	As (in^2)	Mcr	1.33 Mu	a	Mr	As Modified
1	Ia	288	0.2102	123.49	148.65	0.309	111.77	0.209
1	Ia--	288	0.1850	123.49	131.06	0.272	98.54	0.209
1	Ib	288	0.2806	123.49	197.37	0.413	148.4	0.2806
1	Ib--	288	0.1157	123.49	82.38	0.170	61.94	0.138
1	Ib*	288	0.3217	123.49	225.57	0.473	169.6	0.3217
1	Ib*--	288	0.0758	123.49	54.13	0.111	40.7	0.091
1	Ic	288	0.1137	123.49	80.97	0.167	60.88	0.136
2	Ia	288	0.5429	123.49	374.32	0.798	281.44	0.5429
2	Ia--	288	0.1444	123.49	102.58	0.212	77.13	0.173
2	Ib	288	0.4762	123.49	330.01	0.700	248.13	0.4762
2	Ib--	288	0.1400	123.49	99.48	0.206	74.8	0.168
2	Ib*	288	0.5609	123.49	386.23	0.825	290.4	0.5609
2	Ib*--	288	0.1253	123.49	89.16	0.184	67.04	0.150
2	Ic	288	0.0039	123.49	2.79	0.006	2.1	0.005
3	Ia	288	0.4642	123.49	321.99	0.683	242.1	0.4642
3	Ib	288	0.5083	123.49	351.41	0.747	264.22	0.5083
3	Ib*	288	0.5111	123.49	353.25	0.752	265.6	0.5111
3	Ic	288	0.0507	123.49	36.31	0.075	27.3	0.061
4	Ia	288	0.7328	123.49	497.95	1.078	374.4	0.7328
4	Ib	288	0.7383	123.49	501.48	1.086	377.05	0.7383
4	Ib*	288	0.7384	123.49	501.54	1.086	377.1	0.7384
4	Ic	288	0.0282	123.49	20.24	0.042	15.22	0.034
5	Ia	338	0.5443	144.93	375.25	0.800	282.14	0.5443
5	Ib	338	0.3300	144.93	231.29	0.485	173.9	0.3300
5	Ib*	338	0.3732	144.93	260.68	0.549	196	0.3732

5	Ic	338	0.1586	144.93	112.61	0.233	84.67	0.190
6	Ia	338	0.4362	144.93	303.24	0.641	228	0.4362
6	Ib	338	0.4979	144.93	344.47	0.732	259	0.4979
6	Ib*	338	0.4813	144.93	333.43	0.708	250.7	0.4813
6	Ic	338	0.0187	144.93	13.43	0.028	10.1	0.022
7	Ia	338	0.5825	144.93	400.46	0.857	301.1	0.5825
7	Ib	338	0.6549	144.93	447.68	0.963	336.6	0.6549
7	Ib*	338	0.5385	144.93	371.47	0.792	279.3	0.5385
7	Ic	338	0.0687	144.93	49.08	0.101	36.9	0.082
8	Ia	338	0.1819	144.93	128.88	0.267	96.9	0.218
8	Ib	338	0.1964	144.93	139.05	0.289	104.55	0.235
8	Ib*	338	0.1684	144.93	119.43	0.248	89.8	0.202
8	Ic	338	0.0394	144.93	28.20	0.058	21.2	0.047
9	Ia	128	0.3164	54.89	131.06	0.465	98.54	0.3164
9	Ia--	128	0.3609	54.89	148.65	0.531	111.77	0.3609
9	Ib	128	0.4870	54.89	197.35	0.716	148.38	0.4870
9	Ib--	128	0.1959	54.89	82.38	0.288	61.94	0.1959
9	Ib*	128	0.5622	54.89	225.57	0.827	169.6	0.5622
9	Ib*--	128	0.1276	54.89	54.13	0.188	40.7	0.153
9	Ic	128	0.1925	54.89	81.00	0.283	60.9	0.1925
10	Ia	128	0.1567	54.89	66.23	0.230	49.8	0.155
10	Ib	128	0.1417	54.89	60.00	0.208	45.11	0.155
10	Ib*	128	0.1455	54.89	61.58	0.214	46.3	0.155
10	Ic	128	0.1474	54.89	62.38	0.217	46.9	0.155
11	Ia	128	0.9912	54.89	375.25	1.458	282.14	0.9912
11	Ib	128	0.5747	54.89	230.22	0.845	173.1	0.5747
11	Ib--	128	0.2042	54.89	85.80	0.300	64.51	0.2042
11	Ib*	128	0.6580	54.89	260.68	0.968	196	0.6580
11	Ib*--	128	0.1331	54.89	56.42	0.196	42.42	0.155
11	Ic	128	0.2704	54.89	112.65	0.398	84.7	0.2704

The red values for Mr are less than the lesser of:

1) 1.33 $M_{strength}$
2) $M_{cr} = \gamma 3\ \gamma 1\ S\ fr$ (k-in.)

Therefore, the area of reinforcement shall be modified to cover the lesser value.
The new (As) value shall be calculated using the following equation by applying the value of lesser moment:

$$M_n = A_s f_y \left(d - \frac{a}{2} \right)$$

M_n is the lesser value mentioned above
For example: for section No.1: the lesser moment value is 123.49 k.in, getting the new
As= 0.209 in^2

Maximum reinforcement values as per AASHTO LRFD as follows:

As per AASHTO LRFD Article **5.7.2,** the maximum reinforcement ratio (ρ max) when:

c/d ≤0.375 & $c = \frac{a}{\beta_1} = \frac{A_S f_y}{0.85 f'_c b \beta_1}$

β1 = 0.85 for f'c =4.0 ksi.
As = The maximum of As & Asmin

The following table shows the values of c/d considering the minimum as values identified in the previous step:

Section #	Combo	d (in)	c/d	Notes
1	Ia	10	0.036	OK
1	Ia--	10	0.036	OK
1	Ib	10	0.036	OK
1	Ib--	10	0.024	OK
1	Ib*	10	0.036	OK
1	Ib*--	10	0.016	OK
1	Ic	10	0.024	OK
2	Ia	10	0.037	OK
2	Ia--	10	0.030	OK
2	Ib	10	0.037	OK
2	Ib--	10	0.029	OK
2	Ib*	10	0.037	OK
2	Ib*--	10	0.026	OK
2	Ic	10	0.001	OK
3	Ia	10	0.037	OK
3	Ib	10	0.037	OK
3	Ib*	10	0.037	OK
3	Ic	10	0.011	OK
4	Ia	10	0.038	OK
4	Ib	10	0.038	OK
4	Ib*	10	0.038	OK
4	Ic	10	0.006	OK
5	Ia	10	0.044	OK
5	Ib	10	0.043	OK
5	Ib*	10	0.043	OK
5	Ic	10	0.033	OK
6	Ia	10	0.043	OK
6	Ib	10	0.043	OK
6	Ib*	10	0.043	OK
6	Ic	10	0.004	OK
7	Ia	10	0.044	OK
7	Ib	10	0.044	OK

7	Ib*	10	0.044	OK
7	Ic	10	0.014	OK
8	Ia	10	0.038	OK
8	Ib	10	0.041	OK
8	Ib*	10	0.035	OK
8	Ic	10	0.008	OK
9	Ia	6	0.046	OK
9	Ia--	6	0.046	OK
9	Ib	6	0.047	OK
9	Ib--	6	0.045	OK
9	Ib*	6	0.047	OK
9	Ib*--	6	0.044	OK
9	Ic	6	0.045	OK
10	Ia	6	0.045	OK
10	Ib	6	0.045	OK
10	Ib*	6	0.045	OK
10	Ic	6	0.045	OK
11	Ia	6	0.050	OK
11	Ib	6	0.047	OK
11	Ib--	6	0.045	OK
11	Ib*	6	0.048	OK
11	Ib*--	6	0.045	OK
11	Ic	6	0.045	OK

All values of c/d do not exceed 0.375. Hence, the reinforcement does not exceed the maximum allowed amount.

Check of Cracking:

Following the same procedure as the previous example.
Apply the equations as per the procedure using an excel spreadsheet, the results are as follows:

Section #	Combo	Ms (K.in)	Ns (K)	d (in)	βs	fss	fss chosen
1	Ia	68.25	2.33	10	1.286	38.792	36
1	Ia--	68.25	2.33	10	1.286	38.792	36
1	Ib	77.9	1.7	10	1.286	38.792	36
1	Ib--	77.9	1.7	10	1.286	38.792	36
1	Ib*	99.11	2.04	10	1.286	38.792	36
1	Ib*--	99.11	2.04	10	1.286	38.792	36
1	Ic	38.73	1.92	10	1.286	38.792	36
2	Ia	163.2	2.33	10	1.286	38.792	36
2	Ia--	163.2	2.33	10	1.286	38.792	36
2	Ib	162.8	1.7	10	1.286	38.792	36
2	Ib--	162.8	1.7	10	1.286	38.792	36
2	Ib*	170.8	2.04	10	1.286	38.792	36
2	Ib*--	170.8	2.04	10	1.286	38.792	36
2	Ic	8.76	1.92	10	1.286	38.792	36
3	Ia	148.3	2.33	10	1.286	38.792	36
3	Ib	162.3	1.7	10	1.286	38.792	36
3	Ib*	163.6	2.04	10	1.286	38.792	36
3	Ic	1.78	1.92	10	1.286	38.792	36
4	Ia	217.7	2.74	10	1.286	38.792	36
4	Ib	219.6	2.5	10	1.286	38.792	36
4	Ib*	219.6	2.61	10	1.286	38.792	36
4	Ic	14.12	1.9	10	1.286	38.792	36
5	Ia	171.5	4.96	10	1.429	27.93	27.93
5	Ib	90.16	1.31	10	1.429	27.93	27.93
5	Ib*	112.2	1.04	10	1.429	27.93	27.93
5	Ic	61.63	3.3	10	1.429	27.93	27.93
6	Ia	137.5	4.96	10	1.429	27.93	27.93
6	Ib	163.3	1.31	10	1.429	27.93	27.93
6	Ib*	153.2	1.04	10	1.429	27.93	27.93
6	Ic	20	3.3	10	1.429	27.93	27.93
7	Ia	189.4	4.96	10	1.429	27.93	27.93
7	Ib	219.4	1.31	10	1.429	27.93	27.93
7	Ib*	180.1	1.04	10	1.429	27.93	27.93

7	Ic	39.7	3.3	10	1.429	27.93	27.93
8	Ia	60.44	5.36	10	1.429	27.93	27.93
8	Ib	70.3	2.03	10	1.429	27.93	27.93
8	Ib*	41.4	1.4	10	1.429	27.93	27.93
8	Ic	22.4	3.24	10	1.429	27.93	27.93
9	Ia	68.25	9	6	1.476	33.786	33.78
9	Ia--	68.25	9	6	1.476	33.786	33.78
9	Ib	77.9	8.72	6	1.476	33.786	33.78
9	Ib--	77.9	8.72	6	1.476	33.786	33.78
9	Ib*	99.11	8.56	6	1.476	33.786	33.78
9	Ib*--	99.11	8.56	6	1.476	33.786	33.78
9	Ic	38.73	2.3	6	1.476	33.786	33.78
10	Ia	30.11	9	6	1.476	33.786	33.78
10	Ib	28.5	8.72	6	1.476	33.786	33.78
10	Ib*	28.7	8.56	6	1.476	33.786	33.78
10	Ic	28.44	2.3	6	1.476	33.786	33.78
11	Ia	171.6	9	6	1.476	33.786	33.78
11	Ib	90.16	8.72	6	1.476	33.786	33.78
11	Ib--	90.16	8.72	6	1.476	33.786	33.78
11	Ib*	112.3	8.56	6	1.476	33.786	33.78
11	Ib*--	112.3	8.56	6	1.476	33.786	33.78
11	Ic	61.63	2.3	6	1.476	33.786	33.78
12	Ia	53.1	9.8	6	1.476	33.786	33.78
12	Ib	72.6	9.93	6	1.476	33.786	33.78
12	Ib*	56.7	9.92	6	1.476	33.786	33.78
12	Ic	1.78	3.5	6	1.476	33.786	33.78
13	Ia	13	9.8	6	1.476	33.786	33.78
13	Ib	27.5	9.93	6	1.476	33.786	33.78
13	Ib*	13.5	9.92	6	1.476	33.786	33.78
13	Ic	0.63	3.5	6	1.476	33.786	33.78
14	Ia	38	9.8	6	1.476	33.786	33.78
14	Ib	107.3	9.93	6	1.476	33.786	33.78
14	Ib*	37.4	9.92	6	1.476	33.786	33.78
14	Ic	2.4	3.5	6	1.476	33.786	33.78

Section #	Combo	e	j	i	fs
1	Ia	33.292	1.073	1.476	23.438
1	Ia--	33.292	1.073	1.476	26.486
1	Ib	49.824	1.238	1.331	18.319
1	Ib--	49.824	1.238	1.331	44.433
1	Ib*	52.583	1.266	1.317	20.002
1	Ib*--	52.583	1.266	1.317	84.893
1	Ic	24.172	0.982	1.684	24.693
2	Ia	74.043	1.480	1.250	17.175
2	Ia--	74.043	1.480	1.250	64.582
2	Ib	99.765	1.738	1.211	16.927
2	Ib--	99.765	1.738	1.211	57.591
2	Ib*	87.725	1.617	1.226	16.091
2	Ib*--	87.725	1.617	1.226	72.031
2	Ic	8.563	0.826	27.959	18.308
3	Ia	67.648	1.416	1.265	18.953
3	Ib	99.471	1.735	1.211	15.833
3	Ib*	84.196	1.582	1.231	17.253
3	Ic	4.927	0.789	-1.661	-14.217
4	Ia	83.453	1.575	1.233	16.078
4	Ib	91.840	1.658	1.220	15.365
4	Ib*	88.138	1.621	1.225	15.679
4	Ic	11.432	0.854	3.958	22.744
5	Ia	38.077	1.121	1.417	21.848
5	Ib	72.324	1.463	1.254	15.649
5	Ib*	111.385	1.854	1.200	13.957
5	Ic	22.176	0.962	1.766	27.161
6	Ia	31.222	1.052	1.508	22.369
6	Ib	128.156	2.022	1.187	14.050
6	Ib*	150.808	2.248	1.175	12.335
6	Ic	9.561	0.836	7.937	25.399
7	Ia	41.685	1.157	1.384	22.166
7	Ib	170.981	2.450	1.167	11.961
7	Ib*	176.673	2.507	1.165	11.679

7	Ic	15.530	0.895	2.361	35.299
8	Ia	14.776	0.888	2.505	19.581
8	Ib	38.131	1.121	1.417	24.806
8	Ib*	33.071	1.071	1.479	17.367
8	Ic	10.414	0.844	5.280	19.226
9	Ia	9.583	0.900	2.290	22.051
9	Ia--	9.583	0.900	2.290	19.331
9	Ib	10.933	0.922	2.025	17.473
9	Ib--	10.933	0.922	2.025	43.447
9	Ib*	13.578	0.966	1.745	20.433
9	Ib*--	13.578	0.966	1.745	90.016
9	Ic	18.839	1.054	1.505	23.645
10	Ia	5.346	0.829	14.409	4.283
10	Ib	5.268	0.828	17.473	3.736
10	Ib*	5.353	0.829	14.179	4.464
10	Ic	14.365	0.979	1.692	22.537
11	Ia	21.067	1.091	1.451	20.138
11	Ib	12.339	0.946	1.851	17.823
11	Ib--	12.339	0.946	1.851	50.162
11	Ib*	15.119	0.992	1.649	20.037
11	Ib*--	15.119	0.992	1.649	99.058
11	Ic	28.796	1.220	1.341	24.959
12	Ia	7.418	0.864	3.317	14.522
12	Ib	9.311	0.895	2.363	19.996
12	Ib*	7.716	0.869	3.081	15.330
12	Ic	2.509	0.782	-1.150	-659.251
13	Ia	3.327	0.795	-2.300	-48.322
13	Ib	4.769	0.819	-32.323	-2.358
13	Ib*	3.361	0.796	-2.375	-40.336
13	Ic	2.180	0.776	-0.880	-376.818
14	Ia	5.878	0.838	6.916	8.036
14	Ib	12.806	0.953	1.807	28.022
14	Ib*	5.770	0.836	7.661	7.282
14	Ic	2.686	0.785	-1.328	-211.633

Section #	Combo	e/d	fs	fss chosen	Notes	As crack	As Final
1	Ia	3.329	23.438	36	OK		0.209
1	Ia--	3.329	26.486	36	OK		0.209
1	Ib	4.982	18.319	36	OK		0.2806
1	Ib--	4.982	44.433	36	fs>fss	0.171	0.171
1	Ib*	5.258	20.002	36	OK		0.3217
1	Ib*--	5.258	84.893	36	fs>fss	0.214	0.214
1	Ic	2.417	24.693	36	OK		0.136
2	Ia	7.404	17.175	36	OK		0.5429
2	Ia--	7.404	64.582	36	fs>fss	0.310	0.310
2	Ib	9.976	16.927	36	OK		0.4762
2	Ib--	9.976	57.591	36	fs>fss	0.268	0.268
2	Ib*	8.773	16.091	36	OK		0.5609
2	Ib*--	8.773	72.031	36	fs>fss	0.300	0.300
2	Ic	0.856	18.308	36	e/d<1.15		0.005
3	Ia	6.765	18.953	36	OK		0.4642
3	Ib	9.947	15.833	36	OK		0.5083
3	Ib*	8.420	17.253	36	OK		0.5111
3	Ic	0.493	-14.217	36	e/d<1.15		0.061
4	Ia	8.345	16.078	36	OK		0.7328
4	Ib	9.184	15.365	36	OK		0.7383
4	Ib*	8.814	15.679	36	OK		0.7384
4	Ic	1.143	22.744	36	e/d<1.15		0.034
5	Ia	3.808	21.848	27.93	OK		0.5443
5	Ib	7.232	15.649	27.93	OK		0.3300
5	Ib*	11.138	13.957	27.93	OK		0.3732
5	Ic	2.218	27.161	27.93	OK		0.190
6	Ia	3.122	22.369	27.93	OK		0.4362
6	Ib	12.816	14.050	27.93	OK		0.4979
6	Ib*	15.081	12.335	27.93	OK		0.4813
6	Ic	0.956	25.399	27.93	e/d<1.15		0.022
7	Ia	4.169	22.166	27.93	OK		0.5825
7	Ib	17.098	11.961	27.93	OK		0.6549
7	Ib*	17.667	11.679	27.93	OK		0.5385

7	Ic	1.553	35.299	27.93	fs>fss	0.104	0.104
8	Ia	1.478	19.581	27.93	OK		0.218
8	Ib	3.813	24.806	27.93	OK		0.235
8	Ib*	3.307	17.367	27.93	OK		0.202
8	Ic	1.041	19.226	27.93	e/d<1.15		0.047
9	Ia	1.597	22.051	33.78	OK		0.3164
9	Ia--	1.597	19.331	33.78	OK		0.3609
9	Ib	1.822	17.473	33.78	OK		0.4870
9	Ib--	1.822	43.447	33.78	fs>fss	0.201	0.201
9	Ib*	2.263	20.433	33.78	OK		0.5622
9	Ib*--	2.263	90.016	33.78	fs>fss	0.407	0.407
9	Ic	3.140	23.645	33.78	OK		0.1925
10	Ia	0.891	4.283	33.78	e/d<1.15		0.155
10	Ib	0.878	3.736	33.78	e/d<1.15		0.155
10	Ib*	0.892	4.464	33.78	e/d<1.15		0.155
10	Ic	2.394	22.537	33.78	OK		0.155
11	Ia	3.511	20.138	33.78	OK		0.9912
11	Ib	2.057	17.823	33.78	OK		0.5747
11	Ib--	2.057	50.162	33.78	fs>fss	0.232	0.232
11	Ib*	2.520	20.037	33.78	OK		0.6580
11	Ib*--	2.520	99.058	33.78	fs>fss	0.454	0.454
11	Ic	4.799	24.959	33.78	OK		0.2704
12	Ia	1.236	14.522	33.78	OK		0.72
12	Ib	1.552	19.996	33.78	OK		0.72
12	Ib*	1.286	15.330	33.78	OK		0.72
12	Ic	0.418	-659.251	33.78	e/d<1.15		0.72
13	Ia	0.554	-48.322	33.78	e/d<1.15		0.72
13	Ib	0.795	-2.358	33.78	e/d<1.15		0.72
13	Ib*	0.560	-40.336	33.78	e/d<1.15		0.72
13	Ic	0.363	-376.818	33.78	e/d<1.15		0.72
14	Ia	0.980	8.036	33.78	e/d<1.15		0.72
14	Ib	2.134	28.022	33.78	OK		0.72
14	Ib*	0.962	7.282	33.78	e/d<1.15		0.72
14	Ic	0.448	-211.633	33.78	e/d<1.15		0.72

Check Slenderness

Slenderness effects shall be considered for interior walls. The first step is to check whether there is a moment magnification required or not, using the following formula:

$$\frac{K\ l_u}{r} < 34$$

lu = 9.0 ft = 108 in.
r = 0.3 * wall thickness = 0.3*8 =2.4 in.
K = 0.65 for interior walls with bottom slab
K lu / r = 29.25 < 34
Hence, Slenderness effect might be neglected and moment magnification is not required.

Despite the moment magnification is not required. However, for the sake of clarity, moment magnification might be calculated as follow:
Maximum Pu = 15.51 kips.

$$C_m = 0.6 + 0.4\left(\frac{M_1}{M_2}\right)$$ Assume Cm = 1.0

$$EI = \frac{\frac{E_c I_g}{2.5}}{1+\beta_d}$$

Reference to AASHTO LRFD Article **5.4.2.4**, modulus of elasticity, Ec, may be taken as:

$$E_C = 33{,}000\, K_1 w_C^{1.5} \sqrt{f'_C}$$

K_1 = correction factor for source of aggregate to be taken as 1.0
γ concrete = 150 pcf. & fc'= 4 ksi.
$E_c = 33000 * 1.0 * 0.15^{1.5} * \sqrt{4}$ = 3834.25 ksi.
$I_g = \frac{b*h^3}{12} = \frac{12*8^3}{12} = 512\ in^4$
β_d = ratio of maximum factored dead load moment to maximum factored total load moment (always positive)
From the model:
The maximum factored dead load moment = Mu(DC) + Mu(EV)
= 5.31 + 0.42 = 5.73 kips.in.

The maximum factored total load moment = Mu max. (Strength I) = 134.55 kips.in.

β_d = 5.73/134.55 = 0.04

Hence, EI = 755052.31 k.in^2

$$P_e = \frac{\pi^2 E\, I}{(K\, l_u)^2}$$

P_e = 1512.18 kips

$$\delta_b = \frac{C_m}{1 - \frac{P_u}{\phi_k P_e}} \geq 1.0$$

,ϕ_k = 0.75

δ_b = 1.014

$$M_c = \delta_b M_{2b}$$

If the moment magnification is required, the factored moment shall be multiplied by δ_b

Transversal Reinforcement Conclusion

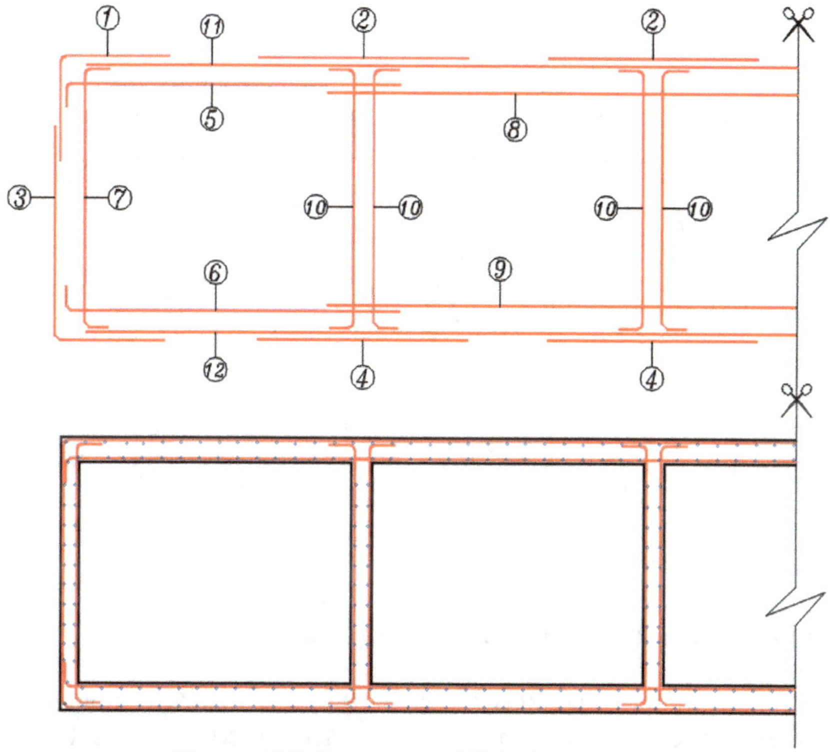

Figure 175. Transversal Reinforcement

Reinforcement areas have been calculated accordingly. The area of reinforcement might be calculated as follow:

- Rebar No.1 covers sections 1 & 9 with area of reinforcement equals to 0.5622 in^2
- Rebar No.3 covers sections 5, 10 (if there is negative moment) & 11 with area of reinforcement equals to 0.9912 in^2
- Rebar No.5 covers section 2 with area of reinforcement equals to 0.5609 in^2
- Rebar No.6 covers section 6 with area of reinforcement equals to 0.4979 in^2
- Rebar No.7 covers section 10 with area of reinforcement equals to 0.155 in^2
- Rebar No.8 covers section 4 with area of reinforcement equals to 0.7384 in^2

- Rebar No.9 covers section 8 with area of reinforcement equals to 0.235 in^2
- Rebar No.10 covers sections 12, 13 & 14 with area of reinforcement equals to 0.72 in^2
- Bars No.11 & 12are representing the secondary (minimum) reinforcement with area of reinforcement equals to 0.25 in^2
- Rebar No.2 covers section 3 as additional reinforcement to rebar No.11. the area of reinforcement equals to (As (section 3) – As (rebar 11))
  = (0.5111 – 0.25) = 0.2611 in^2
- Rebar No.4 covers section 7 as additional reinforcement to rebar No.12. the area of reinforcement equals to (As (section 7) – As (rebar 12))
  = (0.6549 – 0.25) = 0.405 in^2
- Development length, splice length, location of bar termination, and minimum & maximum spacing between reinforcing bars shall be considered as per AASHTO LRFD.

Longitudinal Reinforcement

Temperature and Shrinkage Reinforcement

Reference to AASHTO LRFD Article **5.10.8,** area of longitudinal reinforcement per foot, on each face and in each direction, shall satisfy:

$$A_s \geq \frac{1.3bh}{2(b+h)f_y}$$

Section	b (in.)	h (in.)	As (in^2/ft.)
Top slab	12	12	0.065
Wall	12	8	0.052
Bottom Slab	12	13	0.067

Distribution Reinforcement

The fill depth is lesser than 2.0 ft. Reference to AASHTO LRFD Article **5.14.4.1,** Transverse distribution reinforcement is required in the bottoms of culvert top slab

Distribution longitudinal reinforced limitation is:

$$\frac{100}{\sqrt{L}} \leq 50\%$$

100/√11 = 30.15 < 50% OK

Distribution reinforcement is a ratio from the bottom main reinforcement area

Distribution reinforcement area:

As = (30.15/100) * (larger As of bars 5 &8) = (30.15/100) * 0.7384 = 0.223 in^2

Design of Shear

Figure 172 shows the critical sections for shear as follows:

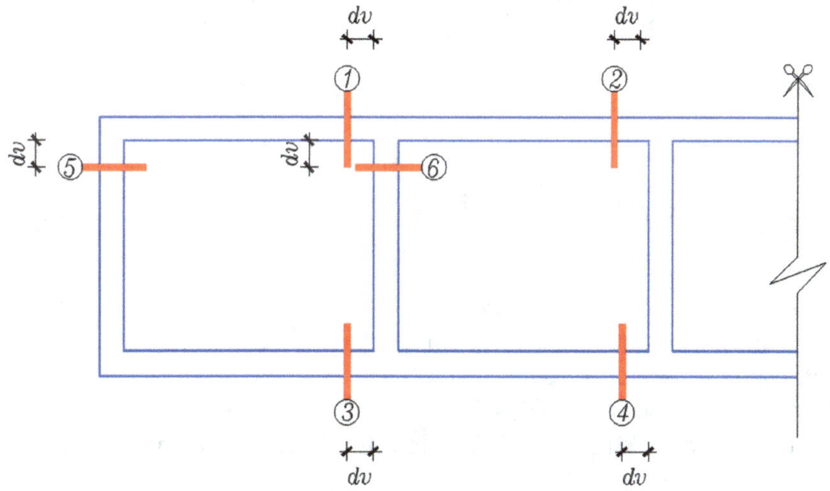

Figure 176. Critical Section Locations for Shear

Note: The designer shall consider the maximum shear value for every slab or wall in distance $\mathbf{d_v}$, whenever the location (right, left, top or bottom). The section locations in the previous Figure are illustrative only.

Calculate d_v

Section No.	Cover (in.)	h (in.)	d (in.)	As (in^2/ft)	a	d - (a/2)	0.72 h	0.9 de	dv (in.)
1	2	12	10	0.561	0.825	9.588	8.64	9	9.588
2	2	12	10	0.738	1.085	9.457	8.64	9	9.457
3	3	13	10	0.544	0.800	9.600	9.36	9	9.600
4	3	13	10	0.655	0.963	9.518	9.36	9	9.518
5	2	8	6	0.991	1.457	5.271	5.76	5.4	5.760
6	2	8	6	0.72	1.059	5.471	5.76	5.4	5.760

Shear Force at distance dv (kips):

Section No.	dv (in.)	Strength (I)			
		Ia	Ib	Ib*	Ic
1	9.588	11	11.55	11.7	1.2
2	9.457	8.7	8.3	8.5	0.95
3	9.600	10.8	10.12	10.14	1.7
4	9.518	6.52	6.1	6.34	1.32
5	5.760	7	3	3.35	4.1
6	5.760	1.18	3.5	1.24	0.01

Check Shear of walls:

Maximum ultimate shear force for walls:
For Exterior wall is 7.00 kips
For Interior wall is 3.50 kips
Reference to AASHTO LRFD Article **5.8.3.3,** concrete shear capacity is the least of:

$$\phi V_c = \phi * 0.0316 \beta \sqrt{f'_c} b_v d_v$$

And,
$\phi V_c = \phi * 0.25 * f'_c * b_v * d_v$
$\phi = 0.85$ (for cast in-situ – shear)
Reference to AASHTO LRFD Article **5.8.3.4.1,** wall size is less than 16 in. and it is not subjected to axial tension, consider $\beta = 2.0$.
$\phi V_c = 0.85 * 0.0316 * 2 * \sqrt{4} * 12 * 5.76 = 7.43$ kips.
$\phi V_c = 0.85 * 0.25 * 4 * 12 * 5.76 = 58.75$ kips.

For Interior wall:
Use $\phi V_n = 7.43$ kips. > $V_u = 3.50$ kips. OK

For Exterior wall:
Use $\phi V_n = 7.43$ kips. > $V_u = 7.00$ kips. OK

Check Shear of Top Slab:

Maximum ultimate shear force for top slab:
For Exterior span is 11.70 kips
For Interior span is 8.70 kips

For fill thickness less than 2 ft., Reference to AASHTO LRFD Article **5.8.3.3,** concrete shear capacity is the least of:

$$\phi V_c = \phi * 0.0316 \beta \sqrt{f'_c} b_v d_v$$

And,
$\phi V_c = \phi * 0.25 * f'_c * b_v * d_v$
$\phi = 0.85$ (for cast in-situ – shear)
Reference to AASHTO LRFD Article **5.8.3.4.1,** wall size is less than 16 in. and it is not subjected to axial tension, consider $\beta = 2.0$.
For Exterior span:
$\phi V_c = 0.85 * 0.0316*2* \sqrt{4} * 12 * 9.588 = 12.36$ kips.
$\phi V_c = 0.85 * 0.25* 4 * 12 * 9.588 = 97.8$ kips.
Use $\phi V_n = 12.36$ kips. > $V_u = 11.7$ kips. OK

For Interior span:
$\phi V_c = 0.85 * 0.0316*2* \sqrt{4} * 12 * 9.457= 12.19$ kips.
$\phi V_c = 0.85 * 0.25* 4 * 12 * 9.457= 96.46$ kips.
Use $\phi V_n = 12.19$ kips. > $V_u = 8.7$ kips. OK

Check Shear of Bottom Slab:

Maximum ultimate shear force for bottom slab:
For Exterior span is 10.80 kips
For Interior span is 6.52 kips

For fill thickness less than 2 ft., Reference to AASHTO LRFD Article **5.8.3.3,** concrete shear capacity is the least of:

$$\phi V_c = \phi * 0.0316 \beta \sqrt{f'_c} b_v d_v$$

And,
$\phi V_c = \phi * 0.25 * f'_c * b_v * d_v$

ϕ = 0.85 (for cast in-situ – shear)
Reference to AASHTO LRFD Article **5.8.3.4.1,** wall size is less than 16 in. and it is not subjected to axial tension, consider β = 2.0.
For Exterior span:
$\phi V_c = 0.85 * 0.0316*2* \sqrt{4} * 12 * 9.600 = 12.38$ kips.
$\phi V_c = 0.85 * 0.25* 4 * 12 * 9.600 = 97.92$ kips.
Use $\phi V_n = 12.38$ kips. > $V_u = 10.80$ kips. OK

For Interior span:
$\phi V_c = 0.85 * 0.0316*2* \sqrt{4} * 12 * 9.518 = 12.27$ kips.
$\phi V_c = 0.85 * 0.25* 4 * 12 * 9.518 = 97.08$ kips.
Use $\phi V_n = 12.27$ kips. > $V_u = 6.52$ kips. OK

Shear is safe

Design of Inlet/Outlet

Edge beam:
Assume dimensions 20"*18".

Wing wall dimensions:
Assume flared wing walls, considering construction joint between the wing wall/Apron slab and culvert's inlet segment.

V = (top slab thickness) + (clear wall height) – 12"
V = 12" + (9'*12) – 12" = 108"
θ = Zero
Assume $\alpha = 30^\circ$
L = 2V / Cos ($\theta+\alpha$)
L = 2*108 / Cos (30°) = 249.415 in. = 20.78 feet
Consider L = 21 feet

Apron slab dimensions:

Consider same culvert's bottom slab thickness.

Toe wall dimensions:

Assume one foot minimum width and also depth from the bottom of bottom slab with 45° inclination.

The inlet dimensions will be as follow:

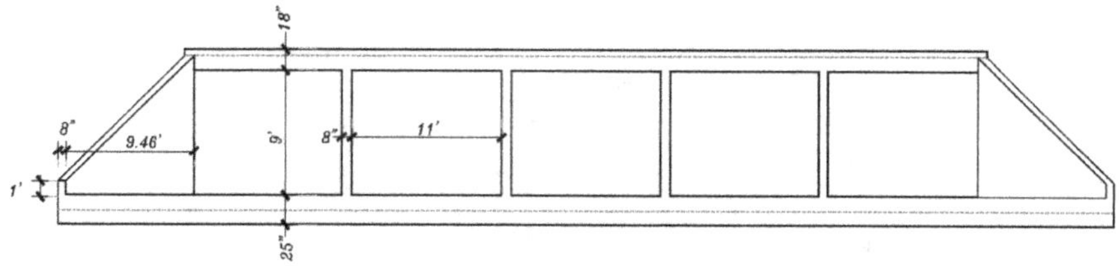

Figure 177. Inlet Front View

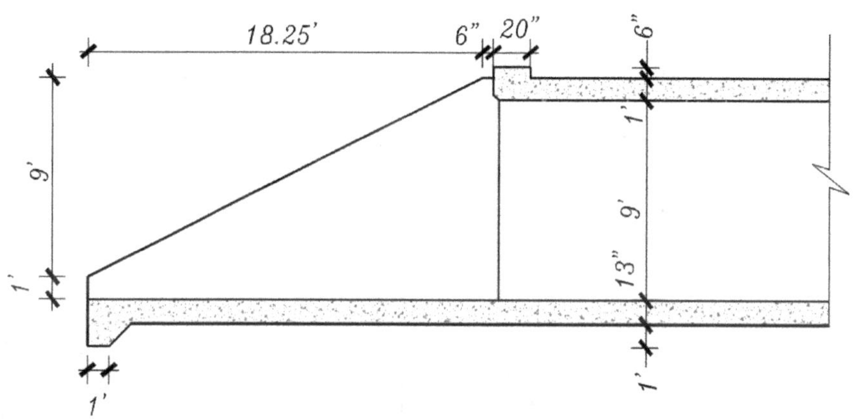

Figure 178. Inlet Section

Figure 179. Inlet Plan

Structural Design

The edge beam will be reinforced with minimum ratios as the culvert is not skewed and no load transferred to the edge beam except its self-weight.

The toe wall will be reinforced with minimum values as per AASHTO LRFD.

The wing wall and apron slab to be designed simply as done in the previous example. However, the wing wall is connected to the culvert's wall and apron slab is connected to culvert's bottom slab. Construction joint might be located in the mentioned connections but the structural connectivity is considered as per the following Figures:

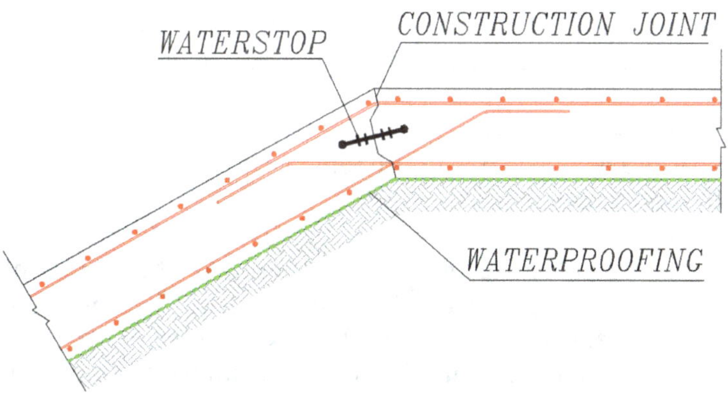

Figure 180. Wing Wall & Culvert's Wall Connection

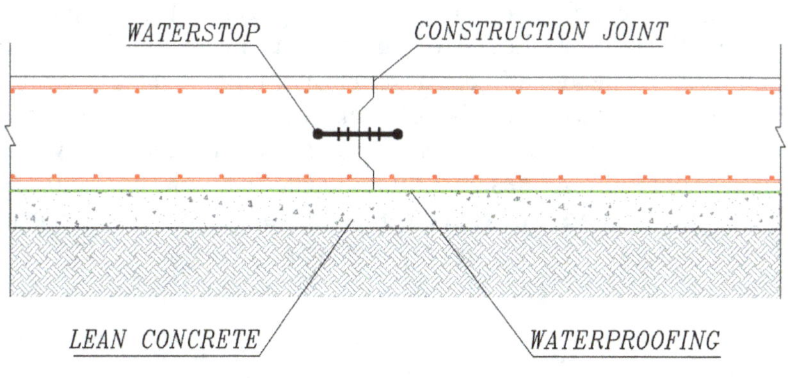

Figure 181. Apron Slab & Culvert's Bottom Slab Connection

10

Conclusion

It is clear from the explanation and the solved examples that the aim of this manual is to make a comprehensive reference for the design of a specific element which is the box culvert and focus on it. The used methods were simple and practical which was the main intention from this manual.

Structural analysis was explained using a specific software proposed by the Author, This book is not intended to explain the program, so the software steps are not explained, and the program can be learned from any other material dedicated to that. The designer might use any other program. Furthermore, the analysis may be done using a two-dimensional strip method or a three-dimensional model, by using frame or a shell elements, also the supporting methods may differ. The designer is free to choose the software and the analysis method if he is aware of the proper analysis method and familiar with the software used.

Structural design and checking, it is based on the terms of the AASHTO LRFD Bridge Design Specifications, which is not different from the references mentioned in the next chapter. Nevertheless, it has been compiled and simplified so that all information is collected in one reference for the engineer which is this manual.

The designer must differentiate between the AASHTO LRFD requirements and the best practices in this manual, as the standard's articles shall be duly respected and the designer might deviate from the Author's recommendations if this based on proper study, experience or many trials. At the end, the designer has the choice to follow the method of analysis and design if there no conflict with the standards or state requirements. The engineering is always based on standards, state-entity's specifications or engineering judgement.

References

AASHTO (2014), LRFD Bridge Design Specifications Seventh Edition, American Association of State Highway and Transportation Officials, 444 North Capitol Street, NW, Suite 249

ACI SP-17, (2014), The Reinforced Concrete Design Handbook, American Concrete Institute, 38800 Country Club Drive Farmington Hills, MI 48331 USA

Bureau of Bridges and Structures Office of Program Development, (2017), Culvert Manual, Illinois Department of Transportation

MoDOT, Engineering Policy Guide, (2022), Available from: www.epg.modot.org

IDOT Culvert Manual (2019), CM 3.4 - LRFD Culvert Design Loads, Available from: www.idot.illinois.gov

WisDOT Bridge Manual (2021), Chapter 36 – Box Culverts, WISCONSIN Department of Transportation

MnDOT (2013), LRFD Bridge Design, Minnesota Department of Transportation, Available from: www.dot.state.mn.us

Joseph E. Bowles (1997), Foundation Analysis and Design, Fifth Edition, The McGraw-Hill Companies, Inc.

Approach Slabs, (2022), BTN 011, Version 2.0, Department of Transportation, Victoria State Government

www.ingramcontent.com/pod-product-compliance
Lightning Source LLC
LaVergne TN
LVHW052315200926
848481LV00002B/576
* 9 7 8 1 9 2 2 6 1 7 5 5 2 *